The Actor Speaks

The Actor Speaks

Actors Discuss Their Experiences and Careers

EDITED BY
Joan Jeffri

INTRODUCTION BY
Andrew Foster

*Sponsored by the Research Center for Arts and Culture,
Columbia University*

*Contributions in Drama and Theatre Studies,
Number 52*

GREENWOOD PRESS
Westport, Connecticut • London

Library of Congress Cataloging-in-Publication Data

The Actor speaks : actors discuss their experiences and careers /
    edited by Joan Jeffri ; introduction by Andrew Foster.
        p.   cm.—(Contributions in drama and theatre studies, ISSN
    0163–3821 ; no. 52)
    "Sponsored by the Research Center for Arts and Culture, Columbia
    University."
    Includes bibliographical references and index.
    ISBN 0–313–29097–0 (alk. paper)
    1. Actors—United States—Interviews.   2. Acting—Study and
    teaching—United States.   I. Jeffri, Joan.   II. Columbia
    University. Research Center for Arts and Culture.   III. Series.
    PN2285.A22   1994
    792′.028′092273—dc20   93–20835

British Library Cataloguing in Publication Data is available.

Library of Congress Catalog Card Number: 93–20835
ISBN: 0–313–29097–0
ISSN: 0163–3821

First published in 1994

Greenwood Press, 88 Post Road West, Westport, CT 06881
An imprint of Greenwood Publishing Group, Inc.

Printed in the United States of America

The paper used in this book complies with the
Permanent Paper Standard issued by the National
Information Standards Organization (Z39.48–1984).

10 9 8 7 6 5 4 3 2 1

CONTENTS

ACKNOWLEDGMENTS

The Research Center for Arts and Culture gratefully acknowledges the contributions of the Andrew W. Mellon Foundation and Actors' Equity Association, which provided resources for the project's research and development, its own Administrative Committee and Advisory Board members, the actors and related experts for their thoughtful guidance, and the members of the staff who carried the project through to completion.

Joan Jeffri, Director
Catherine Sessions, Project Coordinator
Dr. Robert Greenblatt, Computer Consultant
Toby Boshak, Research Coordinator
Rachel Moore, Research Assistant

PREFACE

The interviews in this book were chosen from more than forty personal narrative histories of actors and "related experts"—directors, producers, teachers, designers, casting directors, union representatives, artistic directors and founders of theatres—from all over the United States. Besides forming an important resource of their own, they constitute an integral part of the Artists Training and Career Project, a study of the training and career choices and patterns of actors, painters, and craftspeople conducted by the Research Center for Arts and Culture at Columbia University. Actors are at the heart of this third volume, culled from the study that complements the second, *The Painter Speaks: Artists Discuss Their Experiences and Careers* (Greenwood Press, 1993) and the first, *The Craftsperson Speaks: Artists in Varied Media Discuss Their Crafts* (Greenwood Press, 1992). Through the interviews and a detailed questionnaire sent to 6,133 actors nationwide (4,133 members of Actors' Equity Association, the stage actors' union; and 2,000 non-Equity actors), which garnered a 31 percent response, they were asked to describe in systematic ways the impact of training and career choices on their work, their requirements for doing their work over time, and their career development and satisfaction.

Areas of investigation used first in the interviews and later in the questionnaire have been developed through the creation of a multistage "validation sequence" from early childhood through mature careers. Questions move from initial influences through education, training, and preparation to career entry, peers and colleagues, marketplace judgments, critical evaluation and public response, to career satisfaction and maturity. They also seek information on background and current activity.

By eliciting information about the kinds of validation, as well as the kinds of resistance the actor meets, the Research Center for Arts and Culture (RCAC) has been able to describe the training and career development of actors; contribute to a growing literature on careers that includes research in the scientific, legal, medical, and law enforcement professions but is sadly lacking in the arts; provide important information for advocates and funders; give training institutions a better idea of greatest need for training; give arts service organizations and unions information about appropriate assistance for actors and when such assistance is most helpful; and document the position of the actor as an integral member of society.

These interviews also provide pleasurable reading as they humanize a process and a search. Space does not permit us to publish all the interviews, but all the audiotapes are housed at the Oral History Collection of Columbia University and permission to hear them may be secured there. Data and information from the survey can be obtained directly from the Research Center.

Each published interview begins with a brief biography of the main markers in the actor's life, in education, training, honors, and awards. A photograph of each actor complements his or her interview.

We have tried to represent actors demographically, ethnically, and equally by gender as much as possible. We have encompassed a wide age range and have targeted actors in three broad career stages: emerging, established, and mature. During the study we have been formally advised by a group of related experts and actors to keep our work relevant to the needs and realities of the field.

From this small sampling and from the larger body of interviews, particular comments and insights have stayed with us. The constant battle of the actor to work at his or her art full time was best expressed by one Chicago actress who related a recent conversation with someone she had just met. "What do you do?" asked the stranger. "I'm an actor," she replied. "Oh, what restaurant do you work in?" The irony and pain was echoed in Alan Alda's litany of jobs held while he was trying to survive as a young actor—everything from doorman and cabdriver to clown "at the opening of gas stations and chicken part stores." Advice on how to survive varies widely. There are those like David Drummond who feel actors need to "find something other to do than acting"; those like Fanni Green who feel acting "defines" them; and those like Judd Hirsch who feel that "you somehow have to deserve this in your head." There are complaints about the audience not being trained to judge good acting, about the critics who "come down from the mountain after the war and shoot the wounded," and about unions. One actor in North Carolina spoke about Actors' Equity this way: "Sometimes I feel that *we* have to be protected from *them.*" Ambivalence about the stage actors' union runs throughout these interviews—from people like John Randolph, who grew up in an era during which he helped develop certain kinds of equitability that younger people often take for granted, to Miriam Kressyn, a star of the Yiddish Theatre for whom entry into the Hebrew Actors Union was only through an audition for more than three hundred of her peers. And cities themselves were characterized. Chicago actor Dan Oreskes said, "New York is the place to get somewhere. Chicago is the place to *work.*"

The concept of a career is different for actors than for the painters and craftspeople we interviewed earlier. While investment in the work is of primary importance to all three, actors often feel they cannot get to work without a career. The ambivalence that actors—particularly women and people of color—feel about taking roles that are demeaning or stereotypical complicates career choices. Actors talk a great deal about fate, superstition, and roles that seem to have one's "name on them."

The interviews in this volume represent a history of theatre in the United States for the past three-quarters of a century, from the actor's point of view. They encompass culturally specific theatre, religious theatre, experimental avant-garde theatre, as well as classical theatre, traditional repertory, stock, community theatre, educational theatre, Off-Loop, Off-Broadway, waiver theatre and the Great White Way. As Jason Robards replied when I told him the project was focusing on *stage* actors, "What, all ten of us who are left?" While the reality is not quite that bad (although it sometimes seems so on Broadway), one objective of this book is to illustrate that theatre is everywhere in the United States and that, although the business and production of theatre have become more complex, the appeal of "two boards and a passion" remains.

The interviews were conducted by Research Center Project Coordinator Catherine Sessions and myself, with assistance from staff member Toby Boshak. I am most grateful for their work and conscientiousness. The introduction that follows is written by Andrew Foster, playwright, former actor, and arts manager. I greatly appreciate his hard work, his love of the material, and the excitement he generates.

This work would not have been possible without the substantial aid of the Andrew W. Mellon Foundation and Actors' Equity Association. Even more so, it would not have been possible without the cooperation of actors and experts nationwide, whose lives have made this story and who have given generously and willingly to make this project happen.

INTRODUCTION

Andrew Foster

1650–1800

Theatre as Crime

Although there were elements of theatre in the rituals of Native Americans, and although the first European plays presented in the New World were staged in French (in Canada) and Spanish (on the banks of the Rio Grande), organized colonial theatre primarily began with the arrival of second-rate English actors and bankrupt English stock companies on American shores. These artists were not warmly greeted. England's religiously persecuted had already settled in many parts of the colonies, and although in some areas the effects of long years of prejudice brought about a new social tolerance, in others puritanism reigned.

Regardless, theatre was generally frowned upon. The earliest record of this disapproval was the recorded arrest of three Virginians in 1665. Their crime: performing a play. Although these three were judged not guilty, antitheatre legislation continued to appear. In 1709, the province of New York enacted a law that forbade playacting along with cockfighting. In 1774, the Continental Congress actively discouraged "every species of extravagance and dissipation, especially all horseracing, and all kinds of gaming, cockfighting, exhibition of shews, plays, and other expensive diversions and entertainments." Well into the nineteenth century, many states had "blue laws"; in 1818, Connecticut's prohibition on theatrical entertainments and circuses led to the midnight arrest of Mr. and Mrs. Bartley, English actors who had just finished an evening of readings performed for Hartford's elite in the ballroom of the city's finest hotel.[1]

The records are not one-sided, for they also expose a remarkable appetite for entertainment, the highest form of which was readily acknowledged to be theatre. Illiterate commoners were desirous of this escape from their difficult lives; for the educated class, there was a literary cachet. Even the politicians, while publicly condemning the stage, attended. In 1714, four years after the state outlawed acting, New York's Governor Robert Hunter wrote the first American play to be published. And George Washington, regardless of the Continental Congress's edict, remained an avid theatregoer throughout his life.[2]

Aided by boredom and hypocrisy as much as by love of art, colonial theatre survived the legislative hammer and flourished. Roving acting companies toured the Philadelphia area as early as 1723, against the strong feelings of the Quakers. Boston and Charleston, together with New York and Philadelphia, enjoyed sporadic but ever more frequent theatrical activity.

In all these settings, scattered performances gave way to extended engagements. In 1749, a company led by Englishmen Walter Murray and Thomas Kean played a warehouse in Philadelphia for some or all of the month of August, following up with a six-month season in a three hundred-seat room in New York. In 1751–52, this company, as well as another group from England led by William Hallam, played a newly built theatre in Williamsburg seating four hundred. Around that time, other permanent theatres sprang up in Philadelphia, Annapolis, and Charlestown.

A series of ever larger houses opened in New York City. In 1768, the John Street Theatre debuted. The auditorium held one thousand people, in a city of twenty thousand. The effect of such a facility on a populace that was used to catch-as-catch-can production was noted by a character in Royall Tyler's play, *The Contrast*. Describing a performance at the John Street, the character said, "They lifted up a green curtain and let us look right into the next neighbor's house."

Lessons in Lean Management

In reality, the settings at the John Street were quite primitive. The actors played in front of the proscenium; sparse painted flats describing the play's locale were behind, at the rear of the stage. The candlelit performances were fierce and passionate but unrealistic, full of amplified gesticulations and broad humor; the text was referred to, more than followed. This was true in New York, and truer still in smaller cities. Where stages were not available, readings were the vogue. Where playscripts were not available, texts were approximated or imagined.

Actors traveled in companies or singly. Individual acts were theatrical five-and-dime stores, consisting of impersonations and magic tricks, singing and doggerel rhymes. Companies performed well-known English plays and were led by a manager-actor; there was no separate administration. Companies tended to split income through a system of shares. These groups were lean and hungry, heavily entrepreneurial, pausing only long enough to milk a town of a night or two's tickets, then leaving "one step ahead of the bill."

Theatre and bar owners may have been stiffed, but audiences got their money's worth. An evening consisted not of a single play, but of a number of pieces: a tragedy, entre-acte singing or dancing, and a one-act or full-length farce—to end with laughter instead of tears.

The business grew at a furious pace. Companies formed, split in two, split again, journeyed to smaller and smaller towns farther out on the frontier. On the more highly populated seaboard, traveling circuits of professional caliber developed: Boston–Providence–Albany–New York, Charleston–Richmond, Philadelphia–Wilmington–Baltimore.

By 1800, New York and Philadelphia had developed as primary centers, with grand theatres. Still, every municipality in every state had some kind of performance space, and they were all similar in one way: they were fragile and destructible. Even New York's grand stages tended to be flimsy, built in a few days, accidentally burned to the ground nearly as fast, and soon replaced by ever-more-elaborate facades.

Entertainment was the point, not buildings. Actors performed under an incredible variety of conditions, from sheds to tents to ballrooms to two-thousand-seat palaces—all on a single tour. At the turn of the century, these professionals had one thing in common: they were almost all foreigners. Theatre was not English dominated; it was quite simply English. There was, however, one excellent colonial omen: the audience was American and growing in leaps and bounds. It was in this audience that many of the great early American actors were born.

1800–1900

The Rise of the American Actor

Soon after the turn of the nineteenth century, major English stars began traveling to the United States—many invited by the innovative New York theatrical manager Stephen Price. By the late 1820s, the list included George Cooke, Thomas Cooper, James Wallack, Junius Booth, Edmund Kean, Charles Matthews, and William Macready. The great actresses were more loath to make the ocean crossing. Young Fanny Kemble was soon to arrive, but many others—such as the legendary French tragedienne Rachel—would not undertake the voyage for twenty years.

Stars played New York, Boston, Philadelphia, and Washington for extended engagements, and a host of smaller cities for three or four performances. They often traveled alone, associating themselves at each stop with a theatre's recently formed "stock" repertory group of underpaid and unknown American actors. The star's attitude toward these players was generally condescending and paternalistic. Many visiting luminaries refused to rehearse, or only mechanically recited lines in advance of performances. Many fired local performers for practically no reason at all. In most cases, the locals paid for this professional disrespect; they were judged by their public as incompetent and unworthy of the great English artists. By 1820, even New York audiences had become spoiled, rejecting productions that lacked a major star or a novelty headliner, such as a child Macbeth.

The adoption of the star system held many consequences for the lives of individual actors—stars and journeymen alike. By diminishing the audience appeal of local talent, the system hindered the development of resident companies; box-office success depended not on a solid ensemble but on a visitor's name. The hype attending on that name created public expectations of quality that could not always be satisfied. Small-town critics complained about the performances of the stars as bitterly as they railed at the inexperienced local bumblers.

Even in this competitive and destructive setting, great American actors began to appear. Lacking clear career paths or guidance, they rose to fame through inspiration, perseverance, and sheer talent. Some struggled within the beleaguered stock system. In 1825, Englishman Edmund Kean played Othello in Albany. The role of Iago was performed by a young American, Edwin Forrest. Kean was so impressed that he took Forrest with him to Philadelphia, where he prophesied that the young man would rise to great eminence. He was right; but Edwin Forrest could in no way be called Kean's discovery. His road to success had been too rocky for too many years with too little recompense. Forrest was Philadelphia born to a poor family. He had to make his own way from the age of thirteen. Although he excelled at apprenticeships in a variety of trades, he seemed called to the theatre, reportedly from seeing the eminent Thomas Cooper at the Chestnut Street Theatre.

Forrest debuted in William Wood's Walnut Street Theatre in 1820 and was warmly received, but his first engagements were not a financial success. After conferring with Wood, he embarked on a long and grueling apprenticeship out West. In 1822, he was engaged for eight dollars a week to perform in a theatrical circuit traveling to Pittsburgh, Lexington (Kentucky), and Cincinnati. When that venture failed nearly a year later, Forrest traveled to New Orleans and played in famous actor-manager James Caldwell's company for two seasons, gaining eighteen dollars a week and recognition for his "robust" style.

After three years in the South and an attempted duel with Caldwell, Forrest returned north to the engagement in Albany that led to his introduction to Edmund Kean. Less than a year later, his fortune turned. He appeared in a benefit at New York's prestigious Park Theatre in one of Kean's favorite roles, Othello. His rise from that point was meteoric.

Earlier in 1826, also at the Park, New Yorker James Hackett made his acting debut under very different circumstances. Born of an aristocratic family, Hackett became enamored of a stage career early in life. He attended performances at the Park—partially owned by a cousin—and married a Park Theatre showgirl when he was nineteen. Still, only the burden of financial hardship after a bad investment convinced his relatives to allow him his dream. Untrained, Hackett appeared with little success in a dramatic role; several days later he undertook an evening of mimicry—his true talent—and made an immediate impression.

Forrest and Hackett were America's first native-born stars. They traveled very different roads. Forrest's name—and, indeed, his life—would become synonymous with tragic melodrama. Hackett developed an altogether different style, working from the example of the English comedian and mimic Charles Matthews. He developed a series of monologues—an evening's monodrama—using English plays transposed to American settings. His very first endeavor in this line was a huge success and, within a year, led him to perform in England. Upon his return, he was not only a star himself; he found several other Americans busily copying him with great success.

One of these was a Massachusetts actor who paid a much greater sum in theatrical dues than Hackett. Born to an educated but not overly rich family, George Handel Hill wrote extensively about his life and times. Hill first witnessed theatre, of a sort, during the visit of a traveling actor-magician-singer-comedian to his Massachusetts school, circa 1820: "Potter was a colored man, gentlemanly in his address, adroit in the management of his show . . . and no bad member of society." Although called a ventriloquist, Potter impersonated the famous, sang, and served up tricks, such as "the dancing egg, the ring in the pistol, and the pancakes that he fried in his hat without fat or fire."[3]

Hill was greatly excited by the entertainment and repeated it to his friends, to great effect. He found other ways to pursue the satisfaction he felt in performing: "By the aid of blankets, patch-work quilts, boys and girls from my uncle's, the parson's house, I had constructed a theatre, and acted parts of Richard the Third."[4] He traveled to New York City in the 1820s, but met with no success. He joined a troupe of touring actors upstate.

> The vicissitudes of a stroller's life fell to my share—playing in halls and barns, sometimes to numerous audiences, composed of every class of persons. . . . [A]t others, spare indeed were the numbers assembled; and though our advent into the village had been noticed with a grand flourish and display of bills, our departures were silently accomplished in the darkness, and our whereabouts studiously concealed from inquiring friends, who expected remuneration.[5]

Early in his career, Hill fumed over an unsuccessful engagement in *Julius Caesar* in Philadelphia.

> I was dissatisfied with the part; there was no name in the bill. The representative of the masses and without a name, Citizen..........Mr. Hill. . . . I determined from that moment to play parts with names, and if possible to do something, in my way, that should make my name remembered.[6]

Hill faced the kind of managerial manipulation and social ostracism that are well known to actors of many eras. On one successful audition: "He said I was the best comic singer he ever heard . . . and he had me at his own price." His personal life suffered as well. He engaged to be married "on the condition that I should leave off acting . . . a terrible sacrifice, yet I submitted." Nonetheless, his fiancee's friends "forbade me, on any account, to visit the house."[7]

Soon after his disaster as the uncredited Citizen in *Julius Caesar*, Hill played Hackett's trademark role as a "Yankee" character, receiving even greater acclaim than his progenitor. He went on to develop and perform his own original Yankee sketches of American life.

Hackett and Hill, along with a few others, brought high drama home to their followers. They may well have had a similar effect on American audiences as that of German houses hearing opera in their native tongue: a wonderful mix of guilt, consternation, and delight. In his autobiography, Hill sums up his feelings about life as an actor, with a typically American blunt reticence: "My professional life and its accidents are the result of the exercise of free will."[8]

Forrest, meanwhile, achieved international renown. He played all the classic dramatic roles to stunning acclaim and illuminated some of the earliest American dramas with his energy and emotions. His acting style was direct, and so was his challenge to the established stars of the day. He was not content to conquer New York, but strove to capture the English crown as well. In so doing, he brought about the first major English–American acting rivalry, capped by one of the most infamous theatrical occurrences of the 1800s.

The rivalry began in 1827, when the brand-new Bowery Theatre offered the young Forrest an engagement while William Macready played across town at the Park. Forrest not only matched Macready's Shakespearean roles; he performed the leads in plays specifically written for Macready. Nonetheless, the two remained somewhat friendly acquaintances until the 1840s, when events propelled them into the limelight not as actors but as representative symbols of the common man and the elitist, the nativist and the foreign oppressor, the quintessential two-fisted American and uppity Englishman.

On May 10, 1849, these events led to an act and an aftermath that summed up the limitations and dangers of an actor's life, and not only in the nineteenth century. By that time, Edwin Forrest was considered by many an overbearing and arrogant man, certain of his position as the people's performer and incensed that some found the intellectual Macready the greater actor. Abused by English critics on a final tour of that country, Forrest blamed a "Macready conspiracy." Always outspoken, he expressed his anger by standing and hissing Macready during the Englishman's performance of Hamlet in Edinburgh, Scotland, in 1848.

For the next year, personal letters publicly printed in American newspapers heightened the controversy and widened its implications. The "common" citizen of the United States was tired of all forms of English domination. With this rivalry, the English theatrical monopoly became the last straw.

Macready disregarded the building wave of anti-English feeling and toured America in 1849. In each city he played, the conflict built, taking on class overtones. The social elite—more reliant on English leadership—abandoned Forrest and his increasingly unreasonable emotional state. The lower classes supported him utterly. This support became political hay for New York's newly formed Tammany Hall. A group of politicians espousing "nativism"—a violently chauvinistic patriotic movement—announced a "civil action" on the final night of Macready's New York engagement.

Edwin Forrest was not a part of these plans, although he did nothing to stop them. Perhaps he did not recognize the depth of the public emotion; perhaps he could no longer judge events. He was mired in a long and bitter divorce suit, born out of his Othello-like jealousy. Performances were often followed by an appearance in front of the curtain in which Forrest condemned his wayward wife. Critics were more likely to dwell on this personal scandal than compliment his increasingly overblown acting.

As his life spiraled out of control, so did the rivalry with Macready. Strangely, the comedic James Hackett found himself in the middle. Actor-manager Hackett had taken on the sponsorship of Macready's New York performances. Even though he was known to be neutral in the ongoing quarrel, Hackett believed that the principles of free speech demanded freedom to perform. He spoke forcefully of this on the night of the final performance, but he was preaching to believers—an audience of socially elite Macready supporters.

Outside the theatre, a riot ensued. Twenty thousand "commoners"— encouraged by Tammany Hall lackeys—fought to take the theatre. Uniformed troops were called in. Twenty people were shot to death and hundreds injured in the night-long battle. Inside, protected by a cadre of police, Macready performed the historically unhappy tragedy *Macbeth*.

The controversy surrounding the battle and the titillation over his personal affairs made Forrest a rich box-office attraction in the ensuing years. His standing as a serious actor, however, suffered. The curtain speeches clarifying his personal innocence got longer; his performances lost their edge. What had been strengths early in his career were now mocked. His own extravagances, along with the passage of time and fashion, led many to condemn that robust style. George Curtis, writing in *Harper's* magazine, may have summed it up best: "That human beings, under any conceivable circumstances, should ever talk or act as they are represented in the Forrest drama . . . is beyond belief."[9] Continuing his tours to smaller and smaller towns and audiences, Forrest ended his professional life as he began—a strolling player out West.

Edwin Forrest was an early example of the heights to which an actor could climb in America. But those heights were dangerous indeed, and never included real social acceptance. Although he was given medals and banquets, he was seldom invited to a respectable socialite's home. His life was an example of the actor's ongoing vulnerability to overexposure, social whimsy, character judgment, ostracism, psychic isolation, and self-destruction.

The Actress

The 1800s were a story not just of American actors but of actresses as well. Even as the first two leading men made their rocky way through the century, the first American actresses of great repute appeared on the scene—again, from widely disparate beginnings.

Charlotte Cushman was born to a distinguished but poverty-stricken Boston family in 1816. Intelligent and forward, she was also born plain—"a tomboy," she later said. Like Forrest, Charlotte Cushman saw Thomas Cooper on stage at an early age and was, from that time, determined to perform for a living.

As well as acting with unusual force, she sang beautifully. In 1834, when she was eighteen, she was employed to sing duets with an English opera star at Boston's Tremont Theatre. The diva, Mary Ann Wood, was impressed and talked Cushman into training for the profession. During the following season Cushman made her debut in the opera, traveling to New Orleans to continue her engagement. Within the year she ruined her voice. The ubiquitous James Caldwell advised her to become an actress. At the end of the season, she performed Lady Macbeth to great acclaim and traveled to New York to work for twenty-five dollars a week at the Bowery Theater.[10] At the time, she was supporting her mother, younger sister, and brother. When the Bowery burned down only weeks later, she once again left New York and accepted engagements in Albany, Detroit, Buffalo, and Boston.

The next season saw her back in New York as a stock company member at the Park—at a weekly salary of twenty dollars. Over the next four years, she played more than thirty leading roles and many lesser ones. She played Goneril and Cordelia to Forrest's Lear, and Ophelia to Charles Kean's Hamlet. In 1840 she moved to the National Theatre in Philadelphia, also securing a job for her younger sister, Susan. Two years later, she became acting manager at the Walnut Street Theatre—the first actress-manager of the American stage.

Stardom did not come easily to Cushman. Many of her eccentricities—such as playing male roles—brought public criticism, at least from men. Her career progressed, but at a snail's pace compared to that of Hackett or even Forrest.

In 1843 she played Lady Macbeth opposite Macready, who found her interesting if unpolished. After retaining her for the rest of his tour, he convinced her to travel to Great Britain. To Charlotte Cushman, the trip was a great gamble. After a decade of acting, her finances were still insecure and her notices variable. She was her own most vociferous critic, always looking to better her performances and despairing of ever living up to her craft. Nonetheless, she made the trip and, after several grueling weeks, secured an engagement. Her success was immediate and immense. To her own surprise, she was acclaimed as a tragedienne without equal. As with many American performers, Charlotte Cushman needed a European stamp of approval before being fully accepted in her own country. She was the first American to receive that approval unreservedly, and she returned home in triumph.

Anna Cora Mowatt was as different from Cushman as Hackett was from Forrest. Mowatt was born into fashionable New York society. Her reasons for going onstage were economic, like Cushman's; however, poverty struck her much later in life. It was Mowatt's husband who brought on their difficulties. When his business and health failed, Anna Cora was already an accomplished writer and deeply interested in the theatre. She too had attended at an early age—to see Fanny Kemble in *The Hunchback*.

At age twenty-one, Mowatt attempted to address her family's financial troubles by performing a series of readings—a slightly oblique approach to theatre that she felt would salvage her reputation. She further protected herself by debuting in Philadelphia. Nonetheless, old friends shunned and criticized her. Retreating from society, she wrote numerous articles and a novel under an alias, admitting the latter after it won an award.

Her husband's next business venture also failed, placing them under greater pressure. She determined to write a play. As well connected as Hackett, Mowatt received a quick reading and a quicker production. Her play, *Fashion*, was an immense success; it is still looked upon by many as the first great American satire.

Anna Cora Mowatt wrote about her decision, the year after *Fashion*'s premiere, to become an actress.

> I should never have adopted the stage as a matter of expediency alone. . . .
> I reviewed my whole life and saw, that, from earliest childhood, my tastes,
> studies, pursuits had all combined to fit me for this end. I had exhibited a
> passion for dramatic performances when I was little more than an infant.[11]

She encountered stiff resistance.

> The instant my projected appearance was announced, I had to encounter a
> flood of remonstrances from relatives and friends—opposition in every
> variety of form. But tears, entreaties, threats, supplicating letters could only
> occasion me much suffering—they could not shake my resolution.[12]

Like Forrest and Cushman, Mowatt took acting seriously.

> Incessant study, training—the discipline of a kind which the actor/student alone can appreciate—were indispensable to perfect success. I took fencing lessons . . . used dumbbells . . . exercised my voice.[13]

In 1846—her first year on stage—Anna Cora Mowatt performed two hundred nights. Many considered her Charlotte Cushman's equal or superior, although their styles were sufficiently different to obviate comparison. Both were thrust upon the stage by circumstance as well as desire, and both embraced the discipline as well as the fame.

Mowatt played professionally for seven years, after which she reentered a society that had decided she was, after all, respectable. Hers was one of the few cases in which personal courage brought public admiration and acceptance. She died far too young, in Europe. Cushman lived on, giving years of "farewell" performances, always returning to the stage after brief or long absences to a warm welcome, playing male or female roles as she desired.

Hackett, Forrest, Cushman, Mowatt—these were four of America's first great actors and actresses. Their common inspiration was English, their career paths and training were pure trial-and-error, and they provided an inspirational transition for a generation of purely American performers.

Theatre on the Frontier

It was not just the English who toured America. Stars like Mowatt, Cushman, Hackett, and Forrest all traveled. Their tours were extensive, expanding as the country grew. Initially, though, well-paid actors stuck to the Eastern Seaboard and the Old South, perhaps making an occasional foray a bit inland.

Miles to the West, though, hundreds and eventually thousands of American towns too small to attract these stars desired professional entertainment as much as their city cousins. Most frontier communities embraced theatre at the earliest possible opportunity: Pittsburgh in 1790; Lexington (Kentucky) and Cincinnati around 1800; Nashville in 1807; St. Louis in 1814; Houston in 1838; San Francisco, Sonoma, Monterey, Santa Barbara, and Los Angeles in 1847–48 (evidently all due to Colonel John Stevenson's Seventh Regiment of New York Volunteers); and Salt Lake City soon after the Mormons' arrival in 1848.

First performances were almost universally given by local amateurs—all men, either unnamed "young gentlemen" of society or army groups like Stevenson's (which seemed, according to the records, to have an incredible amount of spare time on their hands). There seldom were theatres. These towns used warehouses and icehouses and stables as performance spaces. Audiences were generally quite tolerant. Unlike the highly critical and competitive East, there was room out West to try and fail and try again.

Groups of actors identified possible new markets and set out to get there—not always the easiest of tasks. When they did arrive, the rate of failure was enormous, leaving it to individual members to attempt some slightly different approach and once again move on to supposedly greener pastures. As individuals, these frontier actors of the early-to-mid 1800s are the hardest to characterize fully. The quality of their private lives is unknown; their careers, a mass of inconstancy. They disappear from sight with alarming abruptness. The little that has been recorded of their travels and trials is a testament to physical courage and entrepreneurial boldness.

St. Louis

Actors traveled West long before a major Eastern economic upheaval in the 1830s forced the issue. English-born William and Sophia Turner were early examples. She appeared in New York, Montreal, Pittsburgh, Lexington (Kentucky), and Cincinnati—all by her late teens.

By that time, St. Louis residents had enjoyed solely amateur entertainment. Even that had only begun with Eugene Leitensdorfer's extremely tentative 1814 versions of "The Magic Picture, Moses' Rod, Dancing Eggs ... and other sports too long to detail here." Leitensdorfer had few pretensions, criticizing his own act in a public disclaimer: "He is not as well prepared as he will be in the future."[14] He had no competition. At the time, St. Louis was considered the most isolated American city, with no similar-sized community for hundreds of miles. Thus, on December 30, 1817, the two thousand residents were understandably excited when the Turners and their troupe of "professionals" completed the arduous trip down the Ohio and up the Mississippi.

Sophia Turner, in particular, was well received. An anonymous letter to the *Missouri Gazette* includes a compliment on "Mrs. T's deep knowledge of the human heart, and her admirable skill in controling pulsations."[15] The troupe performed in a single-room structure, originally built as a blacksmith's shop but later used as a courthouse. Although their eight-month tenure seems successful from the limited notices now available, the company dissolved in early fall.

At that time, almost all company members disappear from theatrical notation, never to be mentioned again. Sophia may have performed later in minor roles in New York, but even that is questionable. Disappearance was the constant fate of the average frontier player—and, in fact, a historical trait of the American theatre artist. Playwright Dion Boucicault summed it up later in the century when, after writing four hundred plays and appearing in numerous productions, he noted to a friend: "I write for a monster that forgets."[16]

St. Louis enjoyed the attentions of a second troupe in 1820, led by the estimable Noah Ludlow, who not only disregarded the Turners' prior performances, but claimed in his memoirs that they never occurred. In the prior two years, Ludlow had presented short seasons in Natchez, Huntsville, and Nashville. Like the Turners, his company traveled by river—down the Ohio to the Mississippi, then upstream by cordelling (a method in which a boat is hauled by an onshore rope). After this lengthy trip, they barely began performances before another troupe arrived. Competition was impossible, so the two groups merged. During the month of April, more than twenty different plays were performed by this talented combine. Yet only weeks later—faced by dwindling box-office receipts—they departed.

Another group arrived the next year, and failed. In 1827, James Caldwell came up from New Orleans. In ten years, St. Louis had more than doubled in population, to five thousand. Caldwell must have thought it a perfect acquisition for his growing theatrical empire. Regardless, he only lasted until August. Effort upon effort to create an ongoing presence would continue to be frustrated for the next eight years. Institutional success was not to arrive until Ludlow and comedian-manager Sol Smith entered a partnership covering Mobile and St. Louis in 1835. Within two years, they had a new theatre and the first certifiable box-office hit: *Cinderella* managed a run of seven consecutive mights—an amazing feat in an era of limited audiences and constantly changing repertory.

Success may have encouraged Smith and Ludlow, but it did not make life for the actors that much easier. Early in the fall of 1837, the St. Louis season came to a close, *Cinderella* notwithstanding. The troupe left for their annual winter stint in Mobile, fourteen hundred miles away. Upon arriving, they discovered a company in place. Once again, a merger occurred; and an unlucky half were immediately sent back upriver to St. Louis, in winter conditions. They arrived in January to play in a theatre built specifically for summer temperatures. The correspondence is enlightening. Here, for instance, is Sol Smith to Ludlow:

> The people cannot study sufficiently fast, being nearly all novices. . . . Then we have no wardrobe. . . . [T]here has been very near rebellion in the corps.

> . . . It is cold as thunder. . . . [S]o cold, the lamps won't burn. . . . —all for
> [a box office of] $15.50—Isn't it horrible?[17]

This was the lot of the frontier actor: no objective measure of talent, no career path short of trials and errors, no economic stability, constant dangerous travel under difficult physical conditions, lack of technical support, lack of scripts to study, lack of community acceptance, and, finally, unending change. And still the American appetite for theatre continued to grow.

In the year 1818, St. Louis—population two thousand—witnessed thirteen performances of as many plays. By 1827, the population had increased to five thousand. The number of plays produced was thirty-seven. In 1838—twenty-five years after its first amateur performance—this city of twenty thousand people witnessed more than three hundred performances of more than 180 comedies, tragedies, and afterpieces. Only a season after the disastrous winter described above, a company of "novices" learned parts in as many plays as a modern actor might in a lifetime.

By 1839, St. Louis was thought of as a fine theatrical venue. Transportation had improved enough that the premier actor of his age—Edwin Forrest—debuted in the city that so recently had been a frontier outpost.

Houston

In 1837, Houston still awaited professional entertainment. The populace was eager; one entrepreneur, a Mr. Carlos, actually began to build a theatre in advance of a company. Mid-year, G. C. Lyons published an ad in the *Telegraph and Texas Register* of the upcoming arrival of his new troupe. It never came; the schooner *Pennsylvania* capsized in a gale, killing Lyons and all but two of the players.

Ignorant of both the sinking and the new theatre, another troupe successfully made the voyage west in 1838. Led by one Mr. Corri—ballet dancer and actor as well as manager—the ensemble consisted of the following members:

> Mr. Barker, late of the St. Charles, New Orleans, and Mobile Theatres; Mr. Alex Jackson, late of N.Y. and London; Mr. H. Sargent, late of the Mobile Theatre; Mr. H. S. Newton, late of the Tremont Theatre, Boston; Mr. Jas S. Ormund, late of the Philadelphia Theatre; Mr. G. W. Chambers, late principal dancer of the Mobile Theatre; Mr. Horn, late of Mobile and New Orleans Theatres; Ms. Emma Barker of the St. Charles, Mobile and London Theatres; Mrs. Hubbard, from the Camp Street and Mobile Theatres; and Madame Thielman from the St. Charles, New Orleans.[18]

Houston was disappointed that the troupe was not direct from New York—a feeling that would be echoed many times in the next hundred years, discrediting any number of regional actors. Theatre owner Carlos actually served notice in the local paper that he had no belief in the group's credibility, but warned the community that the drama must be supported even if the players failed.

The drama was well served. By the end of the first month of performances, public reaction led both Corri and Carlos to put notices in the paper of their separate intentions to build grand new theatres the next year. Neither theatre was completed. In fact, by 1840 little further mention was made of the overwhelming majority of this troupe.

It is possible to track the moves of a few well-known actor-managers like Ludlow and Smith, or follow for a short time a situation like Corri's, but individual players surface only sporadically. While some commentary can be made on the nature of their training and craft, it is literally impossible to grasp their private lives. Hundreds of these troupes existed; thousands of actors pursued an invisible career for an unknown number of years. This constant flow of star-struck pilgrims was repeated in every town in thousands of miles of frontier territory from 1820 to 1880.

By mid-century, New York had become the undisputed leader of American theatrical cities and a world center as well. Competition was fierce and business was robust, but winds of change were blowing in the wings—ready to remove in a decade the classical style of acting and stock system of theatrical presentation that had reigned for the century. Many factors were involved in this change; of them, the explosion of theatre on the ever expanding frontier was one of the most important. In particular, the sudden rise of San Francisco as a bustling entertainment center held great consequence.

San Francisco

Unlike the lengthy process in St. Louis, San Francisco theatre thrived from the start. Less than three years after the area's first amateur performance in 1849, the city's first professional house was built. Through embezzlement and destruction by fire, San Francisco lost and then rebuilt a bewildering number of theatres in the following two-year period. In fact, the whole town was burning during those initial years of the Gold Rush—burning down in millions of dollars' worth of fires, and burning up with gold fever.

Ticket prices were high and salaries were higher. Performers and musicians could make fifty or a hundred dollars in a night. Even if the cash disappeared the next day in cafes and gambling houses, the amounts were amazing. Eastern actors caught on early. George Handel "Yankee" Hill talked about the city in its 1850s theatrical prime.

> The Jenny Lind, Adelphi and Metropolitan in the 1850s—were able to attract leading actors from the East Coast for lucrative starring engagements, even though this meant either a long voyage around South America or an arduous and dangerous trip across the Western plains and mountains.[19]

Junius Brutus Booth was one of the early birds, arriving with his son Edwin in 1852. Junius was not to repeat his many theatrical successes in California; in fact, the round trip killed him. For son Edwin, the entire state would be a gold mine. Edwin had already experienced a lifetime of theatre anecdotes while acting as dresser for his eccentric father. He had debuted in Boston and played New York, if briefly. Now, out West, he took up his own theatrical standard. After performing with his father, Edwin toured the camps of Nevada. Listing himself in the San Francisco city directory as "comedian and ranchero," Booth was willing to perform any piece, attack any genre. He was unpredictable; he was exciting. In late 1853, a theatrical unknown—Mathilda Heron—arrived and teamed up with Booth at the Metropolitan, playing Juliet to his Romeo and Ophelia to his Hamlet. Heron left the audience breathless; Booth electrified them. The public was ecstatic. These two were out to change the theatre world.

Successful though they were in that goal, they never again appeared together. Each marched to a different drummer. Before either was to have a major impact on the American stage, Heron got married, divorced, and saw Europe, and Booth went to Australia. Both were to become representative of San Francisco's policy of discovering its own stars and then sending those stars east to New York.

These two were not the only professionals playing the area. Top Eastern establishment stars, and unknown actors as well, performed throughout California and Nevada for adoring audiences of miners. The pay was fabulous, the work and travel hard, the employment substantial. At the region's heart, San Francisco became a major entertainment center nearly overnight.

Through the mid-1850s, the opening of rail lines past Chicago and the improvement of transocean service created great upheavals in the entertainment industry. The Industrial Revolution was in full swing, and its advances were seen as being of great benefit to the stage. Legitimate theatre enjoyed a period of singular domination as the most important entertainment industry and the most active performing art. Society changed along with technology, and with it—even driving it along—came a new theatrical aesthetic and a new economic reality. Starting in the late 1850s, declamatory acting, classical romanticism, and the stock/repertory system would be replaced by naturalism, a growing social realism, the road company, and the extended run.

Naturalism, the Road, the Actor Trapped in a Role

Heron and Booth were not only symbols of a new westward-oriented career path; they were representative of an important step in the movement toward a new style of acting. Naturalism had barely begun to surface by the 1850s, for a number of reasons. Prior to mid-century, subtleties in acting were not supported by technical stage means. Bad lighting, poor scenery, terrible acoustics—all these led the classical actor to rely on an instrument that could physically control an audience that might not be able to see or hear well. Nor was realistic material available; the broad comedies and overheated melodramas of the day required an overbearing execution. Shakespeare's plays, as well as those of a few other talented dramatists, offered a much greater range of interpretation, but a tremendous challenge to the established English standards was implicit in altering the traditional characterizations.

In 1857, that challenge occurred with the arrival in New York of Heron and Booth. Heron's vehicle—an adaptation of Dumas' *Camille*—offered the audience a vision of the real world that, to her, had to be matched by a new style of acting. As for Booth, he developed Shakespearean interpretations that were vastly different from those of the elder generation.

Forrest and Cushman were outraged by the disrespectful newcomers. The public, however, responded with enthusiasm. Critic William Winter raved about Booth's Hamlet: "When you saw Booth's Hamlet you saw a noble exemplification of that art—the ideal of a poet supplied with a physical investiture and made actual and natural, yet not lowered to the level of common life."[20]

The word *natural* had been used in reference to his father's art as well, but more as an elemental force: "His art was, in a high sense, as natural as the bend of Niagara; as the poise and drift of summer clouds; the play of lightning ... or the sea, storm-tossed, sunlit, moonlit or brooded in mysterious calm."[21] Edwin himself claimed a simpler distinction: "I make less noise."[22]

Meanwhile, in 1854, Heron's debut performance in San Francisco had caught the audience by surprise.

Her tone and face do nearly the whole work, and her features speak as audibly as her voice. Her best acting is done while listening to others. . . . She is not like an actress treading the boards with clever pomposity and laborious passion, but a little girl who has caught some half-dozen of you in a room, and . . . is telling you the pitiful story of her woes.[23]

In New York, one audience member reacted even more strongly to her Camille. She was "not only terrible in her lifelikeness, but at times offensive."[24]

Audiences found Dumas' *Camille*—especially in Heron's challenging interpretation—difficult to accept emotionally. This street courtesan was simply too realistic, and all lower-class types had long been omitted from most plays. Dumas was not alone in trying to change that. Writer-actor Dion Boucicault's *Poor of New York* opened in 1857, mixing rich and poor thematically and offering a series of astounding sets and stage effects in support. Boucicault would have a substantial impact on the aesthetic changes of the next quarter century. As a playwright, he wrote a series of "social realism" plays like *Poor of New York*; additionally, he brought lasting fame to another naturalistic actor, Joseph Jefferson III. Jefferson gained raves for his performance of Boucicault's adaptation of *Rip van Winkle*: "From the rising of the curtain on the first scene until its fall on the last, nothing is forced, sensational, or unseemly. The remarkable beauty of the performance arises from nothing so much as its entire poise and equality."[25]

The new wave of naturalists would coexist with the classical generation through the difficult Civil War years. Edwin Forrest and Charlotte Cushman both played to warm welcomes in 1857 and following seasons, but the stylistic tide would turn ever more strongly against them. Perhaps the change in style was part of a ripple effect of a new era of social awareness; perhaps it had more to do with the newfound technical capabilities in the theatre. Or it could be that naturalism was in part an answer to the scattershot career path of the American actor—the attempt to perform on inbred ability without the advantages of long years of training.

Clara Morris was a poor girl from Cleveland who stunned audiences in the fall of 1870 with her emotional honesty. Of her own untrained approach, she said merely that she acted from her heart. The aesthetics of naturalism ran parallel to the lifestyles of the American-born actor.

Economic and operational change also struck in the 1850s and 1860s, and Dion Boucicault once again had a hand in it. For a hundred years of American stage history, the numbers of available audiences and sheer tradition had enforced a constantly changing repertory of farces and dramas, melodramas and musical skits. Audiences chose from hundreds of plays year after year, with occasional contemporary additions. Actors were favored in one piece or another—Edwin Forrest in *Metamora*, for example—but each played a changing repertory, regardless.

In the late 1850s, longer and longer runs of successful plays on Broadway brought home the truth that the massive stock repertory might no longer be the only answer to box-office success. Dion Boucicault was among the first to realize the implications. Many had wondered at the incredible growth of the railway—from six thousand miles of rail in 1849 to thirty thousand miles in 1860. Boucicault may have seen this as well and understood it in practical terms: it might be possible to tour a whole company, and not just a star. He therefore sent out on tour one of his 1860 Broadway hits, *The Colleen Bawn.* During its performances at any given theatre, the existing stock company was displaced. The experiment was a success, for audiences clamored to see the "real" New York company in the latest hit.[26]

Throughout the next decade, the road company grew in importance, ripping at the fabric of small-town acting lives and displacing a young national acting corps with more consistent Broadway professionalism. By nature, the road changed the ethereal connection between artist and management that had existed for a century in the person of the actor-manager. Road business was business—not theatre. The important questions centered on finance of a high order: gross figures; travel expenditures; columns of numbers on a scale unprecedented for the art form that a hundred years earlier had been outlawed by an act of Congress. Numbers of this magnitude were best handled from a distance, by a financier in a booking office in New York.

The separation of artistic and business sectors in the theatre had already begun. Many impresarios earlier in the century had acted only as a sideline. On Broadway, managers were already just managers—no longer actor hyphenates. But the road sped the change and made it in many ways irrevocable. The theatre looked more and more profitable to American business interests, and the actor lost more and more control over his or her life and art as a result. Edwin Booth noted this in a letter to a close friend, written after a European tour in 1862: "Art degenerates below the standard even of a trade in America." He refers in the same note to the inevitability of aiming at "the almighty dollar."[27]

In addition to bringing a new economic reality, the road added the final bars to a new artistic cage for the actor: the endless run. Mathilda Heron and Joseph Jefferson were first in a long line of actors to be trapped in a role. Jefferson performed *Rip van Winkle* for more than twenty years, and

Heron was reputed to have earned more than one hundred thousand dollars from ceaseless tours of *Camille*, her pièce de résistance. Neither complained, but Edwin Booth was not so discreet. During his record-breaking one hundred performances of *Hamlet* on Broadway in 1864, he was desperate for release: "I felt that the incessant repetition was seriously affecting my acting."[28]

Years later, Eugene O'Neill referred to the inherent artistic limitation of the long run—and perhaps specifically to his father's crushing second life as *The Count of Monte Cristo*—when he said, "Actors are conceived by and born of the parts they are permitted to play."[29]

To the actor with a memorized repertoire of a hundred roles, long runs and tours of a single show seemed an unending boredom. It was certainly unending in Heron's case: "Camille" was inscribed, in silver, on her casket.[30] To the "new" management, proven properties were proven receipts; and by the turn of the century, theatre was the province of the manager. *Camille* may have died with Heron, or may have buried Heron. Regardless, the extended run prevailed well into the next century.

The Boston Museum

The road killed stock companies and the careers of local actors all over the United States. It also killed another, more limited and utopian alternative: the resident theatre.

A true resident company might be distinguished from stock as having much longer terms of acting service. The audience comes to know the actors—the whole company, not just the leading man. Broadway had not allowed this approach in the nineteenth century. Turnover between competing groups was too great. Individual actors were certainly followed and adored, but in different houses under different circumstances.

In Boston and Philadelphia, however, resident companies flourished for the second half of the century. These groups augmented their offerings with the same "star" visits as did stock groups all over the country, but their own actors were estimable and respected within the profession, and their own company offerings were as eagerly attended as those of their critically praised New York visitors. For the actor, life in this kind of company was a very different kind of life.

The sixty-year history of the Boston Museum began in 1843—as a theatre, not a museum. The twelve-hundred-seat house was called the "Museum" mainly to allow an end-run around Massachusetts blue laws. From the start, this was an ambitious undertaking. The fifteen to twenty players performed as many as three plays a night. In early years, audiences saw shows like *Nicholas Nickleby*, *As You Like It*, *King Lear*, *Wild Oats*, *London Assurance*, *Joan of Arc*, *Oliver Twist*, *School for Scandal*, and *The Drunkard*. During the first four seasons, leading man William Warren appeared in a total of 206 different roles. Warren was the preeminent member of the company. Over a forty-two-year engagement, he played more than six hundred roles at the Boston Museum, and was noted as being peer to the other greats of his day.

William Smith was the actor–stage manager. Of hyphenate Smith, the *Boston Herald* would say fifty years later, "He was a gentleman and a scholar, well grounded in the whole range of English literature. He was a most accomplished actor, at home in any branch of his profession."[31]

The stability of the venture gave those who found acting eccentric much to think about. One skeptical backstage visitor noted that "a more work-a-day, matter-of-fact place it would be hard to find."[32] Most of the actors stayed with the company, year in, year out. The level of training and work-ethic was perceived as very high. "Actors and actresses . . . were bound to know how to speak, how to elocute, how to deliver their sentences, how to move, how to fence, how to dance and how to carry their talents over the footlights."[33]

Boston loved knowing the actors and following their lives, on and off stage. Company members were greeted on the street and congratulated for their work. The group was respected outside Boston as well, many company members performing successfully in other venues. Mr. and Mrs. G. C. Howard, for example, left to play *Uncle Tom's Cabin* in the famous Troy, New York, run—one hundred performances in a town of nine thousand people.

Eventually, the Museum faltered under the economic pressures of the road, ceasing its resident operations in 1885. It became a booking house for road shows. Like Philadelphia's fine Arch Street Company, it never achieved a success equal to its years as a true resident theatre. For the American actor, the loss of the Boston Museum was substantial. Professional life there had been more stable, more rewarding, and more plainly comprehensible as a career. Nonetheless, members of the Boston Museum existed under the same basic social limitations as actors elsewhere. One sharp observer noted that "William Warren, almost alone of the actors in the Stock Company, was accepted in Boston society."[34]

Society: Respectability and Whoredom

As an American social institution, theatre had tottered between acceptance and condemnation for more than two centuries since that early

Virginia arrest. Actors, as a group, had paid for their uncertain standing more than any other artist. In fact, regardless of all the changes that rocked the nineteenth-century stage, the issue of the immorality of the acting profession remained a constant.

Actors suffered from this career prejudice. Women had a more difficult time than men, minority actors a more difficult time than white, and minority women a more difficult time than anyone else. It was certainly with an air of defiance that George Hill, for instance, referred to the "colored" magician Potter as being "no bad member of society."[35] Most actors needed to prove this, seemingly every day. Repeated over and over again in the first half of the century was one or another variant of the standard religious warning: "When a Christian enters the theatre he must leave Christ at the door."[36]

There was some good reason for this warning, but it had little to do with actors. The plying of the trade of prostitution in the third tier of theatre boxes was standard in the nineteenth century, in America and on the Continent. This was one of the reasons why women seldom attended plays, particularly early in the century; when they did, they arrived with a vanguard of respectable gentlemen for protection against advances or insults. Actresses, as a rule, had no chaperones and so were considered no different from whores. Of course, the performers were far too busy acting to be vulnerable to the physical reality of such a charge; nor did any actors, historically, ever enjoy profit participation in such concessions. They would seem, therefore, innocent of the charges. Society—madly avoiding the mirror—condemned them just the same.

In her memoirs, Anna Cora Mowatt had many things to say about the social standing of members of the acting profession. She knew she would at least have to refer to the forbidden third tier: "I allude to the demoralizing effect of allowing any portion of the theatre to be set aside for the reception of a class who do not come to witness the play. But this is a difficult subject for a woman to touch upon."[37] Mowatt once had her own negative moral assumptions about actors; they were challenged when her play was produced. Watching a rehearsal from the back of the house, she was astonished at the hard work, the intensity, the concentration, and the integrity of these odd people. It did not match the image her own social circle propagated. In the end, she added "my feeble voice to those already raised against the wrongs received by the stage, the drama and the profession."[38]

These voices were few; some of them were original, indeed, in their expression. Brigham Young's community of Mormons was devoted to light, moralistic stage entertainments. They constructed a grand theatre in Salt Lake City before completing schools or city offices. One visitor tells us more of the Mormon leader's approach: "Young understands . . . that you must elevate the actor. . . . To this end . . . he places his own daughters on the stage as an example and encouragement to others."[39]

Regardless of innovation or defense, the primary truth of the nineteenth century was that the actor was a social misfit. Accepted for as long as a community found it convenient, the actor's behavior was always to be examined, and the consequence for disapproval was ostracism or expulsion. Even the greatest aficionados may have been uncertain of the nature of the actor's internal makeup. Artists in related fields wondered; Walt Whitman referred to insanity as perhaps a necessary part of theatrical greatness. Within the confines of the greenroom, actors wondered who they were, and why. Those who loved and lived theatre went to great lengths to discover the answers.

The eminent English actor George Frederick Cooke died drunk and almost friendless in New York, attended to the last by a greathearted theatre patron, Dr. John Francis, who attempted but failed to save the performer. Cooke's bones were buried in a common grave. A decade later, the great Englishman Edmund Kean saw this as a tremendous insult. Even as he was being forced out of New York by personal scandal, Kean insisted on paying for a monument to Cooke. The difficulty lay in finding a resting place for his remains: actors and churches were like oil and water.

Difficult as it was, Kean convinced the minister of the famous St. Paul's Chapel in lower Manhattan to place the monument in the church graveyard. (For an actor's remains to be inside the church was considered totally unacceptable.) Kean enlisted Doctor Francis's help in disinterring Cooke's remains. With the skeleton before them, they could not restrain an essential curiosity. Cooke's performing magic had been legendary; they must have wondered what part of that magic remained. The doctor—an amateur phrenologist—removed Cooke's skull for his own study and gave Kean the great thespian's forefinger for luck.[40]

For the next century, this actor's head and finger took part in quarrels, wagers, rehearsals, and opening nights. The head has been a notable if uncredited success time and time again as Hamlet's Poor Yorick. Offstage, it has been poked and prodded and perhaps scientifically compassed. But for all the phrenological research expended on the skull, it is unlikely that anyone has any greater understanding of how an actor's unique talent and desire to please the public add up to his ongoing status as a social outcast.

Transitional Years

By the latter half of the nineteenth century, nearly five thousand theatres[41] served towns and cities in the United States, each offering hundreds of performances per year, each employing a company of five to twenty actors in addition to the touring stars. By 1890, this way of life was a part of the past—killed by transcontinental booking syndicates and rail-transported road companies. Control of the theatre had fallen into the hands of a small group of money men.

Technological change had brought great success to the stage—improvements in lighting and special effects, transportation, printing. This success had created tremendous growth. The growth increased financial investment, and the accompanying image of theatre-as-business necessitated great operational changes. Through it all, the individual American actor struggled. Introduced at the beginning of the century as an apprentice, this actor had nurtured, created, managed, altered, and finally lost control of his or her professional life.

The state of the business was nonetheless rosy, with nary a cloud on the horizon. In 1880, a notion that the theatre would be threatened by technological obsolescence within a few decades would have seemed as absurd as the idea of a man on the moon in the Depression-struck world of the 1930s.

1900–1930

Theatre as Industry

By the turn of the century, the player's life had been turned upside down. No longer was theatre an individual artist's enterprise; it had become a profit venture revolving around real estate. For the first time in two hundred years, the American stage was a building more than an art form. The actor was no longer a criminal—just an anonymous accomplice. The stars of the day were newly arrived financiers. Some felt that the Industrial Revolution had met the theatre head-on—and won. If so, the creation of the "Syndicate" was essential to that victory.

In 1896, the Theatrical Trust had been formed by some of the leading booking agents of the day: A. L. Erlanger and Marc Klaw, Charles Frohman and Al Hayman, and S. F. Nixon and J. F. Zimmerman. The Syndicate—as it would popularly be called—forced independent theatres everywhere to book tours solely through their conglomerate. By 1900, the group controlled enough major theatres to achieve a virtual monopoly. Their power grew exponentially.

Syndicate offices in New York became the headquarters of the professional stage, and made New York City the sole producing center. In some cases, this takeover merely emphasized ongoing changes long under way. New York had already become the preeminent American theatrical city. The resulting need to book shows instead of produce them in-house had led to annual pilgrimages to Manhattan that exhausted independent theatre owners. Many saw Klaw and Erlanger's forced centralization as relieving a chaotic booking nightmare. As for actors, the new system offered a much greater chance for stable year-round employment. But this ruthless efficiency was not introduced for the betterment of the American stage. Actors and managers alike soon discovered that the Syndicate achieved substantial monetary returns by treating the theatre as an assembly line.

Contracts were no longer negotiable. The Syndicate unilaterally declared the booking terms for independent theatres, demanded a percentage of ownership in independent productions, and forced contractual terms on bewildered actors. In all cases, they cut these figures to the bone; if the results were unsatisfactory, they would decree new terms for contracts already signed. The production and performance of plays was to be based on a new and severe financial accountability—and only the Syndicate would profit.

This monopoly did not respect the artistic content of the shows it sent on the road. Companies traveling under the Syndicate banner were advertised as the "New York cast." In fact, this was seldom the case. Often there were several simultaneous tours of the same show—all featuring actors who had seen Broadway only in their dreams. Syndicate in-house producer Charles Frohman soon realized that there was little downside to advertising such unknowns as major discoveries. Frohman became famous for giving these untrained novices leading roles in mediocre shows and hyping the resulting products as smash hits—all at substantial payroll savings. The decrease in quality was noticed by audiences everywhere, and was resented by theatre owners as well.

As the implications sank in, many rebelled, but theatres that refused one Syndicate booking were never allowed another chance. They remained empty, fell into bankruptcy, and were purchased on favorable terms—by the Syndicate. Independent producers remained, but most were independent in name only. When it came to touring, there were few independent options. By 1904, the Syndicate owned or controlled hundreds of theatres nationwide, including nearly all legitimate first-class houses in every major city.

Some actors rebelled almost immediately upon the Syndicate's formation. In 1897, six of the leading performers of the day signed an agreement to boycott Syndicate houses, but these stars were not reacting as much to an essential loss of artistic control as to the particulars of their own financial future. Within two years, all but one of the signators had succumbed to special Syndicate arrangements. To a considerable extent, the heart and soul of the American theatre at the turn of the century resided in that one last rebel.

The Odyssey of Mrs. Fiske

During the late 1890s and throughout the first decades of the twentieth century, Minnie Maddern Fiske took up the mantle as leading lady of the American stage. Actively involved in all aspects of production—as actress, stage manager, writer, and producer—her accomplishments were extraordinary, but by 1900, unfortunately, nearly anachronistic. The Syndicate did not want the artist to be more than a cog in a well-oiled machine. Mrs. Fiske would have nothing of such limitations.

Her remarkable odyssey through the American theatre began when she was born to a professional actress in 1864. As an infant, Minnie went to work each evening with her mother: "I learned to love the smell of the theatre—that odiferous medley of gas, paint, and mold dear to the hearts of all true children of the stage—as familiar to them as the salt breeze to the sailor."[42]

When she was three, she made her debut in *Richard III*. She was a notably successful child actor, learning the old stock tricks from the elder generation.

> When I was twelve I had a large repertory of widely contrasting parts that I might be called upon to play with very little notice. Sometimes I would be cast for the Widow Melnotte in *The Lady of Lyons* and the next night Little Eva in *Uncle Tom's Cabin*. . . . On successive nights I would be Lucy Fairweather in *The Streets of New York* and Peanuts, the newsboy in *Under the Gaslight*.[43]

She turned away from the old-fashioned acting style she saw in these early days and was drawn as a teen to Edwin Booth's special brilliance. As she matured she "looked to life off the stage and to the new science of psychology for guidance. . . . She played with her back to the audience. She threw away lines."[44] Fiske was influenced not only by Booth, but by the creed of writer-actor William Gillette, who wrote (and practiced) *The Illusion of the First Time in Acting*, and the social realism of writer-actor James A. Herne, whose productions of the downbeat *Margaret Fleming* and lower-class *Sag Harbor* were called "absolute truth to life."[45] Following these examples, Mrs. Fiske carved out her own territory of uncommon realism. Sometimes it was revolutionary in its sheer simplicity. Of one performance, an acting colleague said, "Oh, to be able to *do nothing* like that."[46]

With that comment, the idea of the "natural" in American acting entered the twentieth century. Eighty years before, "natural" had referred to an essential and stormy power; forty years before, to an elegant and refined but still larger-than-life intensity. Now, with realistic staging and precise electric lighting and increasingly powerful scripts embodying the new social realism, a peak theatrical memory would be Mrs. Fiske in her "do nothing" scene, cradling a beaten lover's head in her lap silently for ten minutes. Around her hurried the nightly goings-on of a lower-class barroom, but "gradually one could watching nothing else; one became absorbed in the silent pathos of that dumb, sitting figure."[47]

Well before that very special *Salvation Nell*, Fiske had been propelled to stardom by two spectacular performances—in *A Doll's House* (1895) and *Tess of the D'Urbervilles* (1897). She was adored by audiences and as controversial to the critics of her day as were the Duse, Edwin Booth, and Edwin Forrest to theirs. Norman Hapgood, who at first rejected her unique approach, eventually stated that he would carry images of her performances to his deathbed.[48] Alexander Woollcott said, "It was not merely that you could not choose but hear: you could not choose but believe."[49]

Mrs. Fiske was devoted to the play, not to herself as star. In fact, she despised the "star vehicle." Some of her roles were not classic leads at all, but secondary parts that struck her as especially appropriate. Her company was chosen for excellence, not to enhance her personal stature or hide her shortcomings. Company members were regularly cited by the public for doing the best work of their careers under her freehanded guidance. As for Fiske herself, regardless of the size of her role, her technique was just as thorough and performance just as inspired.

She had strong views on dramatic material as well as acting style. She supported new American writers with commissions, and her expectations were always high. Once again, her views were not in accord with those of the Syndicate. Charles Frohman replied to Fiske's clarion call for challenging drama by saying that material had to be carefully selected to soothe the primary audience: tired businessmen. She replied, "The complete imbecile will always be able to find appropriate entertainment."[50]

Fiske was valued for her courage as well as her talent. In opposing the Syndicate, she nearly threw away her stardom. But if she embodied the

American theatre's style, she had its guts as well. Like the frontier barnstormers before her, she quite simply did not know how to give up. Even after her peers abandoned the 1897 anti-Syndicate agreement, Minnie and producer-husband Harry maintained a policy of no negotiations. As a result, the best theatres—by right of stardom, *her* theatres—were closed to her. For several lengthy stretches of time she could not play New York at all.

She and Harry took what steps they could, creating the Independent Booking Agency in 1902. The seriousness of their purpose comes through in this statement: "This booking agency is not for financial profit in any shape, form or manner, but solely for the convenience, benefit and protection of the attractions."[51] The agency was not successful in slowing the immense Syndicate momentum. The Fiskes were pestered with lawsuits and misinformation publicized by Syndicate hired hands. The couple performed wherever they could, regardless of the difficulties.

In 1907, the Fiskes opened an immense hit: Langdon Mitchell's *The New York Idea*. When they tried to book a national tour, they found themselves frozen out of every desirable venue. They were able to play only one legitimate theatre west of the Missouri; the other stops were quite simply incredible. With their sophisticated and critically acclaimed comedy and a baggage-car full of silk-upholstered Louis XV furniture in tow, Fiske and her excellent first-rate company played Yankton, South Dakota; Albuquerque; El Paso; first-ever theatrical engagements in a skating rink in Ratin, New Mexico; a mining camp in Globe, Arizona; and Tucson and Bisbee, Arizona. They played to full houses everywhere they went—at a third-rate stock house in Burbank, California; a movie house in San Francisco; a church in Seattle; and the Thistle Rink in Edmonton, Canada, where second-act furniture sat outside on a lawn, waiting for intermission. This exhausting eighteen-thousand-mile tour, which played in one reputable first-class house, remains one of the great acts of will in American theatre history.[52]

Late in the first decade of the twentieth century, the Fiskes gained a powerful ally in their fight against the Syndicate. The up-and-coming Shuberts joined the few remaining mavericks under a banner of theatrical independence—and then exhibited an even greater desire for control than their archrivals. Two decades later, the Shuberts would control 60 percent of the nation's legitimate theatres, owning or booking nearly nine hundred establishments. By 1910, the Syndicate's total control was broken; yet centralization endured.

By 1911, conditions solidified that would dictate the course of theatre for the next twenty years. Nationally, the terrific internecine warfare between Shubert and Syndicate interests led to an overabundance of half-empty houses and an ever decreasing quality of product. The road and its "combination company" began a long and utter collapse. Traveling companies in 1900 had been estimated at roughly 339. By 1920, that number would shrink to 39.[53]

New York temporarily flourished. From eighty-seven productions in the 1899–1900 season, Broadway would grow to a record of 264 in 1927–28.[54] This centralization, which fostered the greatest period of native American drama, turned into something closer to isolation. A combination of theatrical mismanagement/misrepresentation and the relentless growth in popularity of the movies exiled professional theatre from the country's heartland. In 1931, Mrs. Fiske—one of America's great troupers—slowly died while audiences watched in sadness and awe.[55] Broadway also began to fade away. In two years (1929–31), the number of active theatre weeks fell from 2,636 to 1,685.

Even before the stock market crash, bad omens abounded. Theatres available for legitimate productions outside the major metropolitan areas suffered a tremendous decline. Estimated at 1,520 in 1910, by 1925 that number was halved.[56] Meanwhile, in 1925, $250 million was spent nationwide on the construction of movie theatres; scarcely any legitimate theatres were constructed outside of New York.[57] This trend was highlighted by the movie industry's habit of purchasing legit theatres merely to close them and thus lessen competition in key strategic areas. Before a single talking picture was released,[58] there were more than twenty thousand movie theatres, as opposed to 674 theatres still offering live productions.

From this point forward, theatre would shrink; conversely, the entertainment industry would grow into an immense giant. In some ways, the actor's life would shrink along with the theatre; more and more it would come to rely on specialized skills. Many media formats would require not a whole actor, but a technique or a body part: the voice on radio, the hand on a television commercial; the few snips that might be all that was left of a performance in a completed film. Worse yet, these formats were at war: the legitimate stage versus film versus television versus radio, each against the others.

The actor would never again regain the artistic control he enjoyed in the first two hundred years of this country's stage history. *Hamlet* and a following short burlesque highlighted by entre-acte singing and dancing— all by the same tired, inspired company—would never again be performed on one evening to one audience. By the second decade of the twentieth century, innumerable actors throughout America understood this, even if it was never completely articulated. Dispossessed by the professional theatre's artistic stagnation and monopolistic practices, they developed new approaches to art, entertainment, and the whimsical pursuit of the actor's life—undeterred by the grim realities. Theatre in America had never been merely a profession. Hated, feared, adored, it would be more accurately termed an "obsession" for audiences and actors alike. That obsession did not die with the road, nor would it die with Broadway. While the professional theatre played with economic fire, a theatre of art grew in the amateur ranks, and the great spread of rural America rediscovered the stock system and the theatre caravan.

The Little Theatre, the Caravan, the Fight Goes on in New York

By 1910—with the battle between the Shuberts and the Syndicate raging—more than one hundred stock companies had revived in small and large towns throughout the country. Most were formed within the preceding two years. These companies tended to exist in the cracks between legitimate and vaudeville theatres, charging less than a dollar for their top tickets. As the road declined, they grew in number and quality. By 1920, *Billboard* predicted that "with existing road conditions every city is likely to have its 'permanent stock' for full seasons." In 1927, *Variety* identified two hundred permanent stock companies in the United States and Canada.[59]

On the art front, Shaw and Ibsen were only the tip of a new trans-European influence. Berlin's Freie Buhne, founded in 1889, Andre Antoine's Théâtre Libre in Paris, the Art Theatre of Krakow, the Moscow Art Theatre and London's Independent Theatre pointed the way toward a new era of challenging theatre in America—a noncommercial era.

Maurice Browne's Little Theatre of Chicago debuted in 1912 in a storage space; the Toy Theatre of Boston, in a stable; the Provincetown Players, on a dilapidated wharf. Conditions were not dissimilar to St. Louis in 1820: budgets were minimal. Company members shared; at Chicago's Little Theatre, each received an initial salary of three-and-a-half dollars per week. The sets for the first Provincetown production cost around thirteen dollars.[60]

Throughout the teens, new Little Theatres were born: Baltimore's Vagabond Playhouse, the Wisconsin Players, the Little Theatre of Indianapolis, and New York's Washington Square Players, among others. This anticommercial movement embraced a host of philosophies and practices: university theatres, community theatres, commercial offshoots, black groups. Some Little Theatres performed standard commercial pieces, but the movement was known for an eclectic unpredictability. From the American premieres of great Greek classics to new pieces by theatrical unknowns, the Little Theatre challenged popular tastes.

In New York, two groups led the way. From 1915 to 1918, the Washington Square Players presented sixty-two short plays and six full-length ones in a variety of small theatre spaces, led by such members as Katherine Cornell and Roland Young. The Players grew into the Theatre Guild, a successful and tremendously influential professional art theatre. After a decade of operations, the Guild was indistinguishable from the commercial world in which it operated, yet the name and the initial principle continue to wield a mythical force.

The Provincetown Players were more determined to remain small, but there was no greater safety in that decision. In bringing to light the first universally acclaimed American playwright—Eugene O'Neill—they came under intense commercial pressure, and disbanded in the mid-1920s.

The life cycle of most of these organizations was short; they died like the poorly clad foot soldiers they were. The actors regained some lost dignity: here they were once again, if briefly, actor-managers. There was a price; seldom were they paid. Salaries brought financial ruin. Nonetheless, the movement—if not the individual proponents—prospered until the Depression. By 1927, more than seven hundred Little Theatres existed; one source approximated that there were perhaps fifteen thousand amateur actors involved in this arena.[61]

Rural America witnessed another theatrical rebirth in the return of frontier barnstormers. Tent caravans playing six to eight months a year toured throughout the South and Midwest. Physically, the caravan was a unique theatrical phenomenon, springing from circus tradition.

> This theatre was set out on a plain. . . . So I said to the actors, "Where does the audience come from?" They said, "you'll see." So, sure enough, late in the afternoon the audience started to arrive. And they came across the plains on horseback and in wagons. And then after them came Indians dragging long poles and tepees after them. And within the time you could practically blink your eyes, they had completely surrounded this tent.[62]

Highly speculative estimates place the number of tent shows in 1925 at around three hundred traveling troupes employing six thousand actors for more than thirty thousand performances given to an audience of roughly eighteen million.[63] These numbers and their implied competition brought another heavy response from the already powerful movie industry. Taking a page from Syndicate books, Hollywood studios invested a substantial sum of money to "buy" legislation banning tent caravans in small American towns. The bribes were often successful.

On one such caravan in the early 1920s, a troupe of journeymen actors heard of another attempt by actors to regain some control over their lives.

> An actor arrived from New York City. He said, "You know what's happening back in New York? You know how we've been treated like dogs all these years? We're not goin' to have it happen to us any longer. We've got a union started. They call it Equity, and all of the people in the country have signed up to join this union, Equity." We knew absolutely nothing about it whatever. But we also painted on our Pullman car which we lived in on the road with the tent show, we painted Equity on our Pullman car.[64]

Even before the turn of the century, actors had expressed great disgust with management abuses and great interest in the collective bargaining process. Throughout the first decade, attempts were made to join the American Federation of Labor; the White Rats Union already held the AFL's franchise for performing artists, however, and a successful deal could not be struck. By the mid-teens, the situation had become intolerable. Luckily, the Shubert–Syndicate war created a division of power in the producing ranks. That schism created a small window of opportunity and the actors jumped through, fighting through a series of strikes and actions to a partial victory. The first signed contract did not set minimum wages or require rehearsal pay, but the actor regained one more small measure of control over his or her professional life.

1930–1980

WPA: A Bright Light in a Dark Time

Disaster struck the theatre soon after the financial panic of 1929. Never in the history of the American stage had one financial downturn had such drastic effect on the acting profession. Always, in the past, there had been an escape: the frontier during the downturn of the 1830s, the thriving road in the panic of 1897. In 1929, however, many factors combined to paint the theatre into a very tight corner.

Nationally, the movie industry was the new champ of the entertainment field. By 1930, the movie was challenged only peripherally by the stage. Broadway could not match ticket prices, nor could road companies; and throughout America, audiences were strapped to pay more than a quarter. The Little Theatre could and did offer an alternative, as did the caravan and the smaller stock companies. Regardless, America entered a period where an overwhelming majority of its citizens would never see a live show. Movie attendance, meanwhile, soared well above one hundred million per year. Many actors began the pilgrimage to Hollywood. It became a stampede in the years after the collapse of Wall Street, as even the one remaining legitimate-theatre haven of New York was taken from the stage. From a record 264 productions, Broadway shrunk to 70 in two years. By 1932, thousands and thousands of theatre artists were unemployed nationwide.

The problem, of course, was much greater than the theatre or the entertainment world. But when the Roosevelt administration took steps to address the problems of millions of impoverished American citizens, for once the artist was not excluded. Of one billion dollars in relief funds announced, thirty-five million dollars was reserved for the arts. On August 29, 1935, $6.78 million of that money created the Federal Theatre Project (FTP)—salvation for thousands of unemployed actors, and a glimpse into the future of the theatre in our country.

The intent of the Federal Theatre Project was not essentially artistic, but was simply to aid people by paying them to do what they could do best. It seemed wasteful to have a generation of professional artists digging ditches when they could be entertaining a shocked nation. Volunteer boards auditioned fifteen thousand theatre professionals (and a host of amateurs as well). Twelve thousand were hired. For actors, this represented a return to the oldest producing system in the country: the share system used by the first traveling American troupes. Every actor shared equally in the FTP, receiving twenty-three dollars per week. Repertory was once again in vogue, but it was a repertory of new plays more than old—plays that reflected the difficult spirit of the times.

Broadway was initially upset by the formation of the FTP, feeling that competition was inevitable. The Project, however, had other theatrical goals; the aim was clearly away from commercial production. The emphases were on new areas: Children's Theatre, Marionette Theatre, Dance Theatre, Negro Theatre, Hispanic Theatre, High School Classics. Tent caravans and community theatres were reinvigorated with the tremendous professional resources available to the Works Progress Administration (WPA). Within a year, there were more than 150 resident acting companies active in twenty-eight states.

Tickets were often free—always less than a dollar. Performers traveled to places that had never before seen a live actor. In one year, one company played 625 performances throughout Wisconsin and Illinois. Marionette shows were seen by 5 million schoolchildren in a single season. By 1939, the FTP companies had played to an audience estimated at 30 million,

60 percent of which had never before witnessed a play. In these years of utter hardship, more than \$1 million of ticket income entered FTP coffers. As in the early frontier years, people were more than willing to pay what they could.

For a decade, movie fanatics and commercial producers had sounded the death knell of live theatre, pointing to falling attendance nationwide. The issue, as FTP proved, was one of high ticket prices—not desire. At the peak of movie industry popularity, there was still a tremendous potential theatre audience. The times and the national trauma allowed for a different kind of understanding between live audience and live artist. The august business journal *Fortune* said it in principle:

> The government's experiments in music, painting and the theatre ... brought the American audience and the American artist face to face for the first time in their respective lives. And the result was an astonishment and excitement such as neither ... had ever felt before.

Fortune then restated it in human terms:

> The Mayor of Valley, Nebraska, a town of 800 inhabitants and 1,000 theatregoers, wrote Mrs. Flanagan to ask if the WPA cast of the *The Dictator* couldn't settle down and live there permanently.[65]

The material performed was often provocative—especially the Living Newspapers, in which actors attempted to deal with the huge issues of the day in a new and powerful way. Audiences were touched; some people were frightened. This was nothing new, as Augustin Daly had discovered upon addressing a shocked audience that had just witnessed his production of *Mrs. Warren's Profession* at the turn of the century: "people having attained their majority should be able to face the problems of life and willingly cast off illusions and youthful legends."[66] Daly was arrested shortly thereafter; a similar fate was in store for the FTP.

The Federal Theatre, short-lived as it was, forged several great advances—among them, the theatre's first attempt as an institution to deal with the issues of racism and cultural equity.

Cultural Equity and the History of the American Stage

The 1790 census of the United States identified more than 750,000 African slaves and thirty-three thousand "free Negroes"—in total, 19.3 percent of the population. Aside from the overwhelming question of slavery itself, these disenfranchised members of society held their own artistic aspirations. They had no access to the theatre: even in Northern cities, free blacks were not allowed entry to theatres, nor were black theatrical forms given institutional standing. Regardless, blacks strove to gain footholds in the theatre world—and upon occasion, miraculously succeeded.

In 1821, against great odds, a black performing troupe called the "African Grove Theatre" played a repertory season of Shakespeare in New York on Bleecker Street. Meeting with some success, the company soon had the wonderful audacity to advertise a roped-off section in the back "for white patrons."[67] This was too much for the racist spirit of the day, and the company was forced to disband. That it existed at all is a testament to the artists' courage and tenacity. That testimony was repeated later in the century by the young black thespians who, led by the example of Ira Aldridge, traveled to England to secure fame and a legitimate acting career.[68]

Domestically, white fascination with black culture assured it a growing influence on mainstream American art even if this influence came, in earlier years, through patronizing and parodizing formats such as minstrelsy. Popularized in the 1940s by Jim Crow Rice, the original minstrel show was a black-face compendium of comic, supposedly black, attributes performed by whites with darkened faces. Later in the century, black groups attempted to reclaim some of the minstrel fame accorded white mimics. Sadly, these performers also wore black-face and employed many of the same clichés as their white predecessors. Similarly, vaudeville, Broadway, and the road developed derivative "Negro" shows that did little to allow free artistic expression on the part of black performers.

The opportunities were limited by law. Blacks could not perform in white shows before 1877; the first black performer to play Topsy in *Uncle Tom's Cabin* appeared in 1879. Nonetheless, the black theatrical presence continued to grow. In 1890, the census reported 1,490 black performers; by 1910, the number had risen to 3,088.[69] Nearly all these performers appeared in musical comedies.

With the Little Theatre movement, things slowly began to change. Harlem's Lafayette Players, Cleveland's Karamu House and its Gilpin Players, and others proved that blacks could succeed in standard dramatic fare and even begin telling their own story on stage. Charles Gilpin's stunning success in *The Emperor Jones* for the Provincetown Players in 1920 was a measure of the change. Another came in 1923, with the opening of the first Broadway production of a black playwright's work. Willis

Richardson's *The Chip Woman's Fortune* was part of an evening of one-acts produced by the influential Ethiopian Art Theatre.

The real breakthrough in altering the status of the professional black theatre artist came with the Federal Theatre Project. Hallie Flanagan said it forthrightly: "freedom from racial prejudice . . . must exist at the core of any theatre for American people."[70] The FTP supported nine major projects featuring black theatre artists: two in New York and one each in Boston, Newark, Tampa, Chicago, Birmingham, Seattle, and Los Angeles. Additionally, smaller cities had black projects working hand in hand with amateur groups.

New York had a Negro unit located in Harlem's Lafayette Theatre. One of the greatest hits of the WPA years was born there: a production of *Macbeth* set in Haiti. Directed by Orson Welles, the production played to nearly 120,000 people in 144 performances (in New York and on tour). Haiti seemed an apt metaphor to black America: a fiercely independent people of color, under attack by a powerful white force. W.E.B. DuBois wrote about the black uprising in his play *Haiti*, along with the resulting attack by Napoleon's forces, and the island's heroic and bloody defense. The FTP performed the mixed-cast play to great acclaim in the Lafayette Theatre. Behind the curtain, the experience was even more memorable.[71]

> I will never forget that first rehearsal: the whites on one side of the stage and the blacks on the other, as though ne'er the twain would meet. . . . I ordered the dressing rooms laid out with equal part pepper and salt. . . . I set up the bows with black and white alternating, hand in hand. . . . The audience nearly lifted the roof off the old Lafayette.[72]

For the actors, "there was a kind of joyous relief about it, as though they had escaped from something which had troubled them and filled them with doubts for years."

Other major successes of FTP Negro units included the Los Angeles version of *Walk Together, Chillun*, Seattle's *Natural Man*, and Chicago's *Swing Mikado* and *Big White Fog*. The young black author of *Big White Fog* later discussed the overall effect of the FTP's involvement.

> It extended to the Negro opportunities such as not even the boldest imagination dared dream previously. At once it supplied an outlet national in scope and scale. . . . It was Federal Theatre that proved the open sesame, providing at once a laboratory and the wherewith for creative enterprise.[73]

In a more tentative way, the FTP also addressed the needs of other minorities, backing a Hispanic company in Tampa, Florida. In so doing, the Federal Theatre recognized the very first performers of the American theatre: Spanish soldiers in New Mexico in the 1500s. Actually, Hispanic theatre in the United States had been alive and well for a century before the FTP, but remained unrecognized by the English-dominated theatre world. In 1847, as English theatre arrived in San Francisco, so did the Alvarez Opera Company en route from Peru. In the 1890s, Hispanic theatre enjoyed its own route of combination companies traveling from Mexico up through the southwest. In the 1920s, Los Angeles and San Antonio supported more than twenty Hispanic theatres. Spanish-language tent shows traveled through the Southwest and Midwest, performing *zarzuelas*, *pastorelas*, and *revistas*. The crushing days of the Depression ended much of this activity. The support of the Tampa unit not only offered hope for the future, but an immediate new tie-in with the English-language theatre through the translation of such WPA works as Sinclair Lewis's *It Can't Happen Here*.[74] As with the Lafayette Theatre and its counterparts, the FTP's support helped set the scene for the new era of Spanish-American companies to come.

The Federal Theatre Project was not without its problems. Administrator Philip Barber pinpointed the difficulty inherent in any government-run program. He noted that the FTP began with four thousand actors and twelve hundred administrators and ended three years later with fifteen hundred actors and fifteen hundred administrators.[75] Nonetheless, actors—especially during the first years of the WPA endeavors—were active front-line members of their society. They were approved even by their government for one brief shining moment. That moment would collapse as the issue of relief became increasingly politicized, and the theatre project was finally voted out of existence amid rising congressional cries of communist sedition.

The year 1930 ended one era, and the FTP began another that came to an unhappy and premature end with the decade. Delayed by World War II, the influences of the government's intervention in the arts would echo down twenty years of legislative time and blossom once again in the late 1950s and the bellwether year of 1965.

The Postwar Years: Naturalism Victorious and the Not-for-profit Alternative

In entering the postwar years, we enter the era of many of the personal narratives that make up the body of this book. It is a territory undiscovered by historical perspective. The enclosed testimonies will speak more tellingly of the issues than could this brief pocket history. All contemporary theatrical tales, of course, should be read with a historical perspective, to illuminate more clearly the way that movements aspire toward similar goals, institutional difficulties arise again and again, and support systems die even as acting is ever reborn.

The postwar years began with a heightening of the division between the commercial and noncommercial theatres in New York and throughout the country. Even as Broadway refused either to completely die or to rise from the ashes, smaller groups proliferated. The birth of New York's Off-Broadway and Off-Off-Broadway came about in the 1950s. Circle in the Square, the Phoenix, and the Living Theatre all began operations around the beginning of the 1950s. By 1957, Off-Broadway produced more plays yearly than Broadway. This success led to a second, smaller rebellion when Off-Off-Broadway appeared with the opening of Caffe Cino in 1958. Regionally, the Arena, the Alley, the Actor's Workshop, and Margo Jones's Theatre '47 represented exciting new trends in commercial and noncommercial operating models.[76] Tyrone Guthrie and his "new" thrust stage, which recalled Shakespeare's Globe, arrived in Minneapolis. And the Lincoln Center Repertory waited in the wings, trying in vain to answer the riddle of a "national theatre."

American playwrights continued the flourish; the wave of prewar greats was followed by writers of equal scope: Inge, Williams, and Miller. The historic structure of actor-manager and resident company was reborn. From the Group Theatre, the Living Theatre, the Open Theatre, and the Wooster Group, to Teatro Campesino, the San Francisco Mime Troupe, and Steppenwolf, the heritage of the artistic-managerial hyphenate remained vital.

Another element began to solidify in the postwar era. For the first time, training became a concrete element of the acting career. Beginning with George Pierce Baker's turn-of-the-century Harvard workshops, more and more universities began to offer undergraduate and advanced programs. With the postwar GI Bill, both college enrollment and the number of academic art programs exploded. American naturalism was an understandable initial focus of many of these programs. By the 1980s, however, many had widened their focus, drawing from international sources to create a new spirit of eclectic professionalism.

Teachers from the theatre of the 1930s and 1940s gained great influence in the film medium, as well. Group Theatre graduates Lee Strasberg and Stella Adler ranked foremost among these mentors. Their ever refined influences of theatrical naturalism achieved a fitting victory in a medium that demands even less than Fiske's art of doing nothing.

Institutionally, the theatre survived the challenge of a maturing film industry that itself had to survive the challenge of television. The second half of the century has been replete with great opportunities for the individual actor, and with greater career confusion. New electronic media continue to crowd the entertainment field, offering the actor a wider and wider choice of direction. The more things change, though, the more they remain the same. The theatre stands alone as a unique acting platform—a primal stage from which all the technological media can broadcast or record flickering images for their own purposes.

In each and every medium, in each and every producing system, the acting profession remains an uncertain and inspirational commitment. This commitment may well remain doubly uncertain for American citizens whose cultural and/or racial heritage fall outside the mainstream European tradition. Certainly, the profession will continue for decades to face and address essential issues of access and excellence relating to the cultural equity of the theatre artist.

As for the endowed theatre, it has its own historical citations. Suggested as early as 1836 by William Dunlap, first attempted on a large scale in 1909 with the formation of the huge and ill-fated New Theatre, attempted again in the years of the Federal Theatre Project, the not-for-profit seems solid and eternal in 1990. Yet no system has ever been immortal. And no system—neither the Syndicate nor the Studio nor the new nomenclature of a not-for-profit arts world—can freeze the actor's heritage of endless adaptation in gesture, posture, emotion, action, role, identity, career, life.

Perhaps these personal narratives can act as one reminder to keep eyes and hearts attuned not to the building, institution, or industry, but to the actor.

NOTES

1. Lloyd Morris, *Curtain Time* (New York: Random House, 1953), 6. This is an excellent overview of eighteenth- and nineteenth-century American theatre.

2. Barnard Hewitt, *Theatre U.S.A. 1665 to 1957* (New York: McGraw-Hill, 1959), 32. Another excellent reference book.

3. George H. Hill, "Yankee," in *Scenes from the Life of an Actor* (New York: Garrett, 1853), 27.

4. Ibid., 42.

5. Ibid., 57.

6. Ibid., 9.

7. Ibid., 87.

8. Ibid., 121.

9. Morris, *Curtain Time*, citing Curtis on p. 96. For more information on the

Forrest/Macready feud, *Curtain Time* is suggested, as is *Edwin Forrest* by Laurence Barrett (see Bibliography).

10. Morris, *Curtain Time*, 110.

11. Anna Cora Mowatt, *The Autobiography of an Actress* (Boston: Ticknor, Reed & Fields, 1854), 216.

12. Ibid., 218.

13. Ibid., 219.

14. William Carson, *The Theatre on the Frontier* (Chicago: University of Chicago Press, 1932), 12–13.

15. Ibid., 23.

16. Morris, *Curtain Time*, 185.

17. Carson, *Theatre on Frontier*, 229–30.

18. Joseph Gallegly, *Footlights on the Border* (The Hague, Netherlands: Mouton, 1962), 20.

19. Hewitt, *Theatre U.S.A.*, 166.

20. William Winter, *Life and Art of Edwin Booth* (New York: Macmillan, 1893), 251–52.

21. Ibid., 31, in a footnote quoting Gould's *The Tragedian*.

22. Katherine Goodale, *Behind the Scenes with Edwin Booth* (Boston: Houghton Mifflin, 1931), 231.

23. George R. MacMinn, *The Theatre of the Golden Era in California* (Caldwell, Idaho: Caxton Printers, 1941), 99.

24. Morris, *Curtain Time*, 183, quoting Adam Badeau, a member of the opening-night audience.

25. Hewitt, *Theatre U.S.A.*, 200, quoting L. Clarke Davis from the June 1867 *Atlantic Monthly*.

26. The odd thing about the historical citation of Boucicault is that most sources agree that he sent his road companies out on the *English* road with New York companies of New York hits, and not to the American hinterlands at all. Regardless, he gets the nod as instituting some form of the road company.

27. Edwina Booth Grossman, *Edwin Booth: Recollections by His Daughter* (New York: Benjamin Blom, 1894), 132.

28. Morris, *Curtain Time*, quoting Booth on p. 201.

29. Claire McGlinchee, *The First Decade of the Boston Museum* (Boston: Bruce Humphries, 1940), Introduction.

30. Helene Koon, *How Shakespeare Won the West* (Jefferson, N.C.: McFarland, 1989), 108.

31. McGlinchee, *First Decade*, 63 and generally, for an in-depth look at the Boston Museum.

32. Ibid., 65, quoting Kate Winslow from *Yesterday with Actors*.

33. McGlinchee, *First Decade*, 47, quoting Clement Scott from *The Drama of Yesterday*.

34. McGlinchee, *First Decade*, 84.

35. Hill, "Yankee," 27.

36. Hunt, "The Nashville Theatre," *Birmingham-Southern College Bulletin* (May 1935), quoting the *Southern Methodist*.

37. Mowatt, *Autobiography*, 445.

38. Ibid., 446.

39. Hewitt, *Theatre U.S.A.*, 170.

40. Morris, *Curtain Time*, ch. 2, for a detailed account.

41. This figure, cited in many sourcebooks, is actually a very rough estimate made by William Winter in his memoirs, *Wallet of Time* (see Bibliography). Nonetheless, it is a telling figure.

42. Archie Binns, *Mrs. Fiske and the American Theatre* (New York: Crown Publishers, 1955), 13.

43. Ibid., 309.

44. Hewitt, *Theatre U.S.A.*, 302.

45. Ibid., 268.

46. Binns, *Mrs. Fiske and American Theatre*, 204. The distinguished actress Miss Mary Garden said this of Fiske in *Salvation Nell* (as recorded by Walter Prichard Eaton).

47. Binns, *Mrs. Fiske and American Theatre*, 204. Eaton's own comments on the scene.

48. Norman Hapgood, *The Stage in America* (New York: Macmillan, 1901), 378.

49. Alexander Woollcott, *Mrs. Fiske* (New York: Appleton-Century-Crofts, 1917), 4.

50. Binns, *Mrs. Fiske and American Theatre*, 198.

51. Alfred L. Bernheim, *The Business of the Theatre* (New York: Actors' Equity Association, 1932), 53.

52. Binns, *Mrs. Fiske and American Theatre*, 178–86.

53. Bernheim, *Business*, 75. There was a resurgence in the 1920s, where there were sixty to eighty companies per year. Jack Poggi (see note 54) breaks these same numbers down into more detail to highlight the immediate reduction of companies playing short engagements in small towns. Small-town America lost the road more quickly and more completely than did major metropolitan areas, certainly before 1920. This helps to explain the quick growth of the Little Theatre.

54. Jack Poggi, *Theatre in America* (Ithaca, N.Y.: Cornell University Press, 1968). It is interesting to note the divergence in statistical numbers on theatre in the early 1900s between Poggi and Bernheim; regardless, Poggi lists Bernheim as an especially valuable source, and the usage of numbers in both texts is clear and concise.

55. Binns, *Mrs. Fiske and American Theatre*, 391–93. Binns tells this touching tale with the help of Carlos Drake, the playwright of *Against the Wind*, in which Mrs. Fiske gave her final performances.

56. Bernheim, *Business*, 75–76. Poggi's numbers, from *Billboard*, are 1,564 and 674.

57. Bernheim, *Business*, 88. Poggi notes, though, that construction was extremely active in New York until the end of the 1920s, when it came to an abrupt halt.

58. *The Jazz Singer*, 1928.

59. Bernheim, *Business*, 93–94.

60. Poggi, *Theatre in America*.

61. Bernheim cites several estimates in his chapter on the Little Theatre.

62. Theatre of the Thirties Collection, Special Collections and Archives, George Mason University Library, Fairfax, Va., interview with Maurice Clark, p. 2.

63. Bernheim, *Business*, 99. Note the widely varying estimates by different organizations. Regardless, even the most conservative figures are impressive.

64. Theatre of the Thirties Collection, interview with Maurice Clark.

65. "Unemployed Arts," *Fortune* Magazine (May 1937).

66. Hewitt, *Theatre U.S.A.*, 293.

67. There are different readings of this. The advertisement in the *National Advocate* could have been placed by the theatre, or it might have been a sympathetic plug or a

nastily ironic editorial. Regardless, at least some of the whites who attended behaved poorly and the police closed the theatre.

68. See Errol Hill's *Shakespeare in Sable* (see Bibliography).

69. Allan Morrison, "100 Years of Negro Entertainment," in *Anthology of the American Negro in the Theatre*, Lindsay Patterson, Ed. (New York: Publishers' Company, 1967), 4–5.

70. Sterling A. Brown, "The Federal Theatre," in *Anthology of American Negro in Theatre*, 101.

71. W.E.B. DuBois, *Haiti*. Errol Hill has noted DuBois's long-time determination for blacks to produce theatre with a black identity. In 1915, appointed to the NAACP's Drama Committee, he said, "We should resurrect forgotten ancient Negro art." In 1926, he established the Krigwa Players, whose motto was "About us, by us, for us, and near us." The demand that minority art stand for something more than the art itself—in this case, for the people as a whole—is a compelling and ambiguous twentieth century issue. With *Haiti*, DuBois compromised a bit. In form, the play was a relatively standard American melodrama and a real crowd pleaser.

72. Theatre of the Thirties Collection, interview with Maurice Clark, p. 14.

73. Brown, "Federal Theatre," 107.

74. Nicolas Kanellos, *Hispanic Theatre in the United States* (Houston, Texas: Arte Publico Press, 1984), 7–12.

75. Theatre of the Thirties Collection, interview with Philip Barber.

76. Poggi's *Theatre in America* offers a solid economic and artistic overview of both Off-Broadway and regional theatre in the 1950s and 1960s. Written only a decade later, in 1968, the book achieves an admirable perspective.

The Actor Speaks

Alan Alda

Mary Alice

Philip Bosco

Al Carmines

Pat Carroll

Miriam Kressyn

Marcia Jean Kurtz

Susan Nussbaum

John Randolph

Jason Robards, Jr.

Mercedes Ruehl

B. D. Wong

One

ALAN ALDA

B. New York, 1936. Attended Fordham University (B.S. 1956). Awards: Emmy, *M*A*S*H*, 1974, 1982; Golden Globe, *M*A*S*H*, 1977, 1978; Emmy, writing, 1979.

Q: What were your initial experiences in acting?

ALDA: My first experience was being brought on stage in a burlesque sketch with my father when I was six months old. It was a sketch that was supposed to take place in a schoolroom, and they brought me on in a high chair. It was sort of a gag prop around the burlesque theatre. My father was touring in burlesque for the first three years of my life, so I spent three years in burlesque, watching comics and strippers—it was a very bizarre beginning for a child. An interesting beginning for an actor, because you see the acting process from the ground up. And you see the people that entertain on stage as hardworking people, who have to lug their stuff from town to town. My father carried a pig with him in the back of his car, when he could afford a car. Otherwise we would travel by train. And the pig was just for some gag at the end of one of the sketches. The pig got a little better treatment than I did. They had to make sure they took care of the pig because the pig got a laugh.

Q: Did you have brothers and sisters, too?

ALDA: No, I was an only child. My mother was mentally ill so it was a difficult childhood in a lot of ways. My first interest in the theatre, in performing, came from watching my father, who was known as one of the best straight men in burlesque. I think later, when I saw my father as a success, that was probably a destructively seductive element because when one of your parents is successful in the theatre, you think that it's just a natural process for you to do it, and it was sort of a shock to me to find out that there were eight years where I almost couldn't get a job, from the time I made myself available as an actor until the time I was actually working regularly. But I had a more important foundation which was that I as a child stood in the wings and watched from the side, where you could see both what went into the performance and what was coming out and reaching the audience. It's different from watching from the audience point of view. It's like watching a magician from the wings. Vaudeville was a very different form of entertainment from burlesque. It was less vulgar and more middle of the road. And a little more sophisticated in some ways and stupider in other ways. But the chance to watch the magician from the side was always an image to me of what it was like to stand in the wings and watch an actor. Because you saw where he hid the pigeons and the audience didn't see that. And you saw how he misdirected their attention. And you began to understand the workmanlike factors that went into making a performance. There was inspiration, but there was also craft. And there was even the craft of inspiration. That foundation really kept me going during those eight years when I couldn't get work as a young actor.

Q: Were you also involved in vaudeville with your father, or were you just traveling with him?

ALDA: By the time he was in vaudeville, I was just traveling with him. Although around that time, I started to perform publicly with him. By the time I was nine, I was performing with him at the Hollywood Canteen, which was a place where soldiers and sailors came during the war to be entertained and all the actors and actresses from movies would go in. And then they'd sit down and have a sandwich while the other people would really entertain. And my father and I would do Abbott and Costello sketches and I was Costello and he was Abbott. I was nine years old and I had buck teeth and I was very fat. That was the first time I realized what it was like to stand in the warm glow of the spotlight and be able to control the laughter of two thousand people. And it was a very seductive feeling. It was a tremendous feeling of power.

Q: Were you hooked from then on?

ALDA: Yeah. Up until then I had wanted to be a writer. We had dozens of books of burlesque sketches. Short scenes and blackouts that my father had collected over the years from burlesque. And we used to perform them. Every Sunday night there'd be a lot of his old friends from burlesque who would come over to the house and I would take part in performing from the sketches and he was careful to only let me do sketches that he thought were clean enough for a boy to do. I couldn't tell the clean ones from the dirty ones in those days. It wasn't like the way it is now. Kids were much more innocent then, and so were adults. Even the strippers were more innocent than your average business person today. The sight of those sketches, and to see that all of that humor and all of that laughter could come out of the words that were written. As funny as those people were, they always started with the written word. And I started writing my own sketches when I was about eight and I wanted to be a writer, before I was conscious of wanting to be a performer. Although they had dragged me on stage many times in burlesque. I had to make a conscious decision when I was in my teens and I had to announce to my father that I wanted to be an actor. I was about sixteen.

Q: How did he feel about it?

ALDA: He was dismayed and tried to discourage me and told me that it was a very hard life, and that it took a lot of energy. And I at the age of sixteen could honestly say to him, I had a lot of energy. I didn't realize I was someday going to be fifty-six and it wouldn't be so easy to say that. But I still do have a lot of energy. I think acting gives you energy, but all my life I've been aware of the special energy of actors. I don't know whether it's manic energy or narcissistic energy or just being given the opportunity to play all the time. I mean, what we do is play. But he was right. It did take energy. And it is a hard life, and it's a very discouraging life. And I discourage young people just as he discouraged me. I don't like to step on people's dreams, but if there's anything else you can do, you shouldn't do this because you pay a big price for the pleasure that you get. And the pleasure is intense. The pure sense of play can take place whether you're doing *King Lear* or *Flugel Street*, and sometimes somebody can be so brilliant at *Flugel Street* that it's an experience that far surpasses somebody who's just pretty good doing *Lear*. I'm glad I had that background in a more vulgar form of performing because, around the time I was eighteen, two years after I made this decision to become an actor, I wanted to be a classical actor. I went to college when I was sixteen to Fordham. I started reading the classics. And it was my ambition to play Oedipus. Then when I was twenty-nine and I was already starring on Broadway, by that time I hadn't played Oedipus, and it looked like I never would. On the contrary, I was in a musical trying out in Boston called *The Apple Tree*. It was a high-class show. It was directed by Mike Nichols, and Barbara Harris was in it, and Larry Blyden and me. Nevertheless, here I was, ready to go on stage in one of the scenes playing a caricature of a rock'n'roll singer, and I had tights on and a fright wig and I looked ridiculous with a stupid expression on my face and I started to cry. Just before they wheeled me on stage. Because I realized that I would never play Oedipus, and instead of that, here I am playing a buffoon. From that moment on, something changed for me, because they pulled me onstage. They pulled this sheet off my head, the audience looked at me and laughed and I did my song, and I gave up something in that moment. I gave up a fantasy of being highfalutin' and I settled for what it was in me to do, whatever I could do well. And the paradox is that since then, I have just looked at what was in front of me and eaten what was on my plate and enjoyed it as well as I could. Oddly enough, the paradox is that I have wound up doing more things that I care about than most people get a chance to. I think it has to do with being true to yourself. But to get back to the original question, my father did discourage me and, nevertheless, tried to help me get work. By that time he had a big career in California. When I was seven he was making movies in California. He made a movie called *Rhapsody in Blue*, which was the life of George Gershwin, and he was a very well known movie star.

Q: Did you grow up primarily in California when you weren't traveling with him?

ALDA: I was born in New York and we traveled all over the country in USO shows and nightclub shows and burlesque until I was about six or seven. At seven, we moved to California because he had a term with Warner Brothers, which was really a slave-labor contract. They paid you nothing and they made him a star, but they took all the money and he made a few hundred a week and they were making hundreds of thousands. At seven, I got polio so I had tutors until I went to junior high school. Then when I was in high school, my father did the original production of *Guys and Dolls* in New York. So by the time I was sixteen and ready to make a transition from high school to college, he was a big cheese on Broadway and he encouraged me to go to college. And helped me get a job in summer stock in Barnesville, Pennsylvania, with John Kenly and the Kenly Players. Everybody sort of knew him as the colorful theatre person in town. There was a little theatre in an amusement park and you'd hear the roller coaster and the ferris wheel outside while you were trying to do your lines. As a young apprentice I built the scenery and put it up and took it down, and also got to play good parts with interesting people. I played the long part in *Charley's Aunt*. And some small parts—I acted with Mae West. And I didn't act with him, but I was there in the wings every night watching Buster Keaton do *Merton of the Movies*, although I was too young and ignorant to know who Buster Keaton was at that point.

Q: Did you ever formally train as an actor?

ALDA: No. I wish I had, I always wanted to. I suffered from two problems. One was money. I didn't have any. And the other one was narcissism. I was afraid that if I studied with somebody, that they would take away my natural genius. Most of which I didn't possess, but I did have talent. That was my third problem. I had a lot of talent. And I could get by on raw talent. If I had less talent, I might have been encouraged to see the importance of training. Because with serious training, with industry, you can overcome a lack of talent. But talent will only take you so far and you have to learn the techniques of acting eventually. They include relaxation and knowing yourself and being able to learn to be in touch with your emotions. They go beyond acting class and they often get into a need for some kind of psychotherapy so you can understand who you are. If you don't know who you are, it's very hard to be an actor. I have seen many, many people who didn't start acting until they were past the age of forty who were much better actors than people who started out as actors from the beginning. Because they've had to relate to real people in real life for forty years. Whereas if you spend all of your life making believe most of the time, and basing it only on limited real-life experience, I don't think you have as much to draw on as the person who really lives and *then* acts. Nevertheless of course, it's amazing to see that each generation of young actors that comes up now, for the past ten or fifteen years, it's amazing how able they are, especially compared to how we were when I was a kid. They're more truthful, they're more relaxed. They're more confident.

One of the things my father told me is that if you know it's funny, they'll think it's funny too. What he meant was, the confidence you have inside you commands the stage. You can be as dry as a bone about your acting and never let on that you know it's funny. But way deep down, you know that this is an experience worth going through for the audience. They won't be able to take their eyes off you and they'll go through the experience. Whereas if you come in uncertain, they'll start reading their programs. Training can speed that process up.

Q: I was going to ask you if you had mentors, other than your father.

ALDA: Well, he was my first mentor. He hardly ever said anything to me you could put in words, except he said, "Always find a place where you can sit down because your legs get tired when you're acting." Very practical advice which I put to good use all my life. And secondly, he

said, a simple thing, what you tell an amateur: "Don't wander around
the stage while you're talking. Just stand still and talk." But I would
look for somebody I could learn from in every production. I mainly
learned from watching. I'd watch the other actors acting. I'd watch them
rehearsing. I'd watch how they achieved concentration. And that mysterious thing of how they enter into the imaginary circumstances, how
they believe or appear to believe that they are that person for that
moment.

And I would watch to see how they achieved it. And I talked to them
about it sometimes. As I began to understand it, I would ask about it. I
would read what other people had written. I read Stanislavski in my
twenties. And I read Michael Chekhov, all of the books about acting at
that time that were very interesting. But because I didn't have some
basic skills, I didn't understand some of the things that they were saying.
I understood them intellectually but I couldn't achieve them. The only
other thing I did that was like training was for about six months I worked
with Paul Sills, doing theatre games which were of course invented by
his mother, Viola Spolin. At that time, nobody was doing it but a few
of us. And it was an extremely important part of my development as an
actor because it was very liberating. It was during those eight years that
I was having trouble getting work, in the early '60s. I was around
twenty-three or twenty-four years old. And I auditioned and got a job
in an improvisational cabaret. The kind of improvising we did in the
first half of the show, we did sketches we had developed from
improvisations in rehearsal. The second half of the show was completely improvised on the spot. The kind of improvising we did was
what I call "guts improvising," where they just shove you out on stage
and you sort of make it up as you go along. You write on your feet. Then
when that season was over, I was back in New York. I managed to get
into a workshop with Paul Sills and we started to do theatre games,
which has nothing to do with making it up, or making up what you say
or writing on your feet. It has to do with establishing the connection
with the other actors and getting your mind off of what you're saying
by virtue of sticking to the rules of each theatre game that you're
playing. And that frees a part of your brain and stuff comes out of you,
both verbal and physical, that you didn't know was in there. And
brilliant things happen, but you have to learn the skill and you have to
learn the discipline of how these games are played. I recommend that
to everybody. I also recommend conventional acting classes of the kind
I was never able to take. A couple of times, I almost decided to work
my way through acting school and then was kept back from it by this

timidity that I was going to be overwhelmed by it. But I also had a family to support. We had three children very early. I married at the age of about twenty-one.

Q: You said when you first started out your dad opened some doors for you and helped you out. Was that an advantage?

ALDA: Yeah, it was an advantage. He was only really able to open the door for me three or four times. One was to get me a job as an apprentice. The next time was when I was twenty-one and we were just married, he got me a job playing a small part in a play he was doing on tour in summer stock. I turned out to be very good in the play. Just on raw talent. But because I didn't have any skill, the producer was dismayed when he saw me read for the part. I saw him put his head in his hands. I thought, "Gee, I wonder if he has a headache." I was so unsophisticated. I thought to myself, "Does he really think I'm that bad?" Because I knew I'd be good in it. I just couldn't do it from the paper, but when I could get up on the stage, I knew I'd be good and I was good. It was a good part for me, and I stood out in it, and it was a good beginning. It helped build my confidence, but I still was unskilled. A few years later when I couldn't get work as an actor except maybe one or two small television parts a year, my father was working in Rome and he got me a job in a play with him doing an English-speaking production in Rome of *Three Men on a Horse*. And later we did a murder mystery there. But those are pretty much the only jobs he got me. Later on, when I was doing *M*A*S*H*, I got him a couple of jobs on *M*A*S*H*.

Q: You started working in your twenties. How did your career start developing then? Was there a big turning point or some big break that came for you?

ALDA: It never seemed to be a big break. I started out while I was still in college as an understudy in a play that Sam Levine directed and the play closed the first night on Broadway, I think. I was able to go out of town with the play and come back and have the play close all during my Christmas break so I didn't miss any of my senior year of college. My junior year of college I spent in Europe, Paris, and while I was there, I went and did one of the plays with my father. And then one of the other plays I did in Rome was later on after I was married. But after I was married at the age of twenty-one, I went to New York and started looking for work. It was very difficult but at least you could go to agents' offices and introduce yourself and somebody would talk to you in many cases. It was called "making rounds," and you went around to the offices. And it was sort of an exercise in frustration because it was the only thing you could do. You would send your pictures out. You would read the trade papers and see who was casting but you'd never get an answer from sending out your picture. I did once. Somebody was advertising for writers, directors, and actors and I answered as all three and sent them some sketches because they were doing an Off-Broadway review. I was about twenty-four. And I wound up acting in this awful thing and directing it and writing some of the sketches. It was a really terrible production. I had worked with Phil Silvers in burlesque when I was six months old. He remembered me fondly and he told his casting director to try to see if there was something I could do. I think I was an extra a couple of times on the show and then once I played a really good part. And I saw it a year or so ago. I went over with my middle daughter, Elizabeth, and we looked at the program at the Museum of Broadcasting. And when I compare that performance to twenty-one-year-old actors today, it's just amazing the difference that I see. And I think that one of the differences is the pervasiveness of training now. There's also a different sensibility that everybody has. People are a little bit more in touch with themselves now and I see that young parents are more aware of the development of their children than parents were when we were kids. And certainly more so than when my parents were kids. You can see it in the acting styles, too. You can see it when you listen to people interviewed. If you listen to an interview from the '50s, people are still talking for posterity or something. Or they're making a recitation. And if you listen to people talking back in the '30s, it's even worse, where they actually assume a kind of phony British accent. People are getting more simple and direct and natural and honest. There's a lot less bullshit. A young actor can hold his or her own against a seasoned actor now, much better than he could twenty or thirty years ago.

When I was twenty-five or so, we went to Cleveland, to the Cleveland Playhouse, because I still wanted to be a classical actor and they did Shakespeare there and I thought that I'd get a chance to train. But they kept putting me in Broadway comedies because I had this comedy skill. And I was very frustrated. We had our first child there and I realized we were only making sixty dollars a week and if we had any more children, I wouldn't be able to afford even a car trip out of there, and we were going to be there the rest of our lives, as many people were. Many people were there for forty years. So we left at the end of the first year. It was on a grant from the Ford Foundation, which was just beginning at that time with a series of grants to strengthen regional theatre around the country. Now, regional theatre is pretty much the equal to Broadway, if not its superior—because so many interesting productions are generated in regional theatre now and not on Broadway, where they can only do what's safe and claptrap, by and large.

Q: Do you still write?

ALDA: Yeah. I'm as much a writer, I think, as an actor. They're very similar processes, too. I'm always disappointed when I see writers and actors express a rivalry toward each other. And it's very common. In the beginning, before you get into rehearsals, the actors are always expressing the belief that this is the best piece of material they've ever read. How glad they are to be doing it. And the writers are always delighted that these great actors are going to be doing their stuff and bringing it to life. After you get into rehearsal, the writers are saying, "Have that actor killed if he can't say my words right." And the actors are saying, "Who wrote this shit?" And they both start to forget that the process is almost identical in both fields. You have to work from yourself. You have to use a sense of truth. You have to find character. You have to find out what the characteristic traits are and how they express themselves in action. Both writers and actors have to follow the rules in Aristotle's *Poetics* of dramatic action. Character is expressed through dramatic action, which is determined by what the character wants to achieve. And it's the attempt to achieve that against the obstacles placed in their path by the antagonist that creates a play. And that leads to the audience's identification.

That attempt to achieve is what both actors and writers are trying to make happen. The problem occurs very often in that writers don't know what actors have to go through to make the part their own. Because the writer has already gone through that process and forgets that it took him or her a couple of years to find who the character was. Now it's so second nature that they think an actor should just be able to come in the door and put it on like an overcoat. Whereas the actor has to go through the same process that the writer did of searching it out and finding a way to make it connect to one's own life, and inner life. And the actors resent in a way having been given all this by the writer out of whole cloth and not being able to be part of the discovery. The biggest problem is expository writing. You're required to say things that don't serve your character's effort to achieve anything, but serve the author's effort to get the audience to know what the back story is.

Q: Are there people that you go to or whose opinions you respect for criticism of your work now?

ALDA: Only my wife. She's grown up with me. We were married when I was twenty-one and she was twenty-four. And she was a musician when we started. She's now a photographer. But she's been an artist of one kind or another all her life. Our taste has developed together and she's watched my development. She knows when I'm faking and she knows what my problems are. She can read my thoughts when I'm onstage. And she can say anything to me about my performance. Whereas my nose might be out of joint if even a director would say the same thing to me, sometimes. Because I don't trust that he's either got my best interests at heart or really knows what I'm going through. If somebody gives you a piece of advice about your performance but they don't know why you're doing what you're doing, they can get you to do something even more fraudulent than you're now doing. Which is not helpful. It just feels uncomfortable.

Q: What about professional critics? Do you read your reviews?

ALDA: I don't read them because they're too painful for me. The reason you need to have confidence when you're acting, and a lot of nerve, is that you probably wouldn't be acting if you weren't extremely self-doubtful. And in need of encouragement and in need of attention. I mean, we crave attention. I didn't want to believe that when I was a young actor. The older I get, the more I'm able to be honest about myself. And the more I see other actors, the more I think it's pretty much a given that we exhibit ourselves partly because we want people to love us. The effort that it takes to act, the turning yourself inside out, the pain it takes, the rejection you face when you're not allowed to act, day after day by people who just think you're too short or too ugly or too Jewish or too Italian, all these reasons they have for not letting you act. When you finally do act you work night and day. And you hardly get any money for it in most cases. It's a very generous thing because what you wind up doing is making yourself naked, up there on the stage. For people's enjoyment, people's pleasure, people's delight. And thank God that something brings them on that stage because if all they faced was the unhappiness that it takes to get there, we'd never have any shows of any kind. You asked me about critics. Critics I find very tough to get anything positive out of. I hate to get praised for my personality, especially now that they've decided I'm a nice guy. I'm an ordinary person. As far as I'm concerned, I'm sort of a decent person. Now that, along with becoming successful, I also got to be known as Mr. Nice Guy, it's a real pain in the ass. So if I do a performance where I really act my heart out and I struggle to give a good performance and they say, well, yeah, you know, he's good in this part because he's so nice he suits the part. It's as though I just walked in off the street and covered them with the slime of my amiability. And that's my only contribution. So that doesn't help me. Nor did it help me when Pauline Kael in some review of a movie—I think it was *Same Time Next Year*—just put me away. She compared me in other performances favorably to Laurence Olivier, Robert De Niro, and Cary Grant and then said I was stupefyingly awful in *Same Time Next Year*. Well, I felt so horrible by her lifting me up and slamming me down like that, that it was difficult for me to drive my car for a couple of months. Because I'd get so distracted I'd have to pull over to the side of the road. I guess I so much needed approval that I stopped reading reviews. But it can distract you. If you're doing a performance every night, if they say, "Oh, there's that great moment he does in the second act," then every time you get to that moment, you're going to think, oh, here comes that moment again. I don't like judgments. It's very tough. I think I must be a very judgmental person myself. I had a very tough childhood with my mother. I guess I'm basically a fragile person although I talk about confidence a lot and stuff. I take genuine pleasure in the experience of the contact with the audience. I don't think of them as judging me. I think of us all as being in the same room together, experiencing this story together. And that gives me a lot of pleasure.

Q: Are there certain periods of work or pieces of work that you've done that you are more proud of than others, or really stand out for you?

ALDA: Oh, yeah, I cringe at some things I see on *M*A*S*H* and I got a lot of praise for that. And some things I think, ah, there, fine. I connected with it. It all has to do with your development, with looking to get better and simpler and shed distractions and get down to the real work, and that's why training is so important, because it helps accelerate that process. I'd have been a better actor sooner, I think, if I had trained. I can remember the moments on the soundstage at *M*A*S*H*, or in theatres where I finally achieved a thing that I had been wanting to do all my life as an actor. I expect that development will go on for the rest of my professional life.

Q: What was it like after doing so much TV and film, doing stage work?

ALDA: Well, I started on the stage. I did a play in London, *Our Town*, the season before I did *Jake's Women*. And that was the first time I was acting on the stage in about twenty-five years. I was a little nervous in London. A couple of times I noticed I was terrified. But it really was where I came from. I always was more comfortable on the stage than I was in front of the camera. And even though I love the moviemaking process, I felt more comfortable on the stage. The hard thing for me making the transition in movies was the necessity of having to just do two lines at a time sometimes. A few seconds of a part and not have the whole play carry you along. It takes a separate kind of a skill to do that, and it's one I had to develop.

Q: I know one question we kind of passed a little earlier was about money. What was that like in your career—?

ALDA: Well, I didn't have any. Now I have a lot of it. But when I didn't have any, it was hard because I had to act in whatever was available. Whatever I could get. It wouldn't matter how crummy it was. And that made me feel bad sometimes. Because I didn't want to be in lousy productions. I wanted to do parts that would help me grow. But I decided that it was important for a young actor to act in anything and everything, and I still think that's true. You shouldn't be too choosy when you're starting out. You should always shoot for the most interesting parts and try to get them, but if you can't get a great part, you should get a good part. If you can't get a good part, you should take a crappy part. I mean, you should just act, just keep doing it. Because I really think it's true that it's how you do it, and not what you're doing, that is the deliciousness of the art of acting.

Q: How much control have you been able to have in your career throughout its span?

ALDA: An amazing amount of control. It surprises me how much I've had, and it also interests me that I have no control. I mean, I don't think actors have much control. That's one of the reasons that we turn to alcohol and other drugs, I think, from time to time, because you're really out of control as an actor. It's one of the reasons why, instead of turning to alcohol, I turn to writing in a serious way—so I can have more control over my life. If people wouldn't give me a part, I could at least write myself a part. The trouble is, I couldn't write myself as good a part as I could write for other people. The problem that an actor has is that you wait for the phone to ring before they'll let you act. And then they tell you what to wear, where to stand, and how to say it. I would make these rounds, trying to put some element of control in my life as a young actor. It hardly led to any jobs. You mainly wait. And it's worse now for young actors, because you're waiting for a high-priced agent to tell you if they think you should exist or not. And you can't go see anybody and say, "Please, is there anything available today?" They don't want to talk to you. But what young people should know, as they're going into this, is that it's not true that there is some magical line you cross when everything becomes okay. The problems that you have now you will have all your life in different, subtler, more sophisticated ways. I mean it's an old joke that Cary Grant would feel, after finishing every movie, that he'd probably never work again. That insecurity that an actor has is inbred. I have that and I think most actors have it. Very few people don't get anxious and think, I wonder if my career is over. I wonder if somebody will call me. Because unless you're an actor-manager, or an actor-writer-director, you're not creating your own situations. There's a tremendous amount of passivity built into the role of the actor which is detrimental to the actor's development as a human being. And leads very often to our behaving like the children that we're accused of being. And then when we do that, we're reinforced in that behavior—because once an actor gets a few feet of film shot on him, then he can start making outrageous demands because it's too expensive to fire him especially if he's getting some money. They say, "Well, they're crazy actors. Don't make waves. Let's give them what they want, then we'll get the thing shot." So your worst behavior is reinforced and our worst behavior has its roots in the infantile position you're put in to start with, by virtue of the way the business works. You're not ever considered one of the intelligent elements in it. The producer, the director, the writer—those are the grownups. The actors are children, and you're infantilized by the system all the way on. And it's not good for them, and it's not good for the business. Not good for art. It doesn't make better productions. It really ruins some productions. So I think actors ought to know what they have to face. That this lack of control that they're facing is a very tough problem, but one not best solved by getting more passive and more childish.

Q: What kind of roles do you want to play now?

ALDA: I always wanted to be able to play parts that express the lives of real people. I'm a little bit fighting my image as this nice guy, which I developed both because of the character I played on *M*A*S*H* and the fact that I got very active trying to sell the Equal Rights Amendment to state legislatures for about ten years. So I really was Mr. Smith going to Washington in a lot of people's minds. The combination of who I seemed to be as a person and who I seemed to be in some of the parts I played just sort of pigeonholed me a little bit. I think, for a while I ought to play real bastards to sort of eradicate some of that and get a broader scope in people's minds. I have seen so many people destroyed by the deeply held belief that as soon as they were successful, all their problems would be solved. It doesn't make you more sexually attractive. It doesn't make you better able to get along with your wife or your husband. It doesn't make you a better father. It doesn't make you a better friend. It doesn't make you a more interesting person. And when they ask you how to solve the problems of the world, it's a big mistake—and one that I've made a few times—where you think that you'll help by giving them the answer to how to solve the problems of the world. It doesn't make you smarter to be successful as an actor. When you're frustrated and not successful, you're working really hard and the work keeps you busy. Then when you get successful, and you realize that nothing has changed, you're still the same schlepper you were before. It can be depressing.

Q: Was it ever hard to balance working a lot with having a personal life?

ALDA: It was hard and it is hard. But I think maybe as I'm getting older now, I'm finally able to have more perspective about it. I went through so many years when I didn't work at all, or worked so infrequently, that I was really hungry to work. After I got very very successful doing *M*A*S*H*, I pretty much said yes to everything that came my way. I think the frustration then was, oh, I can't do three things at once. Actually, I *was* often doing three things at once. But I couldn't do eight things at once and that was frustrating. But I said yes to so many things that I was working all the time and wearing myself out and spreading myself too thin.

Q: Are any of your children involved in acting?

ALDA: Two of them wanted to be and I gave them the same advice my father gave me. Tried to get them not to. And then I did what my father did and I wrote them parts in a movie. They were in *The Four Seasons*. And then I wrote them parts in the television series version of that, which lasted about thirteen weeks and nearly killed me. It was during that time that I turned down being in *The Killing Fields*, doing the part that Sam Waterston played, because I had committed to do this television series. It was a difficult year. My father was dying that year. My mother was dying. And I was running from hospital to hospital and then getting in a limo and writing jokes for this television series that was not working. I was trying to do in a half an hour and on a four- or five-day shooting schedule what we had done in the movie. But I wasn't directing it. The actors didn't know what it was all about. It was a very discouraging situation and it was a failure. My parents died and I didn't do that other movie, but when I look back on it, it was probably one of the most important years of my life because it did me much more good to be with my parents and nurse them through the last year or two of their lives. And to work with my children and to devote time to them and to learn how to write, stay up all night writing and try to make it work. Try to get actors to act, and directors to direct, and other writers to write. It was a lesson that was very valuable to me.

Q: How do you feel about awards?

ALDA: I think they're silly. But as long as they're giving them out, I'll take as many as they've got. It's always tricky when I'm getting an award from a group of critics. I thank them and I usually make some crack about criticism.

Q: What advice do you give to younger actors?

ALDA: I tell them that it takes about fifteen years, maybe more. You do a workmanlike job in less time if you've got some training, which I also recommend. The first thing I recommend is training. With good people. You know, there's a tendency for an actor—just as there is for an ordinary civilian—to say about their dentist, they're the greatest dentist in the world, because once you've entrusted your mouth to somebody, you want to believe they're great. You want to believe that they're the best and you want to believe your *acting* teacher is the best. And I think that young actors have to do good research to find out why these people that they hear recommended are supposed to be good. I recommend getting to know yourself well, and that may include therapy. I recommend getting to know how to do something other than acting so that you can support yourself during those times that it will fall to pieces. And there will be times, even after you're somewhat successful as an actor, when you won't find work. And you almost surely will not be as lucky as I was to have made a lot of money during the time that will tide you over. You've got to know something else. The trick is to be able to survive. Survival is the most important thing actors can do, whether they're just beginning, whether they're beginning to succeed, or whether they're beginning to fade. You've got to be able to survive. And that has to do with mental health and mental stamina and nerve and confidence, resilience, but it also—for most people—has to do with money. Has to do with being able to get money to tide you over. And you got to use your brains for that. You've got to prepare for that. Don't just think it's going to happen. The world, especially these days, is a lot tougher than when I was a kid. You could live on the fringes of art and survive as a part-time waiter. I was a doorman, a cabdriver. I sold mutual funds. I colored baby pictures. I was a clown at the opening of gas stations and chicken-part stores. I did a lot of things. And I also collected a lot of unemployment insurance. It's not easy to live like that now. There isn't a lot of money laying around now. During the '80s there was; now for the next few years, there won't be. You've got to sit down and figure out, in a calculated way, what can you study? What can you learn to do that will give you an income when you can't get income as an actor? And you have to be able to find something that you can do that won't be interfered with when you go to an audition or you take a job, but that you can come back to. I think there's an awful lot acting schools don't tell you about day-to-day survival. I suppose there are people that teach you how to audition. Auditioning is not acting. It's not what you do when you get the part. It's not the same as finding your character and really finding what the values are in the scene itself. And fitting that in with the whole rest of the story. I could look terrific in an audition, but then I had to learn how to act.

Q: Do you still get excited in every role that you're playing? Do you still get that rush when you're starting something new?

ALDA: Yeah, I do. And I'm glad to see that I also say to myself, "How the hell am I going to do this?" I think when you say to yourself, "Oh, yeah, this is that character that I do. I'll do that and I'll give it a little of this and I'll give it a little of that," you might as well be dead. Or you really should be working for the post office at that point. It's when you don't really know how you're going to accomplish something, then you're approaching it like an artist because then you're looking for something unknown. You're trying to discover unknown territory. And that will be creative.

Two

MARY ALICE

B. Indianola, Miss. Attended Chicago Teachers College (B.Ed.). Trained for stage with Lloyd Richards at Negro Ensemble Company. Awards: Tony, Drama Desk Award, *Fences*, 1987; Obie, *Julius Caesar* and *Nongogo*, 1979; Emmy, *I'll Fly Away*, 1993.

Q: I want to start with your very earliest recollections about acting. Do you remember your initial experiences?

ALICE: Well, I don't think of my earliest experiences in terms of acting, but as I look back on it I spent a lot of time alone. I'm the youngest of five children. I grew up in Chicago. My mother and father were both from the South. My father was born in Birmingham, Alabama. My mother was born in Indianola, Mississippi, where I was born—in Indianola. But at about two months my mother and father moved to Chicago so that's where I grew up. I had identical twin sisters who were the oldest children. And then a brother and then another brother and then myself. I suppose that's where the seeds were planted because I spent a lot of time, I remember, alone imagining all kinds of situations that I was in or that my family was in. I did all of my formal education in Chicago. And went to Chicago Teachers College and became a teacher. During my college years I did get involved in what was really a speech class and every now and then we would do skits or improvisations. But I really didn't think consciously of becoming an actor until much much later. But during the time I was teaching, I became involved in what would be comparable to Off-Off-Broadway theatre, in Chicago. I was teaching during the day and doing what was then called "amateur theatre," rehearsing in the evenings, performing on the weekends. And in 1966 I met someone who was very important to me actually finally becoming an actor: Douglas Turner Ward, who founded the Negro Ensemble Company here [New York] in 1967. In 1966 he brought two plays that he had written—*Day of Absence* and *Happy Ending*—to Chicago. Actors' Equity Association, which is the stage union for actors and stage managers, required that the New York company that was performing in Chicago hire a local person. I was the local person. I had to do several small roles in both plays and I was paid twenty dollars a week and I had to do the laundry twice a week. I was responsible for cleaning the costumes. That's approximately twenty-five years ago—it was probably the happiest time of my career as an actor because there was no pressure and there was no real responsibility in terms of pursuing a career. It was a hobby and I did it quite joyfully.

Anyway, in 1966, as I was saying, I was working with Douglas Turner Ward and he told me that he was going to form a company, and if I ever came to New York to look him up. And about seven months later I was in New York. I had been a teacher and I moved to New York in July of 1967. I called Douglas Turner Ward and he invited me to come and audition for the company. Fortunately, he did not put me in the company. I say, fortunately, because he put me in a class that was being taught by someone who I think of as being the most important person as far as me becoming an actor, really. I mean, really becoming an actor in the full sense of the word, pursuing a career and continuing for all of these years. And that's Lloyd Richards.

Q: You've worked with him quite a lot.

ALICE: Well, I've worked with him in different capacities. He's only directed me in one play over a two-year period. But he is the artistic director, as you know, of the Eugene O'Neill Theatre Center, and I've gone up there for the playwrights' conferences since 1968. And I've worked at the Yale Rep when he was the artistic director. And in so many ways, Lloyd is very important to me. First of all, he's the one who "taught" me. (I say "taught" with quotation marks around them because I don't really believe that acting can be taught.) He helped me to develop a craft through which I could act and create different characters. And that has been the foundation for my career because it has given me—more than anything else—strength and support to pursue this profession.

Q: I want to go back just a little bit before we jump ahead to the present part of your career. You said—when you were growing up—that you did a lot of imagining and fantasizing because you were the youngest. What did your family feel about this? Or about your interest later in acting?

ALICE: When I was very young, they didn't know what I was doing when I was alone. I never shared that with anyone. I won't go too much into my family, but because of the situation in my family life I was not, I would say, satisfied. So what I would do was to create situations that my family could be in that would make everybody much happier. I created situations in the home and outside of the home, places that I would go to, people that I could be other than being where I was and who I was.

Q: How did they feel about your getting into the theatre?

ALICE: I still don't know how they feel. I don't know if they quite understand what I do or why I chose to do this. Because I find that the average person does not really quite understand. I mean, average people enjoy what we do—and those of us who are more visible, they see us as stars, and see all of the fringe benefits that actors acquire: money and fame and travel and all of that. But I don't really know if they quite understand why a person becomes an actor. It seems like such an unimportant thing and it is such an insecure thing. As I'm talking now I am remembering something my mother did not quite understand: why I gave up teaching. That was a so-called secure job. I taught all the subjects—third and fourth grade. Eight- and nine-year-old boys and girls. And she didn't understand, I'm sure, me moving away from home. I am the only one of her children who actually moved away from home and did not go back to live. I've never gone back except to visit. Once my father and brother were discussing something that I did for PBS, one of the first things that I did for television after moving to New York. My father was saying, "That's my baby," and blah-blah-blah. I'm sure he was very proud of me. But my brother was very perceptive about the relationship of my work to my family and he said, "Well—she is us. When we see her—that's us!" It was very true because especially in the beginning of my career, I drew a lot on my feelings about my family and a lot of the pain that was in the family went into my work. So that's how my brother related to it. And I suppose on one level, they were very proud of me because, like I said, the average person thinks of an actor on television or in films as being very different from themselves.

Q: Were any other family members involved in any other art form in any way?

ALICE: I would say I'm the only one of my family that I know of and this includes maybe three generations, including my generation.

Q: Were there any other art forms that influenced you when you were
    growing up, or in school?
ALICE: I remember going to the movies a lot, and I remember going to
    see dance concerts. I didn't really see a lot of theatre, though, when I
    was very young. I didn't do my first play until after I was teaching. My
    first play was an all-black production of *Cat on a Hot Tin Roof* by
    Tennessee Williams, and I was teaching at the time. It was in 1962!
    I was teaching in downtown Chicago, and I was downtown with a friend
    of mine doing some shopping and someone handed me a flyer asking
    people to audition for an amateur production of *Raisin in the Sun*. I took
    one of the flyers and I thought about it and I said, "Oh this might be
    fun." But I had to go into the hospital and I had an operation. I really
    kind of forgot about it but I kept the flyer for some reason, and while I
    was convalescing I saw the flyer and I called. By then this group of
    people was in rehearsal, but the young lady who had been cast to play
    Ruth in *Raisin in the Sun* was in New York on vacation and they weren't
    sure she was going to be back in time to open the play. So they invited
    me to come in. I went in after school one day and auditioned and I got
    the role! I got the role and they told me to take the script and go home
    and work on the lines and come back the next night for rehearsal. I was
    very nervous and very frightened of thinking of myself on stage and
    saying all of these lines. I think the thing that frightened me most was
    thinking, "Can I remember all of those lines?" I went to the rehearsal
    the following evening and I returned the script. I said, "I can't do this."
    Fortunately, I stayed with the group as the secretary. I didn't do *Raisin
    in the Sun* until 1983 at Yale! And the people I got involved with during
    that time were really the people who are responsible for me even
    thinking about becoming an actor, in any serious way. This is the reason
    why I really went to New York because two of these people went to
    New York. They were very involved in the theatre. They had gone
    to school and one had gone to Goodman [Theatre Drama School] and
    they were very serious about their careers. And very early on, they saw
    in me something that I didn't even know. They said, "You can act!"
    This was before I had any training so I didn't even know the language.
    But they had a lot of confidence in me and they were the reason that I
    decided to move to New York.
Q: Since you started, as you said, as a hobby, when did you really decide
    to become an actor and how did you know?
ALICE: Well, I liked it from the beginning. Going back to my childhood,
    I always liked being in different situations other than the one I was in.
    So when I started doing it in Chicago it was fun! It was fun! It was

exciting! I could escape. The people I associated with in this group were very stimulating. Then, after I moved to New York, I still liked it and I got caught up in it by calling Douglas Turner Ward and being placed in Lloyd's class. He was such a fine teacher and I met new people. I got a job shortly thereafter, an Off-Broadway play written by Wole Soyinka, two one-act plays: *The Trials of Brother Jero* and *The Strong Breed*. I think this was while Mr. Soyinka was in jail in Nigeria. Things happened very very fast. And I was continually meeting people—writers, directors, actors—and then I was able to join the union about six months after I came. And I worked. Even after I moved here, I took the teaching test here and I got my substitute license. In the back of my mind, I had really planned on teaching here, you know, and just continuing doing this as a hobby. Of course, when I moved to New York, I didn't realize that it was a multimillion-dollar business here! Compared to in Chicago, you know—the Goodman and maybe the out-of-town plays that came to the commercial houses. But for the most part, it was community theatre twenty-five years ago. And the Hull House Theatre was very prominent then. Of course, now they have several very, very commercial houses there.

But when I came to New York it was overwhelming—and of course, then there was the city. I had been to New York in '65 for one week on a theatre tour where you come and you stay in Midtown. And we saw theatre. I saw *Golden Boy*. I saw *Tartuffe*. We went to the theatre practically every night and I really fell in love with New York, but this was two years before I actually moved here. But when I came here in '67 to *live*, it was really a very special kind of time in terms of the country. There was the hippie movement. There was the civil rights movement. There was so much activity here. The city combined with the theatre was so exciting to me and yet I still hadn't thought consciously of making a commitment. Consciously I think I made a commitment in 1979, which was twelve years later, which was when I really felt that I was an actor.

Q: What happened at that time?

ALICE: 1979 was a very difficult year for me emotionally. I remember winning an Obie for a play that I did at the New York Shakespeare Festival, *Julius Caesar*, and a play that I did at the Manhattan Theatre Club called *Nongogo*. It was really my first major award for my work and I looked at this and I thought, "Now what does this mean?" At the same time I'm going through a very difficult time personally. So I had to question, "What does this mean, this plaque?" And I thought to myself, "I guess it really is—not only for these two plays, but for me it has to mean for the body of work that I've done which led up to these two plays and this award." So I really began to accept myself as being an actor at that time.

Q: You've mentioned—when you first came to New York—several people who were really influential, particularly Lloyd Richards as a teacher. Can you tell me a little about how you would describe your technique of what you learned from Mr. Richards?

ALICE: What I got from Lloyd really could be boiled down to two words: knowing thyself. What an actor has is himself or herself: the body, the mind, the imagination, the psyche, the voice—whatever makes up me. This is the instrument and learning how to use this is very important. It's related to knowing oneself—who I really am, how I really think, how I really feel, being very honest in my life so that I can be very honest in my work. How can I bring truth to a character that is written by someone else? How can I tell that person's story if I don't know my own?

Basically, what he did was help me to start that journey so that in my work I could present that. And it was very difficult at first—it had been easy in Chicago. He taught me to do my job and so I'm very proud to be able to say that I do my job. A few years ago I was honored to present him an award at Gracie Mansion. The mayor was presenting some awards to certain artists. It was after I had left *Fences* and I remember standing up there and being so full and I started crying! I couldn't help myself. I was so full and I apologized to him. My memory went back to 1967. I mean, I cannot think of my career without Lloyd being a major part of it. That's what I was saying. And as I said this to him and about him, I just had to stop, and somebody handed me a Kleenex. I finally got through it. They were tears of joy. I mean, all the wonderful memories that I have of this man. He is so very special to me.

Q: We talked about your career up until '79 when you won the Obie. And you've been mentioning *Fences*. Can you tell me a little more about how your career has progressed?

ALICE: I would say that I'm very fortunate. In a way, I'm very glad that my career has gone the way it's gone because my work has helped to shape me, which has helped to shape my work. I see a circle—because the more I work, the more I get to know myself, I think, and put that into my work and then do my work, I'm able to learn something that helps me as an individual. So it's all, for me, just a constant cycle. That, of course, has strengthened me to go forward in this. Because it's been, in some cases, very difficult. And one of the reasons it has been difficult is that I am a black woman and there is less work for nonwhite actors and, of course, there is less work for women. And then, therefore, there's less work for nonwhite women. And then as you get older there's less work for older actresses—I mean, really good roles worth doing. And then, of course, there's less work for nonwhite actors, especially for middle-aged black actresses. There is the additional problem of the image of being offered roles that have to do with being housekeepers or maids—nurturers, not only to white people but nurturers in terms of people in general. And recently, I've had to have constant discussions with my agent about this.

Q: So you don't feel it's getting any better?

ALICE: Not really. There are exceptions of younger black actresses who are given opportunities to play interesting characters. But still they don't work as much. So the work is difficult to come by for most actors, but especially for nonwhite actors because 85 percent of actors are always unemployed anyway. But I must say that I've been lucky—I still work. I think the key for me has been that when I first arrived in New York those first five years, I just did everything. It seems now that there were theatres below the subway system, where everybody had to dress in one little room and it was cold. I remember one time my friend calling me the "Showcase Queen" because I was doing maybe two shows at one time. And I was just working, working, working. No money really. Fortunately, I had savings from teaching so I could afford to do those things. Thank God that I did it, because I grew as an actor so I was able to strengthen my craft and then more and more people saw me. But I've become more selective in what I do now compared to in the beginning.

Q: How do you see yourself being cast now? Or how, most often, do you get cast?

ALICE: Most of the time I'm cast as nurturers: the dorm mother. I'm getting ready to do a series now. I'm the mother. But I want to do this series because it's a very interesting series from HBO and they do good things. Unlike if this were a series for the networks, I would have to be very very cautious about accepting it. But I think it's going to be a good experience. It's a well-written series so I'm looking forward to doing it. And the character is interesting. There are moments when we see "the woman" instead of just "the mother" or "the wife." But most of the roles, I know, are going to be nurturers—mothers primarily, I guess. But I don't mind doing them as long as they're interesting.

Q: Do you still consider, occasionally, giving up theatre?

ALICE: Not really giving it up, but just knowing that when I'm not able to function 100 percent—if I can't remember lines—that will be a sign to me that maybe I'd better start thinking about really deciding about leaving it then. I came with a lot of energy into this profession. When I leave—finally leave it—if I leave it other than dropping dead or getting sick, I want to make the choice to leave it at a time that I feel I can leave it and still have my own good feelings about being an actor. I don't know. I think of myself as being in the process of leaving it now. Even though I'm not really doing anything, you know, to stop my career, in a way I probably am not going up for everything that my agent wants me to go up for. I'm very clear about what I want to do. Sometimes I think when I go in and I may voice my opinions about a character, these people do not want the actor to say things like I say. And I don't want to work for people who limit me and think that I should do those roles. If they do not give me a job because I'm voicing an opinion, those people are really not people that I wish to work for because they're indicating their image of black women to me. These are people that I do not even wish to use my creativity with in their projects.

Q: It sounds like you exert quite a bit of control over your career.

ALICE: Oh, I have to. And I didn't in the beginning. I didn't consciously do this in the beginning because I think—like most actors—I was intimidated by my agent, thinking that they wouldn't love me and send me out on things. They wouldn't want to represent me. And, of course, I didn't do it with the people that I went in to see—the producers and the directors and the casting directors—because then you're afraid they won't love you and won't approve of you and call you in. So there's a lot of fear attached to being an actor. In the past three or four years, I've been very assertive with my career and very selective in terms of what I want to do and what I don't want to do. Fortunately, I can afford to do this so I do not in any way judge actors who may take a job because they need the money, or they haven't worked, or they don't have the visibility. I understand that they have to continue on their journey as I am doing. I only speak for myself. But I do encourage other actors to do this as soon as possible. There's nothing that I have done in my career that I'm ashamed of, that—given that time and that place—that I wouldn't do again. I've always insisted on excellence in my work, and honesty and clarity, and I've been becoming who I am all along.

Q: What has your relationship been to money throughout your career?

ALICE: I didn't start making money until 1987—I mean, real money— until *Fences*. That was my first year of making really very good money. So the first twenty years, I always made money and then, when I wasn't working, I had enough weeks for unemployment. I always had savings. I mean, I've always had money and a little savings—so even though I was talking about the school that I worked at in '72 and '73, it wasn't primarily because of money. It was primarily because work was so slow and I was tired of sitting around the house and I wanted to do something that I took the teaching job. But I haven't had to do what actors call a nine-to-five because I can't pay my rent. I've never really been broke as an actor, knock on wood.

Q: Weren't you nominated for a Tony?

ALICE: I won a Tony for *Fences*.

Q: Did that change your career much?

ALICE: Oh yeah! Winning a Tony was very, very good. I think that's why I got the series *A Different World*. But when you win a Tony on Broadway for a play—and especially a good play, in a good role—it really sort of puts a stamp of approval that you are an actor! So offers come to you. I guess, since that time I think half of the work that I've done in the past five years has come as a result of the Tony. I still audition, though. So the other half is still going through auditioning. But at least half of my work now comes from people just offering.

Q: What acting unions or organizations have you been affiliated with that have been helpful to you in your career?

ALICE: I belong to the three unions: Actors' Equity Association, and Screen Actors Guild, and American Federation of Television and Radio Artists. They don't get any work for you, but they do offer a certain degree of protection. They have worked to try and increase work for black actors, affirmative action, nontraditional casting. They've tried to improve the pension and welfare. They've tried to improve salaries. But basically, the most important thing that they may have done that would affect me directly outside of money would be the nontraditional casting in film and television and on stage. I really don't know how much the unions can do since the unions are not employers. I suppose they could—which they've done—include in the contract agreements that every producer should try to hire as many so-called minorities as possible. But how do you really enforce that? I don't think it can really start with the union. My own personal feeling is that it really has to start, as far as I'm concerned, with the black community. African Americans are basically consumers and we spend a great deal of money in this economy. I think there were figures that were introduced just a couple of years ago that black people are responsible for one-fourth of the ticket sales for movies. We're talking about a multibillion-dollar business, and one-fourth of that money comes from the black community. That's enough for us to produce and distribute our own films. This is where I feel that the solution has to come from, instead of waiting for the powers-that-be in Hollywood to say, "Okay, let's make a movie and

have some black actors in it." Or, "Let's make a black film." It has to
start with people like the young filmmakers, and especially the black
female filmmakers like Julie Dash and a few others whose names I can't
remember who now have films in the can but can't get distributors.

Q: What are your criteria for success as an actor?

ALICE: I'm very satisfied with my career, in a sense. I think I'm successful
in that I haven't given up.

It must have been ten years ago I was talking to Earl Hyman. He was
talking about the theatre and passion for the theatre. And I realized after
talking to him that there were really two elements here: there's the
theatre, there's the work; and then there's show business. And I—along
with probably many others—allowed the show business to overwhelm
me, and I forgot. Sometimes I would forget why I had chosen to be an
actor—which really involves a lot of the work. One can really be
sidetracked because one can get caught up in the show business, and
it's so much of the show business that you have to get through before
you're actually allowed to do the work. And sometimes you're still not
allowed to do the work because of the show business. So I think of
myself as being successful in that I continue to do the work and I think
of myself as most successful because I finally put myself in charge of
my career. But I've also taken charge of my life. And I'm very satisfied
with the fact that I have continued on and that I didn't give up when I
was very discouraged and at the low points. And that I haven't allowed
the "they" in show business to tell me that I cannot dream the impossible
dream. Because I still let no one interfere with the dream. And I think
it's very important for actors to not give up their dreams, even though
I don't think it's important to attain them. My heart has been broken,
but I just got some Krazy Glue and I put it back together and kept going.

Q: Speaking of the "they," how do you feel about critical review of your
work?

ALICE: It took me a long time to realize that they were very important;
the critics are an important part of show business. And sometimes,
they're right on the money. I can truthfully say that after reading some
of my reviews, I understood my characters better. Some of them have
helped me to do my work better. Because I've had directors who
couldn't direct, and because I couldn't see myself, I didn't have that
feedback. I might have missed something about the character or
included something that was wrong. And sometimes after reading a
review, I say, "You know, he or she may be right." I used to read my
reviews immediately when they came out; now I don't. If I'm doing a
play I will wait until after the play closes for about a week. And the

experience of the character is leaving me. Then I will sit down and read the reviews. It's wonderful to read old reviews. They can be helpful— whether or not they're good or bad. Fortunately, I've had some very very wonderful reviews. I mean, they were glorious. Every now and then I'll just sit down and read them. What they do is they sort of help to affirm that body of work that I've done! They help to affirm that I'm an actor.

Q: Are there particular periods of work, or is there maybe one great piece of work you've done, that's been your greatest satisfaction?

ALICE: Well, I think the greatest role that I've ever been fortunate to work on is in a play that I did for television. I've never done it on stage; I've been trying to get it done on stage recently: *The Sty of the Blind Pig*, by Phillip Hayes Dean. It's the most complicated role that I've ever played. It was for PBS. Now, *Fences* was very satisfying, but in a different way. I mean, it was a very good role. It was a hit show on Broadway. It brought a lot of attention to me. It was a very difficult role for me to do, especially on Broadway. I had done it in '85 at Yale. Then we did it in '86 at the Goodman, and then in '87 we went to San Francisco, and then we brought it to Broadway. So on one hand, it was very satisfying to be in a hit Broadway show. On the other hand, it was probably one of the lowest periods in my career. Because my mother and father were dying or were very sick. My father died in April of '87 and my mother died in November. So I was very divided. On the one hand, my career was moving. It was at its highest point and then I was losing the two people who meant more to me than anybody in the whole world.

The thing about *Fences* is that the play in some way dealt with the same themes that I was dealing with off stage—especially death and loss. I was losing my mother and my father, and so it just became very difficult to get on stage and do that. It was very emotional. I remember one night I was on stage and there was this big speech coming up, that big speech when she says, "What about me? I've been standing here with you." I'm looking at Jimmy. And Jimmy is saying what he has to say. And I was standing there and I was saying, "I can't do this. I cannot do this today." Emotionally I was just spent. I had no more to give. My mother had died by that time. And so I'm standing there on that stage. And I'm saying to myself, "What am I going to say?" This is going through my head: "What am I going to say when Jimmy finishes?" And I felt my mother and my father on either side of me. One was upstage of me; one was downstage of me and they said to me, not verbally, but I just felt they were saying to me, "We're all right. We're with you. You can do it." And I did it. I didn't think I could do it. But I had several moments like that where I just thought I couldn't. After my father died and I came back after a week of being off and I only came back because the Tony people were coming and the producers were pressuring me. I remember walking out on stage and I felt like I was in the Twilight Zone. Ray Aranha and James Earl Jones seemed to be on the other side of the world. And the audience—there were thirteen hundred people— they seemed to be receding. I'm walking around there and I have to walk downstairs and pick up an apron and I'm thinking, "Hey, what's the first line?" I went through the whole show like that—sort of talking myself through the show. And Jimmy said to me afterwards, he said, "You were so funny tonight. You were so intense." I said, "I was trying to get through this play." There have been many times in my career where I've had the satisfaction of working on very good projects. At the La Mama [Theatre], I did a wonderful piece by Adrienne Kennedy called *A Rat's Mass*. Up at the Long Wharf [Theatre in New Haven, Connecticut] I did a wonderful play by Richard Venture called *You're Too Tall But Come Back in Two Weeks*. I've worked in a couple of plays by Charles Fuller—*Two Men and the Sign* and in *The Deepest Part of Sleep*—that we did at the Negro Ensemble Company. So there have been wonderful roles that I've had an opportunity to do. Last year in Pittsburgh I did a wonderful new play called *A Sunbeam* by John Henry Redwood that we're trying to get done again.

Q: What is one point that you would make to a young actor who's considering a career in the theatre?

ALICE: Be prepared! And by that, I mean, be prepared in terms of learning your craft. When I speak to young actors just starting out, I always say to them two things. First of all, if you call yourself an actor, be sure you know how to do that. That involves getting the correct training, really learning how to use yourself onstage so that when you go in for an audition you can represent yourself well. And the important thing is not to get the job, but to leave a very good impression. Think in terms of networking—that the more people who know of you, the better your chances of getting work. The second part is knowing that you can act, after you've done the preparation and you, hopefully, get the experience and you begin to know that you are an actor. That's going to strengthen you through all the bad times and the good times. So that you will not be seduced. This is a very seductive profession. And you will not believe everything that people say to you or about you. And that you will learn to keep your own counsel and know when the lies are being told and when they're not being told. You'll be able to discern who is telling you the truth, because there are so many people in this profession who have been ripped off—not just in terms of money, but their hearts. They've been lied to. If you can do the first part, which could possibly lead to the second part, these will cause you—if you want a long career—to keep on going. So, from without you'll be getting the work, and from within you'll know how to conduct yourself—because this is at times maddening for an individual who I feel has not prepared himself or herself. Because there's constant rejection. There's very little approval. I mean, you're approved of and then you're rejected. It's like pulling a rubber band, you know—it can break! And actors do break.

Three

PHILIP BOSCO

B. Jersey City, N.J., 1930. Attended Catholic University, Washington, D.C. (B.A. 1957). Trained for stage with James Marr, Josephine Callan, and Leo Brady. Awards: New York Drama Critics Circle Award, *The Rape of the Belt*, 1960; Obie Award for Lifetime Achievement in the Theatre, 1987; Emmy, *Read Between the Lines*, 1988; Tony, *Lend Me a Tenor*, 1989.

Q: What were your initial experiences with acting?

BOSCO: My very first experience is really quite clear in my mind. It occurred in September of '43. I was thirteen. I was in the eighth grade. I had always been a good reader when I was a child. I had a kind of facility for reading and I began to realize this from the comments that teachers would make as I progressed through school. I went to a Catholic grammar school, St. John the Baptist in Jersey City. There was a nun, Sister Florence. I remember her very clearly because she came to see me in several shows much later in my career. She cast me in the annual play. It was called *The Fairy Cobbler*. And I played a role in it called "Machiavelli The Cat" in which I had this very elaborate cat costume with a long tail. Of course, I stole the show with the tail—as you might imagine. I have a great memory of being congratulated by the parents, and whatnot. I do remember, very clearly, going home with my mother once or twice after the show and people complimenting her and naturally patting me on the head. People have often asked "what made you go into the theatre" and I think it was something like that. I must have

realized how good it felt and how good it made me feel that my mother
and my parents were pleased at my work that I decided to follow it up
and continue it—which is exactly what I did when I went to high school
the following year.

Q: What was your family like? Did you have a big family?

BOSCO: No. At that time, being thirteen, I think I only had one of my
brothers. I had another brother who died when I was very young. But,
at the moment I had one brother. Another brother was born when I was
seventeen. My mom was a housewife. She had no particular career of
any sort other than that, raising the children, taking care of the home,
but my dad was in the carnival business. I grew up in that business. My
father was a carny.

Q: Did he travel?

BOSCO: Oh, all over. All over.

Q: Did you travel with him?

BOSCO: Very much so. Before school age I was with him all the time,
of course. Then as I began school I would naturally be home with my
mother during the winter, the school year. And in the summer time we
went with my father wherever he happened to be. I traveled mostly with
my parents in New England and the Middle Atlantic states. My dad in
the winter would go south—you know, down to the Carolinas and
Georgia—and used to go west sometimes, but primarily it was in New
England for me. And I stayed with my dad. And my dad of course stayed
in the carnival business until I went away to college. Then he kind of
drifted out of it a bit and stuck to carnival-like things—you know, these
Italian feasts that you see around where they have stands on the
sidewalk? Well, then my father kind of went into that.

Q: It's a different sort of theatre in a way.

BOSCO: It is. I've always thought of it as kind of the tail end of the theatre.
You're dealing with people. You don't have a script to memorize necessarily, but you do have a kind of patter that you develop in trying to get
people to come in to play your stand. That was the atmosphere I grew
up in.

Q: How did they feel about your interest in acting?

BOSCO: When I got into high school, my first play that I remember was
Arsenic and Old Lace, which had just opened a year or two before. It
was one of the first plays I saw on the stage in New York. I played
Officer O'Hara in *Arsenic and Old Lace* and I remember my parents
bringing relatives to see me. My mom was born and raised in Brooklyn,
and my father was born and raised in Jersey City. But my mom's siblings
and family all live throughout the Brooklyn and New York area. And

she invited them over and there was all that kind of, you know, "Oh, isn't he cute. How nice." That was my first recollection. We had no real theatrical background. No one in my family was a performer on either side. I mean, there was absolutely no connection whatever with formal theatre or formal show business except as I said in the carnival business.

Q: It sounds like you got a lot of attention and encouragement.

BOSCO: Oh, a great deal. My mother was my severest critic all along. She meant well, and I took her cautions to mind in those days. I remember her saying very often that she was trying to protect me against future hurt and she would say things like, "You know, you really should give some thought into not going into the theatre because you're really not very good-looking. Your nose is too big," and things of that nature. My father was gung ho, and he'd rave about me to his friends. He was totally behind me. My mother was behind me but with great reservation. She didn't want me to get hurt. I think that her reservations about it, and her caution, probably impelled me more to go on to disprove her.

Q: When did you begin to study or train to be an actor?

BOSCO: When I was in high school, I was very fortunate to make the acquaintance of a retired professional actor who probably could be called my "mentor." He was a man of whom I was very fond. The time I first met him I was just barely fourteen and he was in his seventies. His name was James Marr. And he was from Jersey City, from a different parish than I was living at the time—St. Nicholas parish. He took a liking to me and I guess he sensed also some talent in me. He took me under his wing. And I didn't receive any formal training in the sense that I went to classes or studied from texts, but I did a great deal of work with him. Remember now, he was a professional actor most of his life. And he had a son who also was a professional actor at the time, Eddie Marr, who was in quite a few Hollywood films—never became a big name, but he worked constantly. In any event, Mr. Marr guided me. I was in the debating club in those days. I did all kinds of elocution and forensic contests. I was in all of the plays that we did, two or three a year. I was in radio programs, all under his guidance, that we would do at Easter and Christmas. I went four years to St. Peter's Prep, a Jesuit high school in downtown Jersey City. And I was very very fortunate to have him all those years.

Q: Were there any other interests or subjects or other art forms in the high school or college period that were influential as you were training to be an actor?

BOSCO: Not that I'm aware of. If they were they were kind of subliminal or incidental. I didn't consciously train vocally or do any of that. Under

Mr. Marr's guidance (he tried to encourage me to do work outside of the schooltime), I became part of a club. A CYO [Catholic Youth Organization] players—there was a CYO on Bergen Avenue in Jersey City. Also in his parish, in St. Nicholas where he lived, there was an amateur dramatic group which I became part of. I was really quite immersed in it from the time I was fifteen.

Q: What about your peers at that time? Were any of your friends involved in theatre?

BOSCO: Not at all. Whatever friends I ultimately found in that pursuit would be friends that were already doing it. I did then make a close friend named Robert Walk who didn't go on into the theatre, became a businessman of some sort. I lost touch with him. But he was a close friend of mine then during the time I was in high school. He was interested in the theatre, too. We used to talk a good deal about it, listen to recordings a great deal. We used to go to the library and listen to recorded plays, mainly from the British. One that comes into mind was *The Importance of Being Earnest* with John Gielgud which I reveled in, gloried in listening to. And we used to listen to opera and I really got involved in the appreciation of the arts with this fellow Robert Walk. And I had a couple of friends at home in Jersey City, back home in my neighborhood, who weren't interested in the theatre as performers but who loved the theatre and movies.

Q: You were talking about your mentor.

BOSCO: Yes. Mr. Marr. He gave me a book that I remember very clearly as a gift. I was very impressed with it. It was called *Good Night, Sweet Prince*, by Gene Fowler, about the life of John Barrymore. I was captivated with the story. It was beautifully written as I remember, too. It was filled with all kinds of wonderful things about Barrymore who was such a fascinating colorful eccentric man and wonderful actor, of course. If I was studying the role for a play or if I was preparing a dramatic reading for some contest, after that was over, he'd sit in the chair, in one of the schoolrooms at the high school. He'd sit—I can see him now. He smoked, voluminously. He was always smoking. And he'd reminisce about the theatre. He was a wonderful old man and he never got to see me with any kind of success. It's a pity, but he died when I was in the army overseas in 1952.

Q: Was that after you went to Catholic University?

BOSCO: He kind of led me to decide to enroll in the Speech and Drama department at Catholic University in Washington, D.C., which is where I received my formal training. I had gone to Catholic University in 1948, but I was expelled in 1949. By that time I was pretty much gaga about the theatre. And I got to the Speech and Drama department of Catholic University. At that time, it was one of the best drama departments in the country. It had Father Hartke who was the driving force of the whole thing and Walter Kerr was on the faculty, was one of the founding members of the department if I'm not mistaken. Dr. Josephine Callan was a vocal teacher. She was wonderful. Leo Brady, a wonderful friend and a fine teacher, was there. And we ultimately had Alan Schneider as a member of the faculty. A lot of distinguished actors and playwrights have come out of the department over the years. I turned eighteen after I got into D.C. And I remember being so interested in the theatre, I used to spend all of my time at the theatre. Oftentimes I'd sleep in the theatre. I'd sleep on the bench, on the chairs. And I neglected my studies. I was a pretty good student in high school. There was no question of my not being able to do it. It's just that I didn't do it because I was so involved with working in plays or helping to build sets or reading or talking. I was fascinated, and as a result I failed biology and I was taking a senior course in Latin because I'd had four years of Latin in high school. It was very difficult. And I flunked Latin. But the thing that got me thrown out was the third course, for which you received no credit. I flunked gymnasium. I never went. There was no credit for the course and at the time it was kind of a small cause célèbre down there about my being expelled for the third subject, which was not a credit course. Ed McMahon was a friend of mine in those days—the fellow from TV. In fact, I lived with him for a short time. He started a campaign with a huge petition, and hundreds and hundreds of signatures.

Q: Were you reinstated?

BOSCO: No, I wasn't. But they did make an exception. The rules in those days were if you were expelled for academic insufficiency, you were not able to reapply. That was it. But my case was so special because of this gym thing, they did allow me to reapply—which I did after I came out of the army in 1953. I went back and I got my degree in '57 and then I went to graduate school there for about a year. But I never got my graduate degree. By that time I got a job in the theatre.

Q: When did you start working professionally?

BOSCO: My first professional job in terms of being, you know—in the theatre—when you get your Equity card is kind of when you become a professional, no matter how much you've done before. It's when you're getting paid. My first Equity job was in 1954 after I'd come out of the service. I worked in the summer stock company in the suburb of Washington, D.C., called Olney, Maryland—which is still operating today. There was no official connection between the Olney theatre and the Speech and Drama department at Catholic U, but there was a very strong unofficial connection. Most of the people in the department—the teachers, Father Hartke—they were connected with the running of the Olney theatre when I was there. Olney had been a professional theatre long before we got there. I think touring people played that theatre. But when the speech and drama people got connected with it, it kind of was like their summer theatre, as it were. I worked there for about five or six summers.

Q: It sounds like you were really well prepared.

BOSCO: I had a great deal of experience. And I was very lucky—when I first came to Catholic U in 1948, I was one of the youngest people in the department. And I was fortunate to be with a lot of guys, very talented people, who had been in the service. And the disparity between a seventeen or eighteen year old and a twenty-three or twenty-four year old—even though it's only six years, it's still a huge gap. But then I was thrown out and that was a kind of a psychic blow, and I recovered from that, thank God. When I went back in 1953, I was twenty-three and twenty-four then, and I was kind of the old man in the department. And I lucked out because I played a huge number of roles when I was there for the next four years. I was so lucky. I mean, you can take it from Hamlet, to Cyrano and Richard the Third and Shylock and Malvolio. I had a wealth of experience and training.

Q: Can you tell me a little more about how your career has progressed from that early period to now? Start with when you feel you really first achieved professional recognition.

BOSCO: I was in summer stock at Olney for four or five seasons. Then I got my next-level-type job. I began to work at Arena Stage with Zelda Fichandler in what used to be called the "Old Vat." It's not the theatre and the complex that they have now. This was back in '57, '58, '59, in those years. I became a member of that company. I played there before for one or two shows. *Romeo and Juliet* I remember very clearly. And then I became a permanent member of the repertory company there. I was there for two full years and played sixteen or eighteen parts. Then, my first New York–type show happened. A producer in New York who was a member of a triumvirate of producers—Richard Barr, who later became the president of the League of New York Theaters and [who was] a very distinguished producer in New York—was from the area, and his mother lived in suburban Maryland. And she used to see me, unbeknownst to me at the time, on the stage in the Catholic University plays. Of course, there wasn't much professional theatre in Washington in those days, except the odd touring. So we achieved a kind of disproportionate fame—the drama department—because of the dearth of any real serious theatre there. So, we used to get top-line critics in the local paper. We were really very fortunate. In any event, this lady Mrs. Barr, as it turned out, had mentioned me to her son. And he called me one day while I was in Washington and offered me a part in the touring company of *Auntie Mame*. I played Bryan O'Banyon, the Irish poet, on a bus and truck tour. And the leading lady of my company was the now aged actress and somewhat controversial person, Sylvia Sydney. She took an instant hatred to me for some reason. Anyway, that was my first New York job and I toured for eight months with that all around to the Midwest and the East and Canada. And then I had an argument with Miss Sydney or she vilified me in unmistakable terms and I gave my notice. Then I came to New York from Washington and Arena. My debut in New York was in the park—Joe Papp, a play directed by Alan Schneider, *Measure for Measure*. That was my first, in 1960. I'll never forget it. I came to New York on July Fourth for the first rehearsal. I drove up overnight from Washington—my wife was still living in Arlington where we had an apartment. And I parked my car, for the rehearsal, on 81st Street just off Central Park West right in front of the Beresford, and I went into the park. I did rehearse. I came out and they had stolen everything out of my car. The very first day I was here, in 1960. Anyway, that was my first show, *Measure for Measure*. I was lucky to get some pretty good notices in that, and I got an agent out of it. My agent—who then became my only agent for the rest of my career until he died (and I'm still with the office that he founded, but he, of course is no longer with us)—Stark Hesseltine. Alan Schneider was really the one responsible for me doing that show, because he insisted I do it. Joe Papp had turned me down—I think, four or five times—for that part. He said he couldn't see beyond his own prejudice about somebody who could speak well. He said, "Who is this guy? He's phoney. I don't want him." And Alan kept insisting, "I know this guy and I've worked with him in Arena Stage. Believe me. Take my word." Anyway, Alan prevailed, thank God, and Alan was greatly responsible for a lot of my success in the early days. He was very loyal. He always used people that he knew and presumably that he liked or cared about. My first Broadway show was later that same season with Alan Schneider. It was called *Rape of the Belt*, for which I won the New York Drama Critics Circle Award as the most promising newcomer of the year. I kind of got off to a good start.

Q: Have you ever had any periods that you weren't working constantly?
BOSCO: Very few. From that time in 1960 to about 1972, I then did those
    shows in New York. After 1960 I did that Broadway show and I
    auditioned for the Shakespeare Festival at Stratford, Connecticut, and
    I became part of that company. I was there for four years, from '61 to
    about '65. We did three plays, or sometimes four, and we had to start
    rehearsing. We used to play for students in the early part of the season
    before the actual run began for adults. We played what they called a
    "student season" that became increasingly earlier, so by the time I
    finished there in '65 or '66 we were playing pretty much from February
    through September or October. So, it was almost virtually a full year's
    job. And I did the odd show apart from that. I did a lot of television. But
    on the stage I only did one or two other plays of that period of Stratford.
    Then I came back to New York. And I auditioned for the repertory
    theatre at Lincoln Center. And I stayed there for seven years. I was with
    Jules Irving when Jules Irving and Herbert Blau took over when Lincoln
    Center opened—that theatre. They were in charge of that theatre. I began
    the second season that Jules Irving was there and I stayed there from
    '66 to September of '73. You see, I was always interested in repertory.
    Always wanted to work in a permanent company and do different plays.
    I wasn't crazy about and never did, in fact, go to Hollywood because I
    wasn't interested in that kind of work. I didn't want to get on TV. I mean,
    now I do TV, and I've done soap operas over the years. But, I mean, I
    didn't want to make a career out of that. I wanted to make a career on
    the stage: that was my first love and still is. So, I kind of bit the bullet,
    and I was helped in that regard by the willingness of my wife and family.
    They supported me all the way through. Because even though I worked
    all the time, it was still rough going because you don't make a lot of
    money in the theatre. I mean, I chose to do that, so I'm not complaining.
    It's just that it was, in fact, financially kind of difficult. But I also had
    a personal medical problem, which is now under control and I don't
    want to go into it too long. I was unable to travel because I have a
    condition called "panic disorder." That affected my ability to travel.
    I became ill when I'd leave certain things. So, all of those factors tended
    to necessitate my staying in New York. I mean, I wanted to stay in New
    York, but that kind of gave me an added impulse because I really
    couldn't travel without getting ill. As it turned out, looking back, I'm
    glad it happened that way because I wouldn't have been very happy
    doing the kind of stuff that you get involved in which you go to the
    [West] Coast—the sitcoms and stuff.

Q: Do you think these opportunities still exist today?

BOSCO: Very much so. I don't have any personal connection with them. I mean, I've been asked by a good number of theatres around the country—distinguished theatres like the Guthrie Theatre, years ago the Margo Jones Theatre in Dallas and Long Wharf Theatre and other theatres around the country—to go there. But for whatever reasons and my inability to travel, or the poor money that they were offering, I didn't go. But I loved that idea. And there were many successful theatres around the country—in fact, great theatres. The best work is being done in these theatres. There's a very strong regional theatre network out there.

Q: I wanted to ask you about some of the organizations you are affiliated with as an actor, like unions. Which one are you most active in? How do you feel about unionization for an actor?

BOSCO: I'm very much in favor of unions in the abstract. In the abstract sense, the unions, I think, are an important part of the democratic system. And I support them wholeheartedly. I object to the compulsory nature of the unions in show business. Let's speak of Equity now, particularly—the union that governs acting on the stage. You have to be a member of Equity to be able to appear in an Equity production. I find that a little offensive. I mean, I would probably want to be in it given what unions can and do, in fact, do for the benefit of the actor and the benefit of the theatre. I just object to the compulsory nature of it. I wish there were another way to make it available so if you didn't want to for whatever reason, you didn't have to but you would still be able to work. It's a fact that you're not able to work unless you're a member—that rubs me a little bit wrong. And my only objection to Actors' Equity is that they're not the strongest union for the actor. I'm not speaking so much of the present and I'm not even speaking so much from experience, although my experience with the union in terms of settling issues with producers has been very negative from my point of view. I've had several cases which I think by any objective standard would have been a valid and a just case and I was either advised to drop it for expediency's sake or not to pursue it because there's no guarantee that you're going to win. It is very frustrating. And you figure, well, you know, what is your union for? The other thing, in terms of practicality: you cannot get medical benefits that you can get from SAG [Screen Actors Guild] and AFTRA [American Federation of Television and Radio Artists]—obviously much wealthier unions because the money is so much greater. And even though they charge a huge amount of money in dues, you get something back in terms of medical coverage, which makes it all worthwhile. Between the both of them, they pretty much pay all of your medical bills. Now, with a family as large as mine, that's a very important thing.

Q: Are there any other organizations—especially with having such a large family—that were helpful to you as far as providing additional health benefits or credit or insurance?

BOSCO: I got a great deal of personal help given to my family. It was very welcome and very needed in the early days when we had a lot of little children, but it was mostly personal aid. I don't know if I ever partook of any benefits from the Actor's Fund. If I did, it was only in a small way. But I do applaud the Actor's Fund and the Home that they support for old actors in New Jersey. It's a beautiful place. I contribute to them regularly and I think it's a wonderful organization. Thank God I haven't had to use it. But it's nice to know that it's there if you do.

Q: How did you, and how do you now, see yourself as being cast?

BOSCO: Well, I've always objected to these kind of categorizations of leading man and character actor. It suggests that character is kind of less than ideal. You know, leading man—the very nature of the word *leading* is like you're number one. And if you're a character actor, you're just kind of a supporting player. When, in point of fact, what they really are referring to as "leading men" are people who rely on their personalities, rather than any acting ability. People who are thought of as actors of considerable versatility and variety are called "character actors."

Q: Do you think charisma plays a part at all?

BOSCO: Not so much on stage. I think talent comes through on stage. You can be very charismatic in front of a camera and with the lens—you know, however close to you and picking up every gorgeous detail of your beautiful physiognomy or wonderful makeup. Because, in a sense, acting in movies is not really acting at all. It's behaving. You kind of have a personality—at least for the leading people. You have a personality and that kind of pretty much comes across in everything you do. And you can whisper in the dullest kind of faintest tones and be very effective with background music. But you get on the stage, you've got to produce. You've got to project. You've got to be able to reach the back of the hall. It's an entirely different technique.

Q: You've done quite a lot of all avenues—stage, TV, and film.

BOSCO: Lately. The last eight or ten years I've done film. I had done a little bit in some film during the early part of my career. I never liked movies in those days. I had no great desire to do them. But now that I'm getting older, the chances of making considerable money on the stage are very remote unless you luck out with one of the rare hits. There are very few plays done on Broadway. So, if you're not in musicals, you are pretty much relegated to Off-Broadway or regional theatres and what they call "institutional theatres"—nonprofits like Circle in the Square, Lincoln Center—and you don't get a lot of money. Now, having said that, I've been a movie fan all my life. I adore films. And I would love to be in movies as a professional, but probably not as an actor. If I had my choice, I would probably want to direct, you know, or even photograph. That's where the creativity comes in, in film. On stage, you rehearse, and when the curtain goes up after the rehearsal is over, it's you and the audience—you in charge. In the movies it's out of your hands. And the director and the editor and the lighting man are the real geniuses there. They can make fantastic things happen out of little bits and pieces that you've done. You know, in movies hardly anything is ever done in sequence. You can play the emotional ending the first two days you're filming. It's all chopped up. There's no sustainable kind of emotion. It takes great skill for the people who are portraying the roles; it's not acting in the sense that we in the theatre think of it as acting. That's one of the bum things about doing movies. You don't feel artistically satisfied. It's not at all enriching as a work experience.

Q: I wanted to ask you if there is a particular period of your work that you were most satisfied with and most proud of?

BOSCO: To say "satisfied" and "proud" are slightly different. I'm very satisfied doing repertory-type work. I don't think I was more satisfied. When you play a season of Shakespeare like I did up in Stratford, that's beautifully satisfying. You get a chance to get your tongue around those words, get your hands on some of these wonderful characterizations that he's created. And that's very satisfying. I'm proud of a lot of the work I've done in the city—particularly, the Shaw work I've done. And mostly at Circle in the Square, but also at Roundabout. As a body of work, I would pretty much look upon that as one of the proudest of my achievements, if I can say such a thing.

Q: But you've won quite a few awards, haven't you?

BOSCO: I've won a good number of awards, but you kind of take those in stride. They're very pleasing and I'm not being disingenuous when I say it's nice to get them. You feel good, of course. It's somebody saying, "Hey, you're pretty good. Have this award." And that's nice. But how other people react to it is what's really satisfying. It makes you feel good to see people that you care about happy at something that you've done. Maybe after the Tony, people have seen you a lot more— maybe their respect is a little greater, but even that's problematic.

Frankly, I'm against awards of that type in theatre. I wish the awards were more in the style of the Obie, the Off-Broadway awards from the *Village Voice.* Not so much for the kinds of things that they choose to praise, but the way they do it. They don't give an award for the best this and that. They have a series of people or things that are worthy of note in that year—example: The season I won, I won one Obie for the body of my work. Sometimes they don't given an award for the best actor— these are the best performances of the year, by this band of critics. And they'll mention six one year. Maybe twelve the next year. That's the way it should be. I mean, who is to say George Scott in playing *Death of a Salesman* is any better than Nigel Hawthorne playing in *Shadowlands* that he won the award for? They're both wonderful—why do we have to compete? Why not recognize them both as being good? If you want to give an award, give them both an award. It's the competitiveness of it that bothers me, I think.

Q: How do you feel about critics' review of your work, or theatre in general?

BOSCO: I'm one of those cranks who thinks that critics are good for the theatre. I've been very fortunate in getting some nice notices and I appreciate them and you want them. I'm not one of those people who says he doesn't read a review. I read every bloody review that ever comes out. And you don't want to get a bad review, obviously. You figure over a period of time, well, who is saying what; if you value that judgment of that person and that person says you weren't good, you're naturally hurt by it. But, good Lord, you've got to be tough in this racket. Because you get criticism every minute of the day, whether it's a critic or another actor. You're constantly being criticized. And if you can't take that criticism with a certain measure of laissez-faire, then you're in the wrong life—because nobody gets universally good reviews all the time. No one. And the funny thing is: you get 120 reviews. One hundred and nineteen of them are very good; the one that you'll remember is the bad one. You can quote that one word for word. There are very few really good critics around. But I think that they are invaluable to the health of the theatre. Keep you to your craft. Keep your nose to the grindstone.

Q: Has your technique changed from when you were starting out to now? Do you approach your work differently?

BOSCO: I don't think so. If I do, it's imperceptible to me. I don't know if I have any technique at all. I frankly get puzzled when I read so much and hear so much about this method and that method. I don't know if there's any method other than training your voice, which I think is terribly important. We're not as disciplined in the theatre as we should be in terms of vocal training, because I think that's the most critical aspect of an actor in the theatre, obviously. But a good actor is a good actor if he's believable and you can hear him and he has some native talent. You can't invent talent—you either have it or you don't have it. I think actors are born with some something that makes them able to act. You can't learn that. You can get experience; you can get more comfortable on stage. You can become adept at technical things to do with acting—vocal training, movement. You can do lots of those technical things. But if you haven't got it to begin with, you're not going to learn it. Some of the greatest actors we know—people that we admire the most—had very little formal training, maybe none at all. And then again, we've had some wonderful and fine actors who studied and studied hard. I don't know if there's any formula for it. I just try to be real, try to be credible, try to be concentrated, and make sure you can speak properly and all of that. I guess, in short, what I'm saying is, I don't know if I have any technique at all. I'm not aware of it. I just pretty much do it. What I do believe—I've always been against the so-called Actors Studio method, if that's an appropriate way to describe it. Because I think what that has done in practical terms, is it has turned the bulk of the American performing community in the theatre primarily in the wrong direction. Kitchen drama is the result of the Actors Studio. You can do anything that requires you to mumble and contemplate your navel, particularly if you're doing it in the films. I know they'll all scream bloody murder: "That's not what Actors Studio is about!" But we know what it's about. We see the devotees and the results of it. I don't know of any Actors Studio so-called luminaries who have excelled in the classical theater, if you want to use the word *classical*— just to separate it from the kitchen drama. There aren't many. When they try, they have a tough row to hoe. Because they're not equipped to do it.

Q: There's a saying that stage actors can cross over to do film but film actors rarely can cross back to the stage.

BOSCO: Oh, how glad I am to hear you say that.

Q: Do you think it's because of that training?

BOSCO: I can't think of anything more true than that in talking about show business and acting and movies. Absolutely. The examples of that are legion. I don't know. I don't know of any distinguished actors who started out in film without any stage experience and then made the transition to the stage. There may be a handful here and there over the years.

But certainly, in the early days of film, everybody who went into film were actors from the stage.

Q: It seems though, now, that you see quite a lot of film and TV stars that come back to New York to do stage who have never ever done stage before. How do you feel about that?

BOSCO: Well, I have mixed feelings about that. On the one hand, I think it's wonderful for the theatre. Because the nonmusical theatre on Broadway is virtually dead. Any stars that come in are not going to be here for a long time. I understand. I wouldn't want to be in a play longer than that if I were them. I don't mean to be pejorative about it. But, I mean, their careers are not in the theatre. They're movie people. They come in and they do the odd thing. The odd play. And that's great, because it is bringing people into the theatre. It's a marketing strategy. But the theatre is structurally problematic at the moment. It's much too expensive to do. It's much too expensive for the audience. I mean, I've seen figures and heard people talk about a nonmusical play on Broadway— even with one small set—that's anywhere close to a million dollars. I mean, this is outrageous. This is fantastic. And necessitates playing a theatre that has a larger number of seats than you would ordinarily want for a play. And then you have to pay much less to the people—you know, it's just an impossible situation.

Q: How satisfied are you with your career?

BOSCO: Extremely satisfied. I'm very, very happy. I'm very lucky. And I say that honestly.

Q: Do you think luck is important?

BOSCO: I think luck is tremendously important, because take any hundred actors—all could be equally talented, all could have pretty much the same drive and the same sense of commitment and stick-to-it-iveness and whatever it takes to make a success—but 70, 80 percent of those people are not going to make it, by virtue of not being at the right place at the right time! It's like a crap shoot. It's out of your hands. You have to hang in there! That's my motto in the theatre now. "Hang in there!" If you really want to do it, and if you honestly feel you have something to say and want to devote your life to it, you've got to stick to it, because it takes a long time to get going. But it's very rewarding if that's what you want! After all, what is more important in a person's life than doing the work he wants to do? And making some money with it, hopefully, after a while?

Q: You've had many many successes in your career. Have there been any major disappointments?

BOSCO: Oh yes! The successes aren't all that many; there are quite a few, yes, and I acknowledge them and I'm very grateful for them. But there are many many shows that didn't do as well as I'd hoped. You keep going! You try to take it all in, in the same fashion. And in a way, what happens is, to develop an attitude where you can survive the ups and downs in the theatre; you kind of have to give up a little of your innocence; you have to give up a little of the love of the magic of the theatre, because you realize then that it's not all magic, that it's hard work and the backstage thing is not what most people think it is, you know, all these peaches-and-cream and love and lights and fun and games. A lot of times it's miserable and unpleasant, and you're working in places you don't care to work in; the facilities are not right; the people may not be the most pleasant to work with. But you've got to take it all in stride.

Q: If there is one major point that you can make to young actors pursuing a career, what would that be?

BOSCO: For God's sake, get on the stage in front of an audience! I am absolutely fanatical about experience. You've got to get on the stage! You cannot study, cannot waste your time in classrooms and in basements before your mother. You've got to do it in front of an audience, paying or nonpaying! The other aspect I would stress is stick-to-it-iveness; you've got to hang in. If you really want to do it, you cannot be depressed and disappointed—I mean, give up too easily. Disappointment is all over the place. You're constantly being disappointed! And if you can't live with that, then you're in the wrong business, because theatre is just one disappointment after another, mixed in with a lot of the good things! But remember, every time, no matter how big a show is, when you're in a hit and the show closes, you're out of a job! You have to get another job! And if you can't live with that kind of insecurity, then the theatre or maybe even movies is not for you; you have to accept that. Everybody has his own way of perfecting his own way of doing things. That's probably a nurturing process; you know, you get embellished, and you listen to people you admire and what turns you on, and you imitate, you take from what is right for you, and then you go on and you get rid of that. That's the formative stage. And then you've got to get out and do. Keep doing. Be bad. You've got to get the badness out. You learn. You try acting as much as you can, everywhere!

AL CARMINES

B. Hampton, Va., 1936. Attended Swarthmore College (B.A. high honors 1958); Union Theological Seminary (B.D. 1961, and S.T.M. 1963). Awards: Obie for Sustained Achievement Off-Broadway, 1979. Composer, lyricist, playwright, singer.

Q: Can you tell me something about how you first got interested in theatre and in acting?

CARMINES: Yes. I really came to theatre partly through religion. I was very active in my church and at five or seven years old, I think it was, I starred in the first pageant at the church in Hampton, Virginia. I subsequently learned to play the piano and became a musician. I veered between conservatory and going to college; finally, college won out and Swarthmore was my college. I was in my first really professional play at Swarthmore College, Shakespeare play, *The Winter's Tale*. Then I came to Union Seminary in New York. At that time, the Rockefeller Foundation had funded a program in religious drama, headed by E. Martin Browne, who was a director from England of all of T. S. Eliot's plays. And there, I did a great many plays: *The Family Reunion*, I starred in that; and Charles Williams's play *Thomas Cranmer*; a play by Howard Nemerov called *Cain*. I graduated from seminary in 1961 with my B.D. [Bachelor of Divinity] and then decided to go on for an S.T.M. [Master of Sacred Theology]. I needed a job while I was continuing with my graduate work, and Judson Church in the Village [i.e., Greenwich

Village] was looking for someone to assist in preaching and also to begin a theatre. The church had already sponsored a gallery and with very famous artists now showing there. Claes Oldenberg, Jim Dine—people who could buy and sell the church now all began in the basement of Judson Church. From the point of view of "happenings," they got interested in theatre, and so they were looking for someone both to help on Sunday and to help with the ministry, and also to help begin a theatre. I thought it would be interesting, and since I was interested particularly in music and also in theatre, I took the job. In two years I had received my master's degree from Union and I decided that I was a composer. In 1962 I composed my first music—and critics came and informed me that I was a new composer in New York, so I decided I was. When we began the theatre at Judson, we began on a shoestring. Judson Poets Theatre, Caffe Cino, and Cafe LaMama were the first three Off-Off-Broadway theatres. We shared a lot of people, shared a lot of space. Our mentor was the Living Theatre, Julian Beck and Judith Malina. And at Judson, I acted really not from a desire to act, but because they needed people in the plays and at that time we weren't very well known. I actually starred in the first play they had at Judson called *The Breasts of Tiresias* by Apollinaire in a new translation by Louis Simpson. Then I performed in a great many plays, simply as an actor, not as a musician. Derek Walcott plays, Paul Goodman plays, plays by George Dennison. However, my main task became, after 1962, to compose. And I composed over fifty musicals for Judson, over ten Off-Broadway, and I'm having my first Broadway show done next year.

Q: Talk a little bit about your family, your childhood—how you got interested in the things that eventually came out in your work.

CARMINES: My father was captain of a boat on the Chesapeake Bay and he was a very theatrical character. If I inherited talent for acting and probably for music, it was from my father. He was a marvelous raconteur, wonderful storyteller. An unbeliever, an atheist at a time when I didn't know any other atheists except my father. And we would sit on the front porch on Sunday mornings when I was a little boy and he would make comments about the people going to church, which was right across the street from us. My mother was a devout believer and she was a very devout and wonderful woman and very active in the Methodist church. It never seemed to affect their marriage, in a strange kind of way. She left my father alone. He left her alone. Finally, actually, my father did start going to church and Sunday school shortly before he died. But he was a lively and colorful man. When I began to play the piano I began at my grandmother's house, his mother's house. She lived on the street we did. And I began to play by ear and both my mother and father realized that I was talented. My father took me to hear Fats Waller down in Bay Shore, which was the black amusement park. He had to ask permission, of course, from the blacks who worked on his boat. They said it would be all right if I stood behind the rail—so I stood behind the rail. He asked also if I could meet Mr. Waller at the end of the concert. This was in '41. I was five years old. I met Mr. Waller, told him I liked to act and play just like he did. He said, "Learn your scales. Learn your scales." My mother was more like my teacher. My teacher was a very refined, truly refined, cultured influence on me. She took me to hear Horowitz when I was eight years old, to Richmond, Virginia. So I was imbued with both classical and jazz music from the earliest age and I played from the time I was ten years old. I played for everything in the town. I played for the army camps—Langley Field, Fort Monroe, Fort Eustace. I played on television, which was in its very beginning stage. I played on radio. I played to make my living, by playing for a dancing school—that is, my allowance money. So music was the integral part of my life. Religion became an integral part of my life. I became a very fundamentalist evangelistic believer. And when I was a teenager, I did revivals around the state of Virginia. I went and preached in churches all over the state of Virginia at sixteen. And I was a very devout evangelist. Swarthmore changed all of that. Although the fact that I went to Swarthmore said something about my intellectual hunger and yearning, I think.

Q: You have siblings?

CARMINES: Yes, I have one brother ten years younger. I was an only child for ten years. Then my parents informed me I was going to have a baby brother or sister. I was furious. I hit my mother in the stomach. I did not want a sibling. So my parents decided, quite wisely, that they would handle it by letting me name the child. And I immediately became very fond of the unborn child. I named him Ted. My mother said she wouldn't have a son named Theodore, so his name is Edward and I call him Ted to this day. He's now professor and head of the political science department at the University of Indiana in Bloomington. But he was ten years younger than I was. I had asthma as a child and therefore was not athletic. I lived in a town where everyone except for maybe a couple of families lived at the same level economically. There was no sense of middle class or poor class or upper class. We knew that the Darlings were wealthy because they had an estate and we went there for the play on the yard of their estate. But the rest of us all lived in houses on streets and we didn't know how much money anyone had. As a child, I didn't.

I thought we all had the same. Therefore, when I went to Swarthmore on a scholarship, when I was a senior, my dean said, "Maybe you'd like to see the scholarship that you came on." I said yes. And I read the scholarship was for poor boys from the southeastern United States and I suddenly realized they considered me poor. I always thought I was middle class. But my formative years were absolutely egalitarian—apart from segregation, which was absolutely observed totally. When I was a senior in high school, quite independently (not from any teaching or anything, simply by reading the Bible and being a devout fundamentalist), I came to believe that segregation was a sin. I wrote a letter to our hometown paper, stating that this was true. The White Citizens Council called, said they were going to burn a cross in our yard. My father and my mother stood by me, absolutely, although they did not take my opinion. But my father said, "My son has a right to say any damn thing he wants to say." And my mother: "Watch your language, but I agree." And so they stood behind me. My father died in 1955, when I was a sophomore in college. My mother then began to teach school, and the 1954 segregation decision had mandated desegregation, which had to come to our town as well as the rest of the South. And within five years, her job as assistant to the principal was to visit the homes of the children. And within five years, she thought—she said, in fact—"How could I have been so ignorant? I was so stupid. Segregation was the stupidest thing that ever was."

Q: Obviously your parents, and especially your father, were mentors, role models for you. Were there others in your formative years?

CARMINES: Ministers of our church were particularly role models for me. My other role models, apart from my father and my ministers, were women. My mother primarily—and even more primarily, her mother, my grandmother who was the matriarch of a family of eleven children, whose husband had been killed in the first automobile accident in Hampton in 1920. Who was a contractor, a wealthy man. But left her with eleven children to raise and she managed to send the boys to college and marry the girls off, which is what you did in that day. She came to live with us when she was a widow the second time, after her second husband died, and she and I were absolutely inseparable. She was a member of the DAR [Daughters of the American Revolution] and her father had been a soldier in the Confederacy during the Civil War. She was a perfect lady and yet she was a rawboned kind of pioneer woman because she'd had to be after her husband died. She loved washing clothes, ironing. She loved to read, and many of my nights when I was between the ages of eleven and thirteen, we slept in the same room and she read me stories of Presbyterian missionaries from a book she had. She was a great role model for me. My piano teacher was another role model. The ministers of my church. Then my other role models probably occurred in college.

Q: What were your early aspirations?

CARMINES: Well, my first aspiration was to become a piano player, I think, and to become a pianist. Then, when I was adolescent, my aspirations turned toward religion and my aspiration was to be an evangelist, really. However, music and religion were very intertwined. I always included singing as part of my preaching, and I began very young, when I was fifteen or sixteen, to arrange hymns for the choir to sing and with different harmonies than they were used to. But the aspirations, until I went to Swarthmore, were all either toward evangelism or music.

Q: Obviously, your entire life changed in Swarthmore.

CARMINES: Yes, it really did, partly because my father died while I was there and therefore there was one role model that was gone. I remember the first year I was there (when my father was still living), I came home for Thanksgiving. My father said, "Have you had enough?" They had disapproved of me going to Swarthmore. They wanted me to go to UVA [University of Virginia] or Randolph Macon or some college in Virginia, and my mother said, "I never trust anyplace north of Richmond." But I said no. I said, "I've met people for the first time who just want to learn and know for the sake of learning and knowing, not for any pragmatic reason. And I love it, I love it." And that's what Swarthmore meant to me. It meant a hunger for intellectual wisdom that was unrelated to either religion or music or anything. I majored in English literature, minored in philosophy. Became really more interested in philosophy.

I came to Union with the idea of getting my degree in philosophy of religion at Union and Columbia and teaching philosophy of religion. And then, of course, Judson and the theatre changed all that. But I couldn't have gone to a better place for my particular situation.

Q: In the very unique atmosphere that you entered into at Judson and the '60s, did the theatre world seem competitive to you?

CARMINES: In the beginning, it did not, strangely enough. I mean, we didn't know it but we were breaking new ground, of course. We were producing people like Sam Shepard and Irene Fornés, and Paul Goodman, and people who would later be seen as very seminal in the '60s and '70s theatre. But probably more at Judson than at Cino or LaMama, because we were a church, for the first couple of years the church and the theatre stood apart. I mean, we were in the same space but we were wary of one another. We did our theatre Friday through Monday nights, and we did our church on Sunday morning. Gradually, however, the church members began to interact with the theatre by wanting to be in plays, and then some of the theatre people—most of whom were either totally irreligious or secular Jews—began to come to the service because we changed our service to be much more open, and we began to introduce things in the service like people from the congregation standing up and giving their opinion of the sermon, reading something. So theatre influenced religion a lot and, in a strange way, religion influenced the theatre, too.

Q: How did the hierarchy of the church react to this?

CARMINES: Well, in the '60s, they reacted with fear. I mean, not the hierarchy of that particular church—which had always been an avant-garde kind of church—but the denomination was horrified. In fact, we began a dance theatre in 1963 which took off with a lot of steam, and Yvonne Rainer and Robert Morris did a dance where they were nude. And the Baptist denomination requested Howard Moody and myself— Howard Moody was the senior administrator; I was the assistant—to write defenses of our allowing that. There was talk of evicting us from the denomination. However, by the '70s, we became a place that the Baptists included on their tour list because they saw that the interaction between the community and the church had borne incredible fruit. Also, much more liberal people got in charge of the denomination. But in the beginning it was touch and go. We did have a communal feeling, and very little competitive feeling. And I didn't have those feelings about the theatre. I don't think Joe Cino or that place had those feelings. LaMama began to develop them as a lot of money came, and so forth; but in the beginning, and even now, there's no sense of competition there. As things, however, began to move from Off-Off-Broadway to Off-Broadway and Broadway, of course, commercial factors became much more important. And the last two really noncommercial ventures that became big hits were *Hair* and *Chorus Line*. Since then, no matter how something starts—whether it starts at a loft in the Village—by the time it gets to Broadway, it's been groomed and processed and been made highly competitive.

Q: So it has changed radically.

CARMINES: Oh, yes, absolutely. We closed our theatre in 1981 when I left and came to another church. And the feeling of cooperation, community, and joy and delight that was there in the '60s, isn't there now.

Q: Have you been in the position, either early on or since then, to judge any competitions of any kind?

CARMINES: Not to judge, really—although I've recommended people for Guggenheims and that kind of thing—but I've been at college competitions twice as an observer and also I was having a play of mine done by college students. They invited me to be on a panel there.

Q: Do you think there's a particular time in an actor's life when certain kinds of help or certain kinds of training would be beneficial? And can that be generalized across actors?

CARMINES: Well, I've dealt with a lot of young actors. That's true. I mean, to be an avant-garde theatre person—which I am—I'm terribly retrograde when it comes to what I think actors need. I think actors need diction more than they need almost anything in the world. I think there are actors who get to the top of their profession by enormous talent and charm (Brando is one; Sandy Dennis was one), who transcend the need for diction. But finally, for most actors who are going to have to appear in plays by O'Neill and plays by Miller and plays by Shakespeare— diction is needed. I feel that every young actor needs about two years simply on how to pronounce the language. I think it's terribly important. The other thing is, and the thing I missed—I've been in a great many plays, commercial and otherwise, as an actor—but when I was a young actor—I mean, young minister—I didn't have enough "movement." Even though we had the dance theatre in those days, and even modern dance now, doesn't deal with the kind of movement that's probably necessary for theatre people. And I find a great lack in my own self when it comes to simply moving. I just did a play with Bill Gaskill from London, and one of the things that he was remarkable about—in fact, he was shocked about—was that those of us who could speak the language quite beautifully didn't know what to do with our hands. Didn't know what to do with our bodies. Didn't know how to stand. Didn't know how to walk. And to try to teach a person to walk when he's fifty-five years old is a very onerous duty. So I think actors need basic kinds of skills drummed into them for two or three years when they're young. Movement, diction, rhythm, cadence. And finally, actors need a good general education. One of the things that concerns me about the Hammerstein Center at Columbia University finding a new leader when Howard Stein left was that I think it's terribly important for people in theatre to know something about history, to know something about geography. To know something about science. To know something about philosophy. In my own classes, for instance, I will teach a Williams play and then I will say, "Of course, the civil rights movement was happening then." "What do you mean, 'the civil rights movement'?" they'll say. I don't mean they don't know the term; they know what the term is, but they don't know what went on. What the relation between white and black was in a state like Mississippi or Louisiana in 1958 or '59—or '54 when Williams was writing. And the labor movement. I mean, anyone who's going to do a Miller play needs some exposure to the labor tradition in this country. So that kind of training is not only important, but crucial. And it's often absent.

Q: Were there any theatre-related organizations that you were associated with, either early in your career or along the way or now, that helped you in some way, or gave you perspective?

CARMINES: I'll tell you the two theatres that have been most influential on me in the past ten years. One is the Theatre for the Deaf, which I did a play with about seven years ago. Simply as an actor. I had to learn sign language. I had to deal with actors who were deaf.

Q: Why did they hire a nondeaf actor?

CARMINES: The role. It was written by a deaf playwright, but the role was a hearing role and speaking role. The lead was deaf and mute. It helped me a lot. I wasn't very good in the play, because attention to detail—except in terms of music—has never been a strong point with me. And to learn sign language, one has to have a feeling for detail, rather than simply the grand sweep—so that was very important. It helped me in my music and composing, and in acting it helped me. The other theatre that has helped me is Theatre for the Handicapped, Father Rick Curry's theatre. I've directed and written plays for them, and that's been interesting because it expanded me—actors in wheelchairs, actors with cerebral palsy, actors who are blind, actors who are deaf. Actors who are mute. Actors who have no arms. It makes you rethink what you're doing and gives you a wider perspective on how to write and so that was very helpful to me. Then, the one performance that I think helped me enormously—and it was of my own work: a Gertrude Stein opera (based on her novel *The Making of Americans*), which I wrote the music for. I played Gertrude Stein—or the voice of Gertrude Stein. I didn't want to cross dress at that time or play it as a women, but I wanted to play the inner voice of Gertrude Stein, so I had to absorb a lot of feminist thinking—in Gertrude Stein's terms of feminism—in order to play the role. And it expanded me probably more than any other role I've played in many years.

Q: Is there someone or something that you talk to in your mind when you evaluate your professional work?

CARMINES: Well, I have a very dear friend who's a director, Larry

Kornfeld, who teaches up at SUNY [State University of New York at Purchase] and I'm the godfather to his daughter and was best man at his wedding and he directed maybe 70 percent of my work. He's the only person that I talk to fairly frequently about what I'm thinking and feeling in terms of music and theatre and all of that. I talk to Paul Tillich in my mind a lot—who was the first theologian who made it all right for me to be a theatre person, that is, gave me permission to be both a minister and essentially involved in acting and composing and directing and so forth. I was very torn in college about what I was going to do, as I said. One of my assignments in a philosophy course my junior year was to read all of Paul Tillich's *Systematic Theology* and write a paper on it. I read it without stopping, in an upstairs room in the library. I didn't go to meals. I stayed there until the library closed. Came back when it opened. Read it through. Was changed. Was liberated in many ways. Particularly artistically. Tillich was the first theologian I had read who took Picasso, Heine, Goethe, Degas, not as just illustrations, but seriously took them as saying something fundamental about the nature of human beings and life. And through that experience I decided to come to Union Seminary in order to study with him, and also then I followed him around and studied with him down at the New School and so forth. That experience really liberated me to take the arts not as a kind of frill of life, but as part of the deep substance of life. I talk to him a great deal. The other person I talk to is a man I never met, and that's Samuel Beckett, who is my favorite playwright of this century. And he always says the same thing to me: "Pare down. Pare down. Make more minimal. Make more essential." And so I talk with him.

Q: What about peers, when you were growing up, when you were beginning in the ministry?

CARMINES: I don't feel I have any religious peers. By that, I don't mean that I'm peerless in that sense, but I don't think I knew any ministers who really took the arts with as much seriousness. I knew teachers— Tom Driver and Bob Seever at Union and Amos Wilder at Harvard. They are people whose thinking I could jibe with. But none of them did the arts, really. Seever directed some, but essentially they all taught. I didn't know anyone who was out in the actual world, acting, composing, directing on television, and who was at the same time a very religious person. So in that sense I didn't feel I had peers. I had peers as a theatre person. Irene Fornés, Sam Shepard, Larry Kornfeld, Joe Chaikin, Jacques Levy—they were all people that influenced me in theatre.

Q: What do you think actors' perceptions are of what you do now?

CARMINES: Well, it was interesting—I just was in *Comedy of Errors* and the cast, apart from one man, was all younger than I was. Most of them have heard of me, which really surprised me and shocked me. And they said, "Oh, you're Al Carmines. You composed this and so." Or, "You ran the Judson Poets Theatre, the Judson Dance Theatre. My aunt danced with the Dance Theatre"—or, "My father was with the Poets Theatre." Or, "I have friends who knew about you, read about you in college textbooks."

It was gratifying—at the same time, it was dismaying—to be kind of relegated to history. I mean, you know, I take myself with absolute seriousness. I have no false humility about myself. On the other hand, I don't think of myself as a done deed. I mean, you know, I continue to act. I was in a movie with Nick Nolte last year and Susan Sarandon, and I do whatever's available. I'll act Off-Broadway, on Broadway, in a movie, on television. I played two Kojak episodes. I compose. My music is used. But I'm not through. It was a weird feeling, kind of relegated to, "Oh, you are a '60s person." That's what they all said, "You're a '60s person, you know."

Q: Sociologists have a term called "gatekeepers"—gatekeepers meaning the people who let you in and the people who keep you out. Were there people who were gatekeepers in your career?

CARMINES: Yes, there were, in theatre. Most of them were critics, although some were other things. Not in my artistry, there are no gatekeepers there. I mean, you do what you do and then whatever happens to it, happens. But you succeed as an artist in terms of notoriety, in terms of money and so forth, by gatekeepers. And Clive Barnes was the first *Times* critic to take me with absolute seriousness. Although the *Times* had done articles on me before, and Howard Taubman and those people knew I was an interesting composer, Clive Barnes was the first critic to say that I was a seminal person, an important person. And Edith Oliver of the *New Yorker*. Those two critics, and Joe Papp. And also the Metropolitan Opera. They commissioned me to write an opera for the schools about fifteen years ago. I was pleased to be commissioned by them, but I was more pleased to have the opera done and be able to hear it and to be taken seriously not only as a composer of musicals, but as a composer of operas, as they conceived opera.

Q: Let's talk about the relationship to money through your career.

CARMINES: If I hadn't had the ministry, I would have had to get another kind of job. I have never—apart from maybe one year—in my career made money from my works, although my works have won Obies and lots of awards. The continuing income has really come from my ministry. And the perks come from theatre. I think that's very sad, really, but I mean—although in my case, it's not particularly sad—but I've seen people like Sam Shepard, when he was young, reduced to almost nothing. And writing those jewels. And Irene Fornés, working in a clothes factory. And Ellen Stewart, working as a dress designer. In England we would have all been picked up—rightly or wrongly—by government sources for funding within three years of the beginning of our careers. Here, we had to wait. We had to wait until Clive Barnes wrote a favorable article about us, and then the New York State Council on the Arts said, "Well, we'll give your theatre some money." I'm extraordinarily in favor of the NEA [National Endowment for the Arts], the New York State Council, the Department of Cultural Affairs, the Rockefeller Foundation, Ford Foundation, all of those things. I think the attacks on them are unfortunate because I think that, in some ways, they support what is going to be most useful for the future, rather than what's a hit on Broadway.

Q: What do you think is the emphasis the theatre puts on the marketplace today?

CARMINES: I don't think theatre has anything to do with the marketplace. What I think is that some plays that are good are salable and they're still good. I mean, *Chorus Line* was great, apart from the music. And other plays were simply fabulous. Sam Shepard's plays. And they're salable and that's great. There are other works just as great that aren't salable. If you go back and read the first reviews of *Waiting for Godot* when it was done in the city, you see really how crass and how incredibly blind most of the critics were. On the other hand, you know, why didn't they see, why couldn't they see after reading that play, much less seeing it, that it was a work of great, great genius? Genet, Ionesco— so there are works that are unsalable that are fabulous and there are works that are salable that are fabulous. And there are bad works that are unsalable and bad works that are salable.

Q: Do you think one can make a living in the theatre today?

CARMINES: If one is lucky, one can. But for the sake of one's own being and self-esteem, one should never—unless one wants to commit suicide in a certain kind of way—throw oneself on the mercy of the salability of your talent, you know? You could reach a point where you can do that. But no actor or actress, unless they're gifted by God, should depend on their acting for their livelihood and their self-esteem, because audiences can be wrong.

Q: But of course there are so many who do.

CARMINES: I know there are. There are, but I feel sorry for them.

Q: You mentioned some things about the Judson Theatre receiving grants. Have you ever personally received a grant?

CARMINES: I think all the grants we got were through the theatre. I have received grants, but I received them through dancers mostly for whom I wrote scores, that is, "Meet the Composer," or grants from the NEA for a dance work to be commissioned. But I always got them through the dancer and choreographer. I don't think apart from that I got any grants except maybe a small one from the Billy Rose Foundation one year. I got two thousand dollars, I think.

Q: Were those meaningful to you?

CARMINES: Yes, they were helpful. Grants are helpful. Not for the work. You do the work anyhow. But what grants are helpful for are creating an ambience where you feel that the world's not going to dissolve if you do the work instead of taking care of the world!

Q: What kind of control do you think you have over actors' careers?

CARMINES: I really don't know. I'm always surprised when people either in great rancor and anger or in great tenderness say that I have influenced their careers. I don't say that from false modesty; it's simply because I can't imagine anyone influencing my career in that way. What I'm surprised at is the amount of rancor on the one hand, and the amount of regard on the other. I think if I hadn't taken this person, someone else would have done it and fostered their talent; and if I hadn't said no to the person, the next producer would have said no. But there are women who still won't speak to me because I didn't cast them in musicals; and there are men who still say, "My God, you made my life," because I did cast them in a musical. I find it strange.

Q: What do you think the level is of your interaction with the public? Clearly you have interaction with the public in theatre and the church at the same time.

CARMINES: Well, the interaction is two parts. My aim in the interaction is to be as honest as I can be. That doesn't mean always telling the truth, or even always telling everything. But it means that my aim for my own soul is what Sartre said sainthood was—which is transparency. That's a goal. My other goal is to make the theatre and the church, or the theatre and the out of the theater, or the arts and the people that are not artists, less prejudiced against each other. Being at Judson was a wonderful way to begin that process. I mean, I finally am not an elitist, although my taste is often elitist. I don't believe in art for the cream and shit for the masses. And I don't believe that all art is elite. Probably one of the most moving songs I ever heard in my life was in Appalachia about twenty years ago in a one-room shack with a mother singing to her children. As beautiful artistically as Joan Sutherland on the stage, or Maria Callas. Truly, not religiously, artistically as beautiful, as moving, as wonderful. So, what I want to do is create situations where other people come to realize that. I want people in the church to see that art is not some fancy frill hooked onto life, and I want people in the arts to come to see that the crux of what the church is about is not being religious, but being human.

Q: Would you say that, in a contemporary climate, dealing with real social issues is more difficult today than it was?

CARMINES: [*Laughs*] I don't know the answer to that question. It's more obvious today, because the homeless are inescapable, and there are so many of them. On the other hand, how I deal with them as an artist is probably finally going to be more important than how I deal with them as a person in organized religion. That is, as a minister, I deal with homelessness by having a shelter for the homeless in my church. But as an artist, what I did was write a song called "Rags," which had to do with a rag lady who sat on the steps of the church. And I think "Rags" will be around after my shelter has disappeared. I don't know.

Q: Do you have a definition of success? And if so, has it changed through the years?

CARMINES: No, it hasn't changed. Success is—doing the truth. All the other stuff is perks.

Q: As measured by whom?

CARMINES: As measured by God. Although that's too facile an answer—and I really can't let that stand, because I wouldn't say God, really. I would say as measured by history, but history's not big enough. As measured by our conception of God.

Q: What do you view as the next step in your career?

CARMINES: I have a very definite goal as a composer and as a writer, and that is to compose American opera. And to conquer technical problems with that, to conquer the world of recitative, which no modern composers conquer. Not even the classical composers. I've got three operas that I'm trying to have done. I've got several plays that I'm still trying to have done. I don't despair about that. It's funny, because my roommate, and my friends, get very upset because my works aren't done more frequently. That doesn't bother me really. I mean, I want my works done, naturally. But what I want is the energy and the courage to continue creating. And then, whether they're done or not I can leave to God or man or woman or whatever.

Q: What about the teaching?

CARMINES: My whole basis of rehearsals is teaching songs without the music, that is, without the sheet music between me and the singers. But my teaching is in spasms. I have spasms of inspiration and illumination which I share with the class. In between the spasms, we're doing just humdrum work. We're singing the songs by Jerome Kern. Or we're talking about the history of *Showboat*, or we're talking about *Oklahoma!* and the social factors that made *Oklahoma!* such an important musical. Things that almost anyone could do. And then in the midst of all of that, I will have an illumination that only I can have because of my own history and my own talents, and a spasm of teaching will overcome me. But that's how it is, you know.

Q: What would you say was your greatest disappointment for your career?

CARMINES: My greatest disappointment structurally, as a person, may also be—a most important thing. I had a cerebral aneurysm in 1977, which led finally to my leaving Judson, led to the closing of the Judson Poets Theatre, led to my being out of the church for a year, traveling in Europe and singing in cabarets, led to my founding another church, and now to my new church.

"Disappointment" is the wrong word. It was a trauma. It was more than a trauma: it was an earthquake in my being. Whether it was good or bad, it's like saying, "Is a thunderstorm good or bad?" You can't say that. All you can say is the earthquake occurred, and my life took these directions after it. But that earthquake was an occasion in my life that changed the direction that I was moving in, changed my availability to other human beings, changed my idea of the surface of success, changed my feelings of what was important. Not basically, because I've always regarded human relationships as basically important. But it put a spotlight on them.

Q: What about your greatest satisfaction?

CARMINES: My greatest moments of satisfaction come, or have come, when I'm at a typewriter or at a piano, or simply sitting in a chair composing a melody, and the chord comes right or the note comes right. And whether anyone ever hears it, or whether it becomes celebrated, that moment is what it means to be satisfied as an artist. Then the other things are wonderful perks. I love to have people learn my work; I love to have people see my work; I love to have critics rave about my work; I love all of that. I love to be involved in the business of theatre, I loved being in this last Shakespeare play with all those young actors. It was life.

Q: How would you describe your occupation? And is that different from your career?

CARMINES: I guess I'm entering a new phase of my career, so I'm not going to be able to answer that question. I'm going to be teaching at Union next year [1992–93]—my first teaching on the interrelationship of the arts and religion. Depending on how that goes and how that works, I may have found a new career—not a new career, but a fruition of this career.

Q: And until now, what would you say your occupation has been?

CARMINES: Well, it's very humdrum: my occupation is to visit the sick, to preach a sermon every other Sunday, to go to board meetings, go to committee meetings, to bury the dead, to marry people. My occupation as minister's been to do that. My occupation as artist has been to have the piece ready for the chorus to rehearse, to have the piece ready for the soloist to do, to have the scene ready for the class to do, to have the scene ready for the theatre to do. And both of those involve time limits. One involves the business of religion in life, and that involves a time limit: not preaching too long; not making your board meeting go on too long. The other involves art in time, having it ready for people to perform, making it available and easy for people to perform, or making it hard for people to perform. But it involves being involved with time. That's what the occupation is. What the career is, is something timeless.

PAT CARROLL

B. Shreveport, La., 1927. Attended Immaculate Heart College, 1944–47; Catholic University (B.A. 1950). Military: U.S. Army "civilian actress technician." Awards: Emmy, *Sid Caesar Hour*, 1956; Outer Critics Circle Award, Drama Desk Award, and Grammy Award, *Gertrude Stein, Gertrude Stein, Gertrude Stein*, 1980; Helen Hayes Award, *Romeo and Juliet*, 1987; Helen Hayes Award, *The Merry Wives of Windsor*, 1990.

Q: Can you tell me what your very first experiences with acting and theatre were?

CARROLL: My first impression of what the theatrical experience is, is that of being a spectator sitting in some form of a theatre, watching something going on in Juarez, Mexico. We lived in El Paso, Texas; and at that point—it being Prohibition—all Americans would cross the footbridge at five-thirty, six o'clock, to go get *muy tequila* across the footpath. We had a wonderful Mexican maid named Maria Young— a beautiful, enchanting Mexican gal—who asked permission of my parents to take me to a vaudeville in Juarez. I don't remember any of the acts. All I remember was a cornet player standing up in the orchestra with a spotlight on him, playing some mad crazy solo for the cornet. And I remember thinking, "I want to do that. That's nice." And I don't remember whether I wanted to play the cornet or just wanted to be in the spotlight. I must have been three or four. We moved to California when I was five. Early theatrical experiences in California: the greatest was going to see Aimee Semple McPherson at the Foursquare Gospel Church. And I didn't know it, but I was seeing one of the greatest actresses. Aimee Semple McPherson was a lady preacher, evangelist; she started her own church and became the darling of the newspapers because of her theatricality. She was brilliant. I remember this as a child. It was like Lourdes: you'd walk into the church and there would be wheelchairs and crutches and canes and walkers hanging from people who had been "cured." But I'll tell you, up on that stage at the church, she was spectacular. She wore a long white gown and she used to tell people that they had to pin their contributions on the clothesline. Well, you're not going to pin a quarter on a clothesline. So it would have to be a bill of some sort. The woman was brilliant. And her voice was—or it seemed to be—mesmerizing. But it wasn't her voice. It was her self that was mesmerizing. That was something else that affected me theatrically. I do remember seeing shows that there were in the '30s and in the '40s in Los Angeles. One was *The Drunkard*, which ran for something like twenty years. A melodrama with olio acts, and we all got to hiss the villain and cheer the hero. And *Ken Murray's Blackouts* were very popular then too, which was kind of a vaudeville review; and the act that I loved the best was Owen McGivney, who did a quick-change act of Oliver Twist. He would come out in a window or a doorway and he'd be all of the characters, from the women to the men to little Oliver. I was dazzled by that. How did he do that? The thing that impressed me the most about these live shows that I saw—because I was a great aficionado of films when I was a youngster. I mean, I must have seen four to six films a weekend, if my homework was done. The live performances were more exciting to me than film. I adored film. Sitting in that black theatre by myself, just, oh, carried away by everybody. I loved the fact that motion pictures were more of a shaper of my cultural life, I think, than the theatre was, because motion pictures stirred my enthusiasm for history, for biography, for classical music, for dance. So in many ways, I think, I must thank cinema for stirring intellectual curiosity to a point I went on on my own. Being an only child, I was an omnivorous reader and lived in the local library. I adored being in school. I loved learning. As time went by, I'd read everything else in the local library and I stumbled into the drama section one day.

Q: Was anyone else in your family interested in theatre?

CARROLL: Well, my mother and father had worked in little theatre in Louisiana, but that was more a social thing. I think my father possibly had yearnings to be an actor. But in those days it wasn't considered very nice to be an actor. It was socially outré, and people didn't trust you.

But they never proselytized the theatre. They didn't go to the theatre that much, unless it were something like the *Blackouts*. In fact, it wasn't until I fell in love with the theatre that I began going down to the Biltmore Theatre in downtown Los Angeles for touring shows that would come in. So I picked up a book, a play, in this section of the library and I began reading it, and I slipped down to the floor and sat there till I finished it. I was hooked. It was *The Passing of the Third Floor Back* by Jerome K. Jerome, a lesser known nineteenth-century British playwright and novelist. It has a Christlike character who comes to this boardinghouse, and the role that I fell in love with was this young Cockney maid. I took the book out and I went home and I studied, and I said, "I want to do that. I want to be that Cockney maid." So I began reading everything in the drama section. Biographies, history of the theatre, plays. I started with Aeschylus. I read all of Eugene O'Neill the summer I was thirteen. I think most of it went over my head. Because of O'Neill, I began reading Freud—because I began reading literary criticism of O'Neill, in which Freud was mentioned so much. And by golly, at the ripe old age of thirteen, here I was reading Sigmund Freud. Thank God I didn't understand very much of it. But at least I knew that when you get connections, you have to follow those connections. One thing leads you to another. It's somewhat like Sherlock Holmes. After reading everything in the local drama section, of course, I knew I had to act. I literally fell into it. And then I began doing shows at high school and I seemed to have a natural aptitude. I was getting very frustrated, and one day I burst into tears and my mother said, "What is wrong?" And I said, "I want to go into the theatre." I was a fast fourteen by this time. She said, "Well, what do you want to do? Do you want to leave school and go to Pasadena Playhouse?" And I said, "No. Leave my friends? No, don't be ridiculous." So mother said, very wisely, "Well, why don't you look in the Yellow Pages?" And I said, "For what?" And she said, "For little theatre, like your dad and I used to work in." So I started in show business in the Yellow Pages. [*Laughs*]. I did: I looked it up, and there was a place called the Catholic Actors Guild and I called there, and they had an apprentice program where you had to do so many hours workshop and so many hours helping backstage before you could do main-stage stuff. So I worked with them for a couple of years. We'd do one-act plays in the workshop, and working backstage—working on props; doing all the chore work for the theatrical experience. It was very good for a youngster. I immediately saw it was not all the glamor I thought it was. It was hard work. And it was organized work. It took a lot of time and it took a lot of careful thought. And the actor relied on a lot of other people. It was very good for me to learn that. Then I began looking elsewhere around Hollywood. They had a lot of Hollywood showcases at that time, where actors would pay to work in these showcase productions so they would be seen by casting people at the studios. I went to these places and said, "I don't have any money, but I'll be very happy to work because I'm experienced." [*Laughs*] I at least knew what to say I could do and what I was capable of doing. I was still in high school. They saw this bright-eyed kid who was willing to work her fanny off, so they of course took my offer. I'd get to play a tiny little walk-on, or something, in many of these plays. I saw immediately the grubby side of the theatrical profession. This vying for climbing the ladder after you were already on the ladder. I didn't like that very much. I didn't think that was idealistic.

Q: What did your parents think about you getting into this?

CARROLL: They were wonderful. They were supportive. Once my parents knew that this was a passion, my dad in particular said, "I don't care what you do, Pat, but"—he said—"do it to the best of your ability. If this is what's going to make you happy, then we will be happy for you." The only thing they wanted me to do was graduate from college, because—being Depression parents—the college degree represented to them security. And I won a scholarship to college.

Q: Where did you go?

CARROLL: Immaculate Heart College in Hollywood. But I left because I had to go to New York. I was an English major. There weren't too many academic institutions at that time that gave degrees in theatre. But I didn't want to go the academic route for the theater. I wanted to do it now, and I wanted to act. The academic world was not enough for me. So I applied to a place on Cape Cod. It was a summer stock place, but it was called Priscilla Beach Theatre and a lot of young people went there. Dr. A. Franklin Trask, who ran the place, advertised widely in college papers and university papers and *Theatre Arts*, which was the big theatrical magazine of the time, which I adored. I left school to go work at CBS in Los Angeles because I was going to go save my money and go to New York. So I graduated from high school in 1944 and went to college the next year, then left to go work at CBS and I ended up in the sound effects department. Scheduling all the soundmen on the shows, and going up and seeing to all the sound equipment. I began doing part-time radio acting. I'd go out on my lunch hours and go see casting people in radio, and then I began doing the religious shows on Sunday. But it was work and I adored it. I worked at CBS about a year; and then I realized, this is not what I want. I'm not getting any farther.

And I'm not saving that much money. I might as well go back to school. That year did teach me that I still had a lot to learn. So I went back to college, but I lost my scholarship so the nuns up at the college said, "There is a job open at Catholic Girls High School for a teacher." Drama teacher. So I went down and was interviewed by the monsignor who was the principal of the school. Gruff old Irishman named McNicholas. I was eighteen or nineteen. He said, "Well, you come back next week with a course of study, and we'll see." I didn't know what a course of study was. I said, "Oh, yes, monsignor, absolutely"—as if I knew. I went home, called friends of mine who were in teaching, and I said, "What is a course of study?" They said, "What do you want to know for?" And I said, "Because I'm up for a teaching job." They said, "What are you going to teach?" And I said, "Acting, theatre, drama." It's only at that age that you have all the guts in the world to think that you can do anything. I sat down; I did a course of study of what I would want to learn. It was glowing. I loved it myself. The next week I went and gave him the course of study, and I had a job before I left. So I was teaching. I had my classes in the morning and then I taught in the afternoon down there. And it was only at the end of the school year that I had the guts to say to him, "Father this has been a wonderful year and I have adored it, but"—I said—"you sure put me through hell to get this job." Then I came east to do this Priscilla Beach Theatre in the summertime, and I adored it. We ate, breathed, drank, smoked theatre. We worked fourteen, sixteen hours a day. We would do workshop plays. We would do main-stage plays. It was a little barn theatre. Paying audience. And I was doing a play every week. It was wonderful. And toward the end of the summer, Gloria Swanson was coming in to do a package of *A Goose for the Gander*, which was her big summertime show. So Miss Swanson showed up. I knew the name. I had never seen a film of hers. She was dressed in a conical hat with a coif underneath the chin. And just looked smashing. She was a tiny tiny little woman and very grand and very theatrical. She was fascinating to work with. She never spoke to you directly. She always spoke through the stage manager and gave you notes even if you were standing right there. So she was my introduction to movie stars.

Then I was asked to go to Brattle Hall Theatre in Cambridge, Massachusetts, by this same producer, because he had a year-round winter stock company there. Another gal in the company and I decided, "Oh, we're too good for that. We have to go to New York." I was twenty by this time and still very daring. So Jackie, Burkey Cleary, and I left and went to New York. Of course, we went to the Barbizon [Hotel] for

Women because that's where one had to go when parents were proper. Got a job the first day we were there, doing a survey. Hated it. But Jackie went out on an understudy call, and I just schlepped around doing the job and going to the theatre. Within two weeks we were bored with this. So by golly, we decided in two weeks to call the producer and see if the jobs were still open. Jackie did it because she was a charmer. And by God, we got the job. So we went to Cambridge, Massachusetts. I did stock there at that old Brattle Hall Theatre for a year and a half. Summer, winter, spring, fall. In and out, all kinds. We even did a melodrama, which we also doubled at a saloon across from Symphony Hall in Boston. So I was working two jobs. We were getting a fast twenty-five bucks a week. And making some extra money after the show broke. Probably I was making fifty dollars a week. It wasn't that bad, but we had to get our own costumes if they weren't period, so we lived at Morgan Memorial [Thrift Shop, in Boston], buying old clothes and props and that stuff. And by golly, it was hey-diddle-de-dee, the actor's life for me. I was making my way. I was paying for everything with money earned theatrically, and I got my Equity card—which was then, as it is now, the opening door. I had healthy nerves about performing— healthy nerves. There was no question in my mind that this was what I was supposed to be. I knew there was no giving it a try. I was just going to do it, period. And I'm afraid that's the way it's been for the rest of my life. A lot of it has been falling into things by either being there or sheer attrition, but that first year in stock solidified with me that this was my life. I was not dreadfully altruistic about it at that point. My idea was, well, if this is going to be your life, you're going to have to be paid for doing it, because it has to be a livelihood as well as what you enjoy doing. So I got immediately the professional attitude: "How much?" [*Laughs*] It's only been in my later life that how much doesn't make much difference. It's how good, what is it, who's directing it, who are the other actors, I think are more important than how much. It all balances out, you know. I wouldn't give up those early years for anything, because they taught me resilience. They taught me physically saving myself from sheer exhaustion. I taught myself to go to sleep like that. I could sleep anyplace. In talking about it now, I think so much of my theatrical life was my training myself, not relying on other people. Maybe I was too stubborn. Maybe I was too egotistical. Maybe I was too afraid. I don't know. But my early life did not depend on other people at all.

Q: Was there anyone who particularly influenced you?

CARROLL: Yes. We had visiting guests—actors and actresses. And our first leading lady who played with the company was named Louise Kirkland, who was a very well known stock actress at that time. Had done Broadway and worked in every stock company that existed. Louise became our leading lady. We all watched her to see what she did, because *there's* a lady who's been around much longer than we had. Louise's deportment backstage was so wonderful. Louise taught me a great deal about being a professional person, leading a professional life.

And a dear New York character woman named Georgia Harvey. I was a friend of hers till the day she died. Georgia also taught me the independence of being a theatrical, because the fellows in the company would always offer to assist Georgia if she was moving her bags, and Georgia would say, "No, dears, in this business, we carry our own bags." And I thought, "Go for it, old sweetheart." Again, that total-going professional. Independent. Always on time. Deportment backstage, perfection. Those were the people who were my teachers. I probably would not have admired them so much had not their work on the stage been so wonderful.

And when you're doing a different show every week, you teach yourself. The audience is the teacher. You find out what works with them. You find out what silence is about. When people are listening through silence. You find out what laughter is about. You never ultimately find out what really creates laughter. I still don't know to this day, and I've devoted my life to laughter. I still am learning from audiences. I found out early in stock that I wanted to be a very serious actress. I found out early in stock that I had the timing, and I have the psychological profile for comedy. I had an adeptness that I sensed the way a line should be read, although there are five different ways a line can be read—or six—whereby you can get a laugh. I'm always shocked at my youngest daughter, who has different timing that I have, and I swear she can get a laugh doing a reading I never would have thought of. I'm learning from her. But I occasionally yearn to do more dramatic things. When I first came to New York I would go into offices. I'd said I'd do comedy. And I had long blonde hair down to here, big blue eyes, and they said, "No, you're an ingenue." And I said, "No, I am not an ingenue." I said, "I know all those roles, and I hate them. I do comedy." And they said, "No, you don't." So I had great arguments when I first came to New York about what I did.

But after I played stock for a year and a half, I became a civilian actress technician for the army, which meant that I produced, wrote, staged all soldier shows. I had charge of the seven states of the Second Army. I answered an ad, because I was getting tired of stock. I was headquartered at Fort Meade, Maryland, and had charge of the seven states. I toured one show of a hundred men and myself. Wasn't that wonderful? I cast me as the only woman in the show, and wrote some music for it, found some old sketches for it, and we toured the seven states of the Second Army. I did that for about a year. And I had friends at Catholic University and so I used to go up to the university and see productions. Walter Kerr was head of the department then. And I was asked to open a new theatre down in Camp Lee, Virginia, but I had to teach some courses. I did try out a new play there, and I took a course from Walter Kerr—Basic Aesthetics—which was brilliant. God, he was a wonderful teacher. And he was a wonderful director, also. Father Hartke, who headed the whole theatre department at CU, offered me a scholarship and I said, "No, Father, I have my Equity card and I must go to New York." It was very grand. But he said, "Now, if things don't work out for you in New York, you must come back here. I'll always have a scholarship for you." About twelve years later, he called for me to get an honorary doctorate at Barry College in Miami. He said, "Why didn't you ever come back to school?" I loved being at the university; but again, the academic life was not enough for me. It simply was not enough for me.

So I came into New York and began making rounds. I really consider 1950 as the time when I came to settle in New York, to make my life in the theatre here. The first thing I did was Off-Broadway—so Off-Broadway, it was down on 19th Street, a review for a group who had just come down from Yale. Young fellow named Mike Stewart—who later wrote the book for *Hello Dolly*, *Carnival*, and *42nd Street* and a whole bunch of shows—Mike had written a review and I auditioned for these young chaps from Yale and I was immediately hired and we did this review down in the Village. I also concurrently was doing an annual showcase that the stage managers used to do, just called *Talent '50*, or *Talent '51*, or *Talent '52*. They knew a lot of young people in New York were simply not being seen in things in New York, and the Shuberts or any of the theatre owners would loan them a theatre for an afternoon or two and they'd do matinees for agents, producers, managers. And out of *Talent '50*, which I did, Julius Monk at the old Le Ruban Bleu—one of the big supper clubs here—called me and I could barely understand him because he's North Carolina out of Paris by Miami via Palm Beach, but I got enough of it to understand he wanted me to come to Ruban, see what they did, and then he wanted me to perform there. I never thought of performing in saloons. I said, "Well, I don't have an act, Mr. Monk." He said, "Get an act." So I called Mike Stewart. I called

Jim Wise, who later wrote *Dames at Sea*. By golly, I did an out-of-town break in and came into the Ruban in the spring of 1950 and made my supper club debut. I'd never planned this. It happened.

Q: How long did you work there?

CARROLL: I had a career of three years in supper clubs. I went from Ruban to Number One Fifth Avenue, [from] Village Vanguard to the Blue Angel. By 1955, when I got married, I had played probably three or four years in supper clubs. Thanks to those showcases of *Talent '50* and the Off-Broadway review, the work became constant. I was starting to play Tamiment. At Tamiment, you did an all-original review every weekend. And such people as Jerry Bach, who wrote *Fiddler on the Roof,* and Herb Ross, who is now a Broadway–Hollywood producer. Neil Simon wrote sketches there with his brother Danny. Those were my mentors; those were my trainers; those were the people who gave me that next patina of experience and learning. I couldn't have done television without Tamiment. Because it taught me to do things fast, fast, fast. I got married in '55—the '50s were a combination. I made my Broadway debut in '55. A fast live musical review called *Catch a Star.* Then television seemed to take over my life—and I did the *Red Buttons Show* in '53. I had my first child in '56 and also did the *Sid Caesar Hour.* Then I began doing Max Liebman's specials all the time, starting to do commercials, voiceovers. Every bit of work that was in New York, I started to do. During the summer I'd go out in summer stock. Working for many stock producers for whom I'd work for twenty-five dollars. And others were paying me a lot more than that—which I loved. But in 1960 we moved back to California, and I started with the *Danny Thomas Show.* I did six guest appearances on that and stayed for three years. Then began the cycle of television. And my life was full of a growing family, a marriage, and continual work. And I thought, "This is the way it will always be." Never considering that there are changes in your own life; there are changes in the theatrical profession itself.

By 1975, when I was divorced and I had three children, I had a career that was kind of going downhill because now I wasn't a youngster anymore. And what I was doing was boring the hell out of me. And I decided that I had to come to grips with something. What was it that got me into this profession? I thought, "Well, it's not what I'm doing now." And the phones weren't ringing that much, and I thought, "Oh, I see. I've heard about this, but I never thought it would happen to me." So by golly, I began thinking, "You've got to do something to change your career. Nobody else is going to do it. No agent is capable of doing it. Nobody's going to come along on a white charger and change your career." Also at that time, I had to have knee surgery. When I awakened, I knew my life was going to be different because I had never been through such pain in my life. It took me a year to recuperate from that. I had a limp. I was overweight. And that was not a very good prospect for an actress, so I began working on the idea of a one-person show. I thought and I thought. And Gertrude Stein kept coming to mind. I hated Gertrude Stein's work when I was in college. Hated it, abhorred it, and said, "I can write better than that." Of course, the ego that you have when you're eighteen. I called the local library and got everything that was done, everything written, every biography, and I began doing research on Gertrude Stein. And I put a piece of paper in the typewriter and it came out, "Why Gertrude Stein." And I was going to do a concert thing called *Why Gertrude Stein?* A young playwright I'd met in the past called me during this period and said, "What are you going?" And I said, "I'm working on a concert piece about Gertrude Stein." He said, "Oh, my God, I adore Stein. Let me write a play for you." So within two months I'd commissioned him to write a play. I felt I was fairly sure in my research. I thought, "Well, if the kid stumbles, I'll help him with my brilliant knowledge of Stein."

Q: Who was the writer?

CARROLL: Marty Martin from Austin, Texas, and this was '75 or '76. By '78, actually, the play was finished. I worked with him on the second act. The first act as performed was almost the way it came out of his typewriter. Second act had three rewrites. In order to deal with the show on a professional level, I traded co-writing for the copyright so I could do business for the show. I got Mary Ellyn Devery, who was working for the Theatre Guild at the time, to produce the show for me; but my company raised the money and ostensibly produced it, with her as the line producer. We did our initial performance at State College, Pennsylvania, then came in to Circle Rep to share a rep summer with Sam Shepard's *Buried Child.* Did such good business that we rented our own space at Provincetown Playhouse and played over a year. Then did four years on the road. It was a hell of a comeback, and it was also a change in my life because I realized that I had not ever stated what I felt the theatre was about—and that play was what the theatre was about, to me. There was no success or failure predicated in my mind. I just knew I had to do it. Its ultimate success was very gratifying and very surprising, but it also gave me five years' work, which I appreciated. It was work I created.

However, during that five years, a whole new generation of television people had come in. I had been out of town. So I was no farther along in a career, really. I put away the costume, put away the scenery, and I suddenly realized that the almost seven years I had spent away from the mainstream had left me way behind in the game. So I stayed in New York for a while. Nothing much was happening and my mother became ill in California, so I went back to California. I did one season with Ted Knight in his new *Ted Knight Show*. Then I got cast on a valiant series called *She's the Sheriff*, with Suzanne Sommers.

But all during this period, my mother was ill and I needed the money, you know. And I was happy to take anything. But I had this taste for self-determination theatrically. And I started taking risks. I was Stein. That was a risk. It was a big risk. I hocked everything in order to do it. I suddenly thought, "This is mandatory, but it's not the way I want to live the rest of my life theatrical." So my mother died and I said, "Okay, now the kids are grown. My mama's gone." My dad had died in '63. I said, "Okay, I'm just going to take risks and gambles from here on in." And I've continued to do that and I've adored it to this day. From 1975 until now, I've spent most of my life gambling and risking and not doing things for the dollar. The satisfaction has been exceptional. The financial return has been minimal. Fortunately, I'm retired officially from the profession, so I have a base financial pool from which to draw. I suppose, in a way, I can afford my own indulgence and I think I deserve it.

I didn't do my first Shakespeare until I was sixty. And my mother said, "Why did you never do Shakespeare before?" And I said, "Because nobody ever asked me." [*Laughs*] Now you talk about training. When I was doing *Stein*, I decided that it was risky being one person out there. I thought, "I'd better know what I'm doing vocally." So, Mary Ellyn Devery, who had hired Dr. Julia Wing of Temple University for the Al Pacino company of *Richard III*—Dr. Wing whipped that company into shape. I began working with her and the woman is a miracle worker. Brilliant speech coach. She began me on a series of breathing exercises to free and relax my body. She raised my range over an octave. I've never had a voice like the voice I had in *Stein*. I always laughed at Method actors: "my instrument." It really *was* an instrument. I could play it like a saxophone. I could blare it like a trumpet. I could play bass drum on it. And I ascribe that totally to Julia. And in those five years of playing that show, I never once lost my voice. I never once missed a performance. I would even call Julia on the road. I would be feeling something going in my voice and she'd say, "I think you have something wrong in your back." I would go to a chiropractor and she'd be on the money. I said, "What are you—a psychic?" She said, "No, I can tell from the voice what's going on in the body." So I don't do anything, including Shakespeare, unless I call Julia and coach on the phone with her.

I was asked to do the Nurse in *Romeo and Juliet* at the Folger Theatre in Washington, D.C., by Michael Kahn, the artistic director. I thought, "Isn't that funny? That's the one Shakespearean role I always wanted to play." I went into rehearsal, and no one in the company knew I hadn't done Shakespeare before. And most people did not know until after the opening that I'd never done Shakespeare before.

Q: Were you afraid of it?

CARROLL: I was petrified. I began smoking again. I'd stopped smoking for three years. I was scared to death—but oh, my God, how gratifying. Because of my bad knees, I asked to sit on a stool backstage so I didn't have to walk up and down the stairs. Every night I heard actors growing, and I knew I grew myself. And I discovered for the first time what it is not to have a word to say in a scene but to be so totally in that scene and to know that you're important in that scene though you don't have a word to say. It was wonderful. If there's one regret I have in my theatrical life, it's that I didn't start in Shakespeare.

Q: Can you describe a little bit about your technique or how you go about working on a role?

CARROLL: I don't know. First, the words are important, because it's out of the words that I get an idea of what the character may be like. I also read the entire play, which I think is the most important thing. And I suppose I don't even listen to a lot of directors. I know that I'm not always right; but at least my intuitive sense about that character on a page, and how I want to translate that character, is as true for me as anybody telling me what to do. That stubborn Irish streak.

Then, the physicality of that character as I see it. I'm very external. I'm very physical. And I have to latch onto something that's physical for me that says something about that character. Or it could be something vocal, like a dialect or something. I work from the outside almost totally.

Rehearsal is important. People always say, "Well, why do you stick around when you're not needed in rehearsal?" I say, "Because I have to watch." I have to watch and see what other people are doing, because to me it's like painting a painting, and I'm only one figure in that painting. I want to see where I balance out with everybody else. And then I try to live in that painting if I can. It doesn't mean that I am somebody else. I just have all of those external trappings, and I play make-believe. I have fun. When this profession ceases to be fun, I'm out of here.

Q: Are there people whose opinions you respect and rely on to look at your work or review your work?

CARROLL: Quite honestly, no. I know when I feel I'm doing something well. And if I don't do it well, I'll leave it.

Q: How do you feel about professional critics?

CARROLL: I only have one opinion about professional critics. It's a quote from Diderot: "Like eunuchs, they watch it being done every night, but they can't do it themselves." [*Laughs*] There's a necessity for critics, certainly in today's theatre, where tickets cost so much. I wish more of them were like Walter Kerr, who gave an E for effort—although this is not a profession for E for effort. But Walter Kerr could at least—with his good director's eye and with his good theatrical sense— say, well, this was good about it and that was good about it. He was not a killer. He was not getting his own audience reaction from the clever- ness of his critiques.

Q: You said, even when you were very young, you started asking for money. It seems like you've exerted a lot of control in your career.

CARROLL: Well, I have. And I'll tell you, I don't like doing things for nothing. I've worked very hard during my lifetime to learn this craft, to learn this profession; and I'll send money to any benefit, but I don't like to do them, because nobody will do a benefit for me. It sounds very hardhearted, and I don't mean it to sound hardhearted. I'm being honest. When I'm paid. And I don't care what it is, but I must be paid. As someone said, "Like all good whores." [*Laughs*] I suppose in a way that's true.

But it's a fascinating business because "Hope is the thing with feathers." That's why the character people in our profession (of which I am one now) still are the youngest people I know, because they're still hoping that wonderful role is just around the corner. Now I also have the joy of my life in cross-dressing for Falstaff in *Merry Wives*. This did not come off as a feminist statement. I simply had always wanted to play Falstaff, period. I'd seen a production of it at Stratford in the late '60s and I knew I would be called to do Mistress Quickly, but I didn't want to do Mistress Quickly—I wanted to do Falstaff. Michael Kahn had asked me after we did *Romeo and Juliet*. He said, "You know, we have to do more Shakespeare with you." And I said, "Oh, I want to." He said, "What do you want to play?" And I said, "Well, I'd like to play Paulina, in *A Winter's Tale*. I'd like to play a couple of clowns because they're asexual. I'd like to do Amelia in *Othello*. I would like to do

Falstaff in *Merry Wives*." And he said, "What?" I said, "Falstaff." He started to roar. He said, "That's funny." I said, "I'm not kidding." He said, "That's very amusing, Pat." But two years later his general manager called and said, "Pat, we're doing *Merry Wives* in the spring." I said, "Yes, I'd love to play Falstaff." She said, "Can I call you back in the next couple of days?" Michael called me back; he said, "You weren't kidding." Why would I kid about something like that? I knew that I could get away with Falstaff in *Merry Wives*. I would no more think of playing Falstaff in the *Henrys* than I would God. He's totally male. This old rooster has no cockadoodle-doo in him in *Wives*. So it was perfectly all right to play him. And it's not a good play. So anything theatrical you can do to bolster it up, makes great sense.

Q: Did you have fun doing it?

CARROLL: I had a ball. Very difficult to learn to swagger. That's a totally male thing. Women do not swagger. That's a very specific physical manifestation of something internal, and only men swagger. I see my son swagger. I saw my husband swagger. I've seen male friends swagger. I worked and worked because it is the manifestation of what a man who thinks well of himself does. One day it happened in rehearsal.

The production filled me with glee because I asked many people I would meet—actors, particularly men—"Did I upset or embarrass you playing Falstaff?" And they'd said, "Oh, hell, no. After five minutes, I forgot you were a woman." Greatest compliment in the world. I enjoyed the fact that it was well received critically, but that didn't have anything to do with the fact of why I wanted to do it. It was a lot of hard work but, golly, I had fun. I totally enjoyed it. And out of that, Michael had said, "What else do you want to do?" And I said, "I'd like to do *Mother Courage*"—which I am going to start in February 1993. So this has been my season of mothers. I played the Mother Superior in *Nunsense* this summer. Now Mother Fisher in George Kelly's *The Show Off*, and now Mother Courage. How many different characters you get to play! Because we only have a very short lifetime in which to play all the things we want to do.

I hadn't realized that the only place you can pitch yourself against records like athletes do is in the classical theatre. There's no other standard in any other form of theatre that performance can be compared, you know, so that you know that you're going up against the greats when you work in Shakespeare, when you go back and think of all the women who have worked in Shakespeare. What I'd love to do is talk to that actor who played the Nurse in the original production of *Romeo and Juliet*. That's the man I would like to speak to—because he had to be wonderful because, to me, the Nurse is the perfect rounded circle of female characters in Shakespeare. I love the Nurse. I want to do it again. I see why people want to repeat roles in Shakespeare. Because I'm sure there's a passion that comes about about certain roles, and you don't get an opportunity to say that kind of speech anymore in contemporary theatre.

Q: Do you think the marketplace has changed dramatically in your career?

CARROLL: Yes. The marketplace has opened up in television. There are more young actors being hired in television than older age groups. When I started in the theatre, the pay might not have been great, but you had stock companies everyplace, at least on the East Coast. Winter, summer, spring, and fall stock. Also, in New York, when you got here, there were all kinds of commercial opportunities to turn a dollar, like I used to narrate fashion shows. I started doing voiceovers. The commercial outlets for the young performer that are greater today are in voiceovers. Some young performers devote themselves totally to it, because it's a profession unto itself. In the theatre, there are fewer opportunities for the dedicated young actor or actress to work, because there are fewer places doing it. During the heyday of dinner theatre, that was wonderful because there were fifty-two weeks a year that could be devoted to the young actor. I've worked dinner theatres also. And though most critics decried them, I found them wonderful in that they were appealing to people who had not been to a live performance of anything before. Because of the very reasonable price of both food and entertainment, you were getting a whole new audience. And I witnessed that, and I think that's what we need today.

We're losing the youth in this country for audience material, because it's too expensive for young people to go. Unless the parents take them, I doubt if any of them go. Yes, there are fewer opportunities I think for young actors and actresses in the theatre. I don't think you can stir that by forcing it. You can't force culture down someone's throat. And I don't think you can stimulate false employment in the arts. I'm totally against that. If we waited for the demand, I'm sure none of us would work. But the arts are not a necessity in people's life in this country. People would not give up a dinner in order to go to the theatre or the ballet. Maybe young students would; but the normal citizen, I don't think, would give up anything to enjoy the arts. I may be being very cynical, but I think it's true. If it's part of an entertainment that they're planning if they're coming to New York, of course they want to see a Broadway show. There's cachet in that. But to support something in their own community— I doubt very seriously. They will support the sports program that their kids are involved in. I mean, can you think of a little Italian town without some opera company that either goes there or they have because that's part of their living? It's like wine. You can't have life without opera. It doesn't exist. We don't have that passion for the arts in this country. I've been delighted to see that the world of dance has struck more people in the past twenty years. We have more ballet companies being supported in communities. But times are rough financially now. What goes first? The ballet company? The symphony orchestra? The theatre? Because when it's a choice between your belly and the roof over your head and going to the arts—no, people will not do it. And I can't blame them. I'm not making a judgment call here. I'm simply saying, "That's the way it is, folks." And we're living in perilous financial times. So the first thing to go will be the arts, and I don't think we can lay all of that burden on big business. Of course, there are fewer opportunities in this day of November 1992 than there ever have been before. And we see more young striving and struggling actors, painters, dancers in New York City than you do everyplace else. Why, this is Mecca. This is the lodestar. This is where you come. You've got to get that New York title. You've got to get that appreciation from New York audiences. But I think it's far more difficult to be an actor in this day and time for a young person. I think it's madness. I have a younger daughter who's gone into it. She's been working television. She makes more money than I made for the first ten years of my theatrical profession. It's the first time in the history of acting that we've had a slice of the pie. It is—when you think about it—quite wonderful.

Q: On that end, how do you feel about the unions for actors? You mentioned you were proud when you became a member of Equity.

CARROLL: Well, I wish we had higher standards and demanded an apprenticeship like the old guild systems. Young people today are the proud possessors of these things that were fought for years ago—by actors who'd had these horrible things happen to them—so they don't have to think about it. And that's something else that young actors should have: a class or something at the unions to apprise them of the fact that people have fought hard for the rights that you now enjoy so effortlessly. Let's at least respect them by name. I think the unions are mandatory in the big business that the entertainment world is now. What are we—second or third in industry in the country? Entertainment, it's big business now. There's no fooling around. There are a lot of sharks out there. You have to have the protection. I am for unions. I am the recipient of forty-five years of working under unions. I think there have been some crimes committed under their names; but for the most part—

I would say, 80 to 90 percent—it's been good for the workers under those unions. The golden goose is not laying the golden eggs anymore, folks, so I think we all have to be a little sensible. People are not in business for charity. They're in business for profit. And that's why I have a little bit of a problem with not-for-profit theatre; but it has become necessary in many areas, and for many reasons, so I have to go along with it. But my idea was, you either live or die by people coming up and paying for a ticket at the box office—no matter what price that ticket is. I think we're going to see that they're going to have to cut back the ticket prices in New York because people are not going to be able to afford it pretty soon at all. So what are you going to have? Half-empty house and not be able to continue the production? There's going to have to be a breakthrough someplace and I'm not bright enough to know what that breakthrough should be, but I just know that it will have to happen.

Q: What would be your next step that you would like to see in your career?

CARROLL: Well, strangely enough, I have two more one-woman shows that I'm working on. I'm old enough to appreciate that to either live or die by your own standards is wonderful. I like the whole physical thing of being my own boss, and I work twice as hard when I'm my own boss. I also want to do some writing now. I'm working on a couple of things. Being an English major, I think it's only fair to end up with that. Those are just for the next couple of years. Beyond that, I don't think too much. If I'm still doing the things that I want to do, and I'm still discovering new things, I'm way ahead of the game. If I go from season to season now, I am thrilled to death about that. One of the gals in *Nunsense* has a wild bug that wc should all go to Ircland and takc *Nunsense* and go to the villages where they never get entertainment. I'd love to do that. I should have done it when I was eighteen. But if I can still do it physically now, that's the real gypsy life, isn't it? I go to sleep at night thinking about that, and thinking how wonderful that would be. And we could also do poetry readings. We would have another show of American music, besides *Nunsense*. Do a small musical review and then another program of poetry readings.

Q: Is there one piece of advice that you'd give to younger actors—or to you own daughter—about pursuing a career in theatre?

CARROLL: I've always told my daughters, "The minute you start getting bitter, get out of it." There's got to be another way for you to live your life to your satisfaction, to your level. I do feel that sometimes, when you walk away from something, if it's supposed to be yours it will come and tap you on the shoulder. I do believe that happens. But I said to my daughter, "Don't make a time limitation on it. Give your life time to blossom, as well. Don't strangle the other parts of your life for the theatre." We don't find a cure for cancer. We don't solve world peace. We don't do anything that's major important. What we do is alleviate people's life hurts for maybe a couple of hours, and that's not bad. It's like being an emotional nurse. You know, if we can do that for a few hours in the theatre, let scientists solve the problem of cancer. What we're doing for the human beings, I think, is in some ways as important. That's my major piece of advice. When you start to get bitter, walk away from it. It's not worth it.

MIRIAM KRESSYN

B. Russia, 1912. Attended New England Conservatory and Northeastern University in late 1920s. Many early awards, including Youngest First Lady in America in Yiddish Theatre. Other selected awards: Show Business Award, 1973; two Goldies, for Outstanding Acting and for Lifetime Achievement; Drama Desk Award; Sholom Aleichem Award; Workman's Circle Award, 1980s; Forty Years of Yiddish Radio in America, 1988; Goldman-Timberg Award for Contribution to the Yiddish Theatre in America, 1989.

Q: Miss Kressyn, can you tell me a little bit about your early background and your initial experiences with acting in your early childhood?

KRESSYN: My early childhood I had nothing to do with theatre. I had never seen theatre. My early childhood was in Russia, Poland, Germany, Russia, Poland, Germany; those were the First World War years, of course. And I had never seen theatre. We didn't have any formal schooling at first, because Jewish children were not permitted in school. I was born in Bialystok. During the war my father said to my mother, "Take the infant and go to Orla"—a small vacation town in a wooded area—"the war will never reach Orla." So, Mother took the child Miriam and left for Orla. And Orla was on the borderline of a dense forest where the Bolsheviks, the Germans, and Poles were either hiding, chasing, or killing one another. And we were in the middle—running to the synagogue every time shooting started (the synagogue being the only brick building in Orla). The trains were confiscated for the military, so that we were separated from my father. So my mother and I were stuck in the little town without my father or my two brothers. They were recruited to dig trenches for the army. I was raised for about three or four years without my father or the rest of the family—just Mother and I. When I was about four or five years old there was a teacher that came from Bialystok through the Tzisha Schools, a Zionist organization that sent one teacher to the Orla summer school. Incidentally, we had no shoes to wear, so the teacher came without shoes so as not to embarrass the mothers who brought the children to school.

Finally, my father and my brother smuggled their way to Orla and we were reunited at last, until the younger of the two brothers was kidnapped by the Poles—he was only seventeen—to go into the army. He escaped and we didn't know whether he was alive or not. Later we found him hiding in an attic in a barn, under straw (but this is another story). So that was the one year that I had Yiddish schooling, but it was a splendid, revealing, unforgettable year. I loved it. Everything was in Yiddish. However, there were students that used to go to Vilnius— Lithuania now, then Poland—to the university, and a teacher there said to me, "You know that you would make a very good teacher." I was by then eight, nine years old. "I will prepare you, and you will have your examination and see if you can enter the seminary for teachers." I thought that would be a wonderful thing.

We had no library in the town. So we each gave a *groshen* or a *kopicke* which is two pennies or four pennies, and we started buying books for the library. Of course, everybody was much older. I had no peers; little boys, they went to *kheyder* [a Hebrew school, compulsory studies for Jewish boys]—so there were no boys. And little girls, if their parents were too poor, the children went without.

My mother pawned a *perenneh* [feather bed] to pay for my tuition. So I was among one or two youngsters among adults. I had a very receptive mind, like a sponge. Whatever was told to me, I placed it somewhere in the archives of my mind, so that mentally I wasn't a child anymore. I was an overgrown child or an undergrown adult because I really didn't mature until I came to this blessed land and continued my schooling officially in American schools. With my tutor, Dodya Weinstein, every summer I studied—Russian, Polish, German. And every child in Europe spoke four or five languages—Spanish, French. It prepared me for my travels around the world with theatre.

My father went to America before I was born. And brought four of my sisters to America. Mama was left with two boys. He was in America for three years. He couldn't get used to America because, we say in Yiddish, he was "a *learner*"—a man that is an ongoing student of the Torah. He couldn't find a job. They wanted to make a glazier out of him, and he didn't know how to handle glass. He left my sisters in America. He came back three years later. Mother was already up in years, but young enough to have another child. That was me. I don't remember my mother with dark hair. It was always white to me, and very beautiful. We were seven children. I had four sisters and I was born the fifth. Yes, five sisters and two brothers. When I came to America, I didn't want to come.

Q: When did you come?

KRESSYN: We came in 1925.

Q: How old were you?

KRESSYN: Eleven. I didn't want to go to America because it was an enlightenment period for me. Progress came very slowly in a small town like Orla. I was in that—slow (what I thought was progressive)—period. I became a skeptic, "lost" my religion. (You really don't lose it.) My father, brother, studying for the rabbinate. But, no, I had to argue with my father: "What is God?" And, "There is no such thing as God." Now, when I think of it, how could I have the heart to tell my father that "there is no God"—when he was so pious? So that I was brought up "irreligious" in my young mind, religious at home.

When the war finally ceased, I didn't want to go to America. I said, "I can't go to America, because America is bourgeois!" Little communist, you know. I didn't know what communism was, but in theory, it sounded like Utopia. But father said, "My child, we cannot stay here any longer. We are being persecuted. We must go." Naturally I loved my parents, so I came. My oldest brother did not want to come to America, saying, "I'm religious. America cannot live my way and I cannot live the American way." He went to Israel in 1937. So he was the only one of the family left in Poland in 1925. "God is with me," he said, "no matter where I am." I didn't see him until my visit to Israel in 1959.

How did I come to the theatre? Are you familiar with the West End in Boston? Well, the "West End" in Boston was the Jewish "East Side" of New York. We lived at 43 Allen Street, and my sister shared a wall with Musical Settlement. I was singing in my house. And that one wall divided us, and they must have heard me sing. They called me in and asked, "Would you like to study music, singing?" I said, "Yes, I'd love to study, but I have no money." "It's only fifty cents a lesson," they said. "I will not take any money from my family; they're bourgeois." True, they were rich—but they worked twenty-four hours a day! They had delicatessen stores! I was aware of it, but to me they were rich! And it's "Down with the rich." "Well, if you don't have the fifty cents, we'll wait until you'll get it and you'll pay us. Meantime we're going to have an audition." I didn't know what an audition was. What was the audition? On radio. The *Atwater Kent Radio* was giving scholarships, and there were fifteen hundred students—New England children—youngsters thirteen, fourteen, fifteen. I was fourteen at that time.

There was Yiddish Theatre in Boston. I had three brothers-in-law. As I said, they were well off. They were among the "Jewish philanthropists." If a school or a Talmud Torah was needed, they came to Mr. Sheff, Mr. Berger, Mr. Gross, and they always gave. For Yiddish Theatre in Boston—the only one—they donated. On Sundays they didn't play theatre in Boston. Boston was, you know, a blue town. My sister had a very beautiful home, with gardens, in Sharon, Massachusetts. Sunday my brother-in-law and sister used to invite the company to their home for Sunday dinner. The performers used to love it. By the time they left, my brother-in-law gave them salami and corned beef and things to take home. I must have been singing with the children, and Julius Nathanson—star director in the Yiddish "Grand Opera"—asked, "Who is singing?" My brother-in-law kiddingly answered, "My *greene cousine* [immigrant cousin]." He called me over, saying, "You should be in the theatre." "Our little Miriam?" my brother-in-law said. "No. We have other plans for our little girl. She's going to school." I never dreamed of theatre. As I say, I had never seen theatre, so I didn't know what I was missing. I didn't want to "make" money. But if you can play theatre and earn money, and go to school at the same time, that's for me! I went to audition for the chorus. And they were paying at that time five dollars a performance. In Boston at that time they played nine performances a week. And I was suddenly making forty-five dollars a week! So the first thing I bought, I could say a "secondhand"—probably a "fifth hand"—Chickering piano for $150. Now I was studying at the Boston Music School and I had a piano and I was on the way. I was singing in the chorus, so I used to pick out notes on the piano.

Q: You were a teenager?

KRESSYN: Yes, I said I was sixteen because you were not allowed to be on the stage. Suddenly I was notified from the radio station that I won a $7,500 scholarship from *Atwater Kent Radio*. I was dumbfounded. I didn't know. "What does it mean? Do I get the money?" I didn't know. But they told me that you'll be going to the New England Conservatory to study, right next door to Northeastern University. I was a student in music, also registered at the university in night courses. Never dreaming of theatre. The chorus was just a way of making five dollars a performance playing small parts, and studying. That's how I came into the theatre. If it weren't for my brothers-in-law or my sisters, if it weren't for the fact that the company used to come Sundays to relax and eat something, I wouldn't have known about Yiddish Theatre, about earning five dollars a performance, and I wouldn't have had a career in the theatre, nor been professor of Yiddish drama at Queens College for ten years.

Now, I was a little girl who spoke Yiddish fluently, and spoke English—because when I came, they put me in kindergarten at the age of eleven, mind you, because I had never heard the sound of English in Orla or Bialystok. I had a Miss Smith, a very lovely teacher. One of those—slender—tall—with hair piled high on her head, a very sweet-tempered teacher. She may have liked me or had pity on me or something. She would write words on the blackboard, and say, "Repeat after me. Cat, house, or—jew-el-ry." I had heard that word, not "jew-el-ry," because my sisters didn't say "jew-el-ry"; they said "jew-le-ry." And so I said to the teacher—I didn't know whether to put it in a question or what—"No, Miss Smith [*Pause*] 'jew-le-ry.' " [*Laughs*] As though I was correcting the teacher. "No, Miriam. It's jew-el-ry." I listened to the sound. I never make the same mistake twice! My middle name is Mindel. Everybody has a middle name; when they asked my second name, I had heard the name "Marilyn"—to me it sounded like "Maryland." So when they asked me my name I said, "Miriam Maryland Kressyn." The one and only Miriam Maryland Kressyn in this great big universe. I went from this special kindergarten into the eighth grade because I had studied geography and other subjects with a tutor in Europe.

The Junior Hadassah in Boston came to Mr. Nathanson, star director of the Boston Opera House, and said that they want to do a performance of the opera *Shulamis* for the benefit of Hadassah. They want a children's *Shulamis* because it's a novel idea. "Well, I have a young girl that speaks Yiddish very well," said Nathanson. "She sings; she's studying at the Conservatory. She would be your perfect Shulamis." And so they got one of the older performers in the company to direct me in the part of Shulamis. There's a big dramatic monologue. I learned it overnight. Mr. Leon Blank, a guest artist, was standing on the side of the stage, watching me. I finished, and he called me over, pinched my cheek, and said, "*Du vest shoin shpielen theatre* [You will play theatre]." "I, theatre? No." I still had not become imbued with the magic of theatre. I had aspirations to go to the university—to be a lawyer, perhaps. Singing to me was like being born with a voice or having brown eyes.

But not with any special talent. It was my third year at the Conservatory. They started speaking of a "debut." Now, this was a crucial moment in my life.

They put on the record of the opera star Lucretia Bori singing *Butterfly*. We used to practice with a lighted candle; if our breath control was correct while we sang, the candle wouldn't flicker. And my breath control was so perfect, they said, that it enabled me to do the phrasing of *Butterfly* better than Lucretia Bori. I am telling you this because a little thing like the flicker of a candle can decide your entire life. And they decided that I will make my debut in the opera. I still had one more year to study. My teacher's name was Madame Laurenti, a devout Catholic. And she said, "Miriam, you are too young. Besides, you have not studied in Europe. And a singer who has not studied in Europe has very little chance to be accepted at the opera in America." It has changed since. "I have an idea," Madame Laurenti said. "In the spring we'll go to Minchen [Munich]. There they give the *Passion Play*; they are the famous Oberammergau Players. There you will sing; you will make your debut as Magdeline. We'll come back and we'll show them. I'm certain you'll get very good notices and it'll show you were in the opera. We'll have something to go on for your debut. I can just see it—'The youngest opera star!' " I come home and tell my sisters and my brothers that I am going to Munich, and I'm going to sing with the Oberammergau Players. And when they heard "Oberammergau," they said, "What? *Mit anti-Semitin vist zingen. Du vest nicht gein!* [You will not go!]" That stopped there. "Besides, you're not even a citizen." Why was I not a citizen? My father was older, didn't want to bother studying for citizenship. Besides, he was still hoping to go to Israel to see his son the rabbi. I was too young, so I couldn't become a citizen, I had to wait until I was twenty-one. "If you go to Europe, you know what difficulty you will have to come back to America, because of the quota? They will never allow you in." We didn't realize that a "student exchange" is a student exchange. I didn't even know enough to ask what would happen.

So, I remained in Boston, didn't go to Munich, studied at the Conservatory. Until they realized I was singing professionally. I was still in the Yiddish Theatre chorus. While on scholarship, you're not permitted to sing professionally. That was that—finished before it started. Opposite the Conservatory and Northeastern University was a symphony hall, a restaurant, and a cabaret. I went inside and I said, "I want to sing in your nightclub." I gave my name Maryland Crescent. My American middle name—if my great-grandmother, after whom I was named, would have heard her Mindelle became a Maryland, she would have turned in her grave. Crescent—with a C, and a T at the end. So now I am Maryland Crescent. I came in the afternoon unannounced. They asked me, "What can you sing?" "Well, I can sing Russian." I sang "Otchy Chornia" ["Dark Eyes"] and the orchestra picked it up. At that time there was a German picture going on—something about a mother. And it says, "Little Mother, Mutter Hein." I sang that. And I sang the aria from *Butterfly.* "Good, come at night and you will sing for the audience." I came Saturday night. There was a critic in the audience who wrote, "Maryland Crescent sang." No one knew who Maryland Crescent was. But my family knew, and said, "At night, in a cabaret?" "It's not a cabaret. It's in a symphony hall." "What's the matter with you? You're a youngster!" That was the end of my cabaret debut!

In the summer, there was no theatre. I wanted to earn money. So I went in a factory where they make wallets, and they put these little gold edges on the wallets. I was getting eight dollars a week until one of these "gold" things I put in the wrong place—by mistake, of course—and they deducted five from my eight dollars. When I brought home eight dollars the first week, mother asked, "Where did you get the money? What are you doing that we don't know?" I had to tell them; otherwise they would think that I was stealing—worse yet, a streetwalker! God forbid! So that was the end of my labor period. I always wanted to work, so as not to be a burden on my hardworking family. I realized they exploited no one but themselves.

In the meantime when they needed little parts—like boys' parts or girls' parts—in Yiddish Theatre, I was it! Ludwig Satz was one of our very great character comedians. And he came with Stella Adler to play *Der Meshugener* [*The Crazy One*]. They needed a little boy. There were no little boys that spoke Yiddish. They gave me a pair of knickers and a hat. Mr. Satz played my grandfather. And he explained to me, "You come in. I'm your grandfather. And your pants are torn. I put you on my lap, to sew up your pants. And when I stick you with the needle, you have to *shrei* [scream] '*Oy, Zeyde, du shtekhst mir*' [Grandpa, you're sticking me]." What he was doing while I was lying face down on his lap, I never knew—I couldn't see, I didn't rehearse, I didn't know. I didn't know that the audience would laugh. There were such howls that I didn't know what was happening. I thought, "It's time for me to scream." So I screamed. [Laughs] "*Zeyde, du shtekhst mir.*" He jabbed me with his elbow, saying, "*Lig eingelavget* [Lie still. I haven't even touched you yet]." What was I to know? After that scene, I ran away off stage and hid in a corner—because I spoiled his scene. But he found me, and he said to me, "Now, you stupid little so and so, *ost mir tse-kacked the scene. Du vest kein theater nisht spielen* [You messed up the scene. You will never play theatre again]."

There were other small and bigger parts, as I grew older. For instance, Maurice Schwartz, director of the Yiddish Theatre, came with *The Dybbuk*. As a young professional I played the lead—later, the grandmother. I played the girlfriend to Leah, who was the leading part. Then we had a *Drei Kallahs* [*Three Brides*]. That same man that prophesied "*die vilst nisht spielen theatre* [you will not play theatre]" was the leading man at that time. As I say, I don't rehearse. So I come and they tell me, "Now, what you do, now, they dance." You know—I'm the youngest bride. And they dance, like, the Jewish dances. My husband Seymour's brother, Jack Rechtzeit, whom I had not known—or Seymour for that matter—played my groom. We are dancing at our wedding—and suddenly, police come in and put handcuffs on him. I didn't know why, because as yet I had not rehearsed and I didn't know the play. I started crying, "*Hert off! Hert off!* [Stop it!] Why do you arrest Mr. Rechtzeit? He is such a nice person." The audience laughed instead of crying—another scene spoiled. Later, of course, they explained the story to me.

Another incident happened. There was a famous vaudevillian, Nellie Kessman, the one who introduced the hit song "Yossel." The thing that made Joe Papp famous is *Yossel, Yossel*. I was one of the little boys in her play. Eight little boys (all girls, of course), again with knickers and derbies, because it was supposed to be funny. She listens to all the little boys singing *Ich dank dir gotenu, du bist a gooter tatenu*. I still remember it. *Voos die, hust de nie gemacht a schanden spot*. I was the pony, the last one. She lets me sing, then pushed me aside. "*Du vest nit zingen!* [You won't do!]" "Miss Kessman, why?" I was afraid—if I'm not in the chorus, I won't get the five dollars. "Because," she said, "*du redst Litvish* [You speak Litvish]." Litvish is with a Lithuanian accent. "*Reds vie a Litvak, met men lachen foon dier, and foon mier daf men machen, nicht foon dier* [If you sing in a different dialect, they will laugh at you and not at me]." So all the seven sang, and I didn't sing. I was the dummy. [*Pause*] About three or four years later, I came to play in Buenos Aires. I went there for twelve weeks because I had to come back to school. But I stayed on for nine months, I was such a success.—How's that for modesty? I mean, for a Jewish actress who studied for the opera. Boston used to have the finest chorus girls. Later on, they became the Mack Sennett Beauties. Beautiful ballet dancers. So, whatever they did, I used to copy. Not studying. I did a back bend. I picked up a flower with my teeth, did high kicks. Being in the chorus,

I learned how to dance. Here was a Jewish actress who sang arias from the opera *Romeo and Juliette*—with high Cs, et cetera. A *great* big success!—I was appearing at the Ombu Theatre. In the other theatre, they needed an opposition to me. They brought down Nellie Kessman, where she plays a *khazendl* [little cantor]—a little on the burlesque side. That's why she was in vaudeville. I came backstage to compliment her, and I say, "Miss Kessman, do you remember me? I am Miriam, the 'Litvak' with the derby?" She looked at me, and said, "Oh, how you aged!" [*Laughs*] I was eighteen.

So I came to New York to the theatre. Oscar Greene wanted me for his Hopkinson Theatre; Mr. Jacob Jacobs, renowned entrepreneur in the Yiddish Theatre for many years, famous lyricist—he wrote practically all the lyrics that you hear sung in Yiddish Theatre, *"Bei mir bist du schein"* and *"Belz"* ["My Town Is Called Belz"]. My brother advised me, "You're not going to go to Second Avenue. You are young." Mr. Levine—the manager in Boston whom I used to ask, "What do I do now, Mr. Levine?"—remained a dear friend of mine, and I asked again, "What do I do now?" He said to my brother-in-law, "Don't let her go to Brooklyn, or Second Avenue Theatre. She is too young. And the critics will say that she is not mature enough. It's not good for her if she intends to stay in the theatre." Came Aaron Lebedyev. Lebedyev was *the* star. And he said, "I am going to Chicago. And I want you to play opposite me in Chicago." Here both my brothers-in-law, Berger and Sheff, brought me to New York. "How can we let our little sister-in-law go to Chicago alone?" So Mr. Lebedyev assured them, "She will stay with Mrs. Dranova." Mrs. Dranova was a motherly type. "She will take care of her. And I guarantee you that she will be as safe as at home." "Well, if you guarantee"—and he too was naive, in ways. I went to Chicago. My problem was, I wasn't of age and wasn't even in the union at that time. So every young actress in the union claimed my job. So I never even unpacked. I figured that, naturally, if anyone comes and claims my job, they have to give it to a union actress. I was staying in Chicago with my trunk all packed. The director always auditioned all these actresses that came. And said, "It's not Miriam." So I stayed the entire season without having to pack. When the season was over, back to Boston. That season sealed my fate.

While I was in Chicago, in my spare time or backstage I used to write for the "Jewish newspaper." Poetry, not great—they liked it. I had nothing to do. Next year I was engaged in Philadelphia—Arch Street Theatre. This is where I met my husband, Seymour Rechtzeit. And little by little I started playing. I was too young to become *a* star. They were afraid to take a chance. So I went to Europe! I toured for practically nine years. Practically all over the world. In South America, from Buenos Aires to Tucumán, to every little *campo* in the Argentine. And what a unique way to announce that they have theatre that night: they put a firecracker in a can and shot it off! With that unique sound, the vicinity knew it meant Yiddish Theatre. And they'd come with horses. I have a picture where I'm sitting on a *camión*, an open truck that we're all sitting in. I have a kerchief tied around my head so the dust wouldn't get into my hair. But my face and eyes got a goodly share of the dirt road. And so they'd come from all the surrounding towns and villages with a horse wagon, with their children and their dogs. They didn't have theatres. Naturally, they had barns. Since it was the summer, they'd leave the horses and cows out to pasture and let the actors in. Now the stage was on stilts, you know. If we had to make an exit, we had no other place to go but under the stage. Practically in front of the public, hoping no one would notice. And make sure that somebody's standing in front of you so that the audience doesn't see us. In one theatre barn, there was only one small electric bulb hanging. And every time I started to sing, the moths started to gather around this bulb. I would inhale some. We had no orchestra, of course, but we had a conductor at the Excelsior Theatre in Buenos Aires: Mr. Shklaar, a very fine musician-conductor. Samuel Goldenberg came to a town called Mosesville to play theatre. In every play he'd have a scene where he would sit at the piano and accompany himself and sing. He was a very fine pianist and a singer. That piano in Mosesville was broken down. Mr. Goldenberg was slightly hard of hearing, and didn't realize that whatever he said, the audience would hear. When he heard the sound of the piano, he said—what he thought was sotto voce—"*Oy, a krenk oyf ihr the piano* [She should be smitten with the plague with her piano]." Well, when *we* came to play in Mosesville, the lady wouldn't give us the piano. Here was [*laughs*] a conductor sans an instrument—but he stood his ground, conducting. That was the type of theatre we played in—those primitive towns and villages. But they loved it! We, even more!

Q: And you're still not in the union at this point? Yes? Or you are?

KRESSYN: Oh, yes, in the union. After I played Philadelphia, the first year, where I met my future husband Seymour Rechtzeit, the union arranged an examination. They said, "Now is the time to get into the union." They had at that time in the Hebrew Actors Union about 350 performers. They all came; they were the judges and jury. And you had to perform. The committee gave you two scenes—one dramatic and one musical scene. That's an examination. The actors vote. Now, what prima donna was going to give you a yes, when she sees a youngster that is competition? I was eighteen. One scene I had to play a singing, dancing gypsy. I had kinky hair. I had the most beautiful costumes that I could find—red organdy ruffles. In the second scene—it's very dramatic—I sing "Liebe Bloom fin Gan Eden" ["Flower of Paradise"]. And I put it down on the floor, do a back bend, and pick up the flower with my teeth, come up for the finale with the flower with a high C, and the house comes down! Three hundred and fifty people are sitting in the audience. I am on a platform, dressed as a gypsy. Makeup and all that. The rehearsal hall is full. Ludwig Satz is standing in the doorway. And he doesn't know who I am. He doesn't know I'm the "boy" from Boston. I am singing and they're applauding. And I'm dancing; they're applauding. Then the dramatic—I do the scene from the biblical opera *Shulamis*, and Satz turns to the actor near him: *"Ver is dus medele? Ich ken zie usen* [Who is this girl? I can use her]." He comes back backstage, looks at me, and I say, "Mr. Satz, you don't recognize me. I am the one you sewed up the pants, you scolded me for stealing your scene, and you prophesied that I'll never play theatre again." [*Laughs*] After the ordeal I left for Philadelphia. The actors in New York voted. The next day I read the review in the newspaper *The Forwards*. Mr. Ehrenreich wrote, *"M'darf zein a guzlon* [You have to be a murderer] to give the child a no." And there were ten murderers in the auditorium.

Q: They all voted on union membership?

KRESSYN: That's the only way you could get in at that time. Now they don't. If you play, you pay and you're in!

Q: So you were really voted on by your peers.

KRESSYN: Yes, as a matter of fact, you could not play in New York for three years after you're in—only in the provinces: Chicago, Boston, California.

Q: How was your family reacting to all this, through this part of your career?

KRESSYN: [*Pause*] They came to my father and they said, "How come that you let your daughter go to Buenos Aires?" You wouldn't believe what my father answered: *"My hein kind—my medele ken kein schlekhts nit tun* [My little girl can do no wrong]." And I didn't. [*Pause*] When I think of it [*Pause*], the sorrow he must have had when I argued with him, tried to convince him, "there is no God." The fact that I turned professional, that he probably didn't like. And to have grieved him so—and [yet he] had such confidence. To this day, I revere his memory.

Q: So you went around the world for nine years?

KRESSYN: Practically, around—nine years, back and forth. To South Africa, to Johannesburg. South Africa had a trust: the Schlesinger Trust. And they had a monopoly on the theatre—not only on Yiddish theatre—like the Shubert Brothers' Organization. Not only theatres—on tobacco, on chocolates, and every conceivable industry. The Schlesinger Trust—when they sent for me, I didn't have to pay a nickel. They sent you paper, a tag with a green diamond star that you pasted on your luggage, your passport, and everything. That means that everything is paid for.

Q: How were the audiences?

KRESSYN: Wonderful. They were—Jews! Mostly Russian Jews. They had a great Jewish community, wonderful—quite well off.

Q: All this time you were back and forth between Second Avenue and the rest of the world?

KRESSYN: That's right. The rest of the world. Well almost—the only places I was not was in the Scandinavian countries. I wasn't in Australia. Or the South or North Pole, for that matter.

Q: Tell me what was going on on Second Avenue in this time.

KRESSYN: The Second Avenue Theatre my husband and I played—five years with Menashe Skulnick—musical comedy. And it was comedy that I had up to here, because literature it wasn't. You know these musical comedies? Singing. Menashe Skulnick was very funny. We used to laugh more on stage than off stage. But I got tired of it. And I said, "I can't take it any more." I turned to drama. My first dramatic play was *Anna Lucasta*, Jacob Jacobs producer (before the Yiddish Art Theatre).

Then my husband "sold" me for radio. How did he sell me for radio? Prima donnas, as a rule, didn't sing on radio because prima donnas could only sing with a big orchestra to give them support. So they only had, you know, crooners—like Dinah Shore—who had a perfect radio voice. He comes back one day—we were married by then, of course—and he said, "I sold you for radio." I said, "You did what? Why?" "No, not to sing, to write." I said, "Seymour, you mean to write my own material? Seymour, how could you do that to me? I never wrote in my life." He said, "Yes, you did. You wrote for me. You translated all the songs for me that I sing. All these years, you wrote for yourself. You can do it." So I had to write about seven pages in Yiddish, each day a different subject, and include some music. And I started doing it, and for about thirteen weeks I used to read every program to him. He said, "No, this you have to take out, this is too highfalutin' for the audience." I said, "What do you mean? If I like it—I am just an average listener." He said, "No, you're not. Your esteem is a little higher than that. And if you were average, you wouldn't be Mrs. Rechtzeit." One day the manager of the radio station calls me, and he said, "Miriam, I love your writing but it's over their heads. Do you know that our average listener is a fourteen year old?" I said, "But Mr. Keilsen"—I said the same thing that I said to Seymour—"I am not purposely trying to be highfalutin'. If I quote something from the Bible, everybody in the Jewish audience knows what I am talking about. If I quote something from literature, there must be some intellectuals who listen to me. Some of my mail indicates it." But I said, "I'll try." P.S.: for Campbell Soup I was on for five years—fifty-two weeks a year. For Maxwell House we've been on for forty-three years, and ever since then I've been writing. I belong to ASCAP [American Society of Composers, Authors, and Publishers] now. You know how I sign off my news program on the radio? *Ani-hak-tana.* Hebrew—means "Little Me." I don't know how I got there. It was force majeure. I had to make a living. I had to sing. I had to dance. I don't know how I did it. When I interviewed performers, they all told me they went to the dramatic school. I never did. I didn't even dream of the stage. We had an actor, Leo Fuchs, a very talented, funny man. I played with him in a musical comedy, *The Jewish Cowboy.* He used to say, *"Abi ich bin oif der binne* [As long as I'm on the stage]."

Q: Were there particular people—like Maurice Schwartz, maybe—who were influential for your career? In terms of your own development?

KRESSYN: I'll explain. When I finally left Menashe Skulnick and the musical theatre, I left him to go to the Yiddish Art Theatre. At that time we were playing Singer's—not Bashevis Singer [but] his brother I. J. Singer in his play *Brothers Askenazi.* And that I loved! That was theatre. It was literature. It was everything that theatre should be. Then came Jacob Jacobs. When I left Menashe, I said, "I'm not going to play musicals anymore." We were doing very well, Seymour and I. Seymour had eighteen radio broadcasts a week. And I had at least as many. We were making a lot of money! I said, "Honey, I cannot take this anymore. Enough!" Mr. Jacob Jacobs, renowned lyricist and longtime producer, said, "I have a play for you that you must do." I said, "Mr. Jacobs, I am not doing any more musicals." He said, "It's a drama." It was *Anna Lucasta* by Philip Yordan. It was written originally for a Polish company, in Polish. And they couldn't play it because it's about a prostitute and, you know, it's a Catholic country. That's why a colored company played it on Broadway—*Anna Lucasta.* I don't remember now who it was, but it was a great success. Jacob Jacobs bought the play, had it translated. At that time I didn't do any translations yet, because I didn't know I could write. I said, "Mr. Jacobs, I—in *Anna Lucasta*. I'm not the type." He said, "I am paying. And if I am paying you, I think that you can do it." I played Anna Lucasta. And Vernon Rice, a critic at the *Post* wrote, "The youngest leading lady in the Yiddish theatre." And *Anna Lucasta* was one of the biggest dramatic successes that I had until I played in Singer's *Yoshe Kalb*, and joined the Yiddish Art Theatre.

After *Anna Lucasta*, Mr. Schwartz came to me, "It's time that you throw away *der kenig fun gelechter* [the king of laughter]. Your place is with the Art Theatre with Schwartz." With the Schwartz Art Theatre I did a lot of plays. In *Rizpa* I played his concubine. We had a scene where Schwartz (King Saul) is lying on the chaise lounge and I, his concubine, in a garment—like the harem girls. And I tried to be the concubine—I was reclining at his side feeding him grapes. Schwartz had trouble with his legs, and they were bandaged. You know, the Ace bandages. I noticed the bandages were showing. So, very discreetly, I pulled down the royal garment and covered the bandages. He said, "What's the matter, Miss Kressyn, you never saw a king with bandages?" He was in such a mood that he didn't take his part seriously anymore. It fell apart. There was a scene where we walk in the garden. He was very, very tall; and I'm only five foot two, fully dressed. And he must have looked like a giant. He gently pushes me to a stump of a tree; he bends over me, and the audience started to applaud and laugh. You know, Yiddish Theatre had not seen sex on stage, especially in the Kunst Theatre. They thought it was supposed to be funny. Schwartz commanded, "Curtain!" And the curtain came down. After that, we played on the road; we went back to the Singer plays—a great success. But by that time, Schwartz was already a sick man. He died on May 10, 1960.

Q: Did you ever play in English?

KRESSYN: If there's such a thing as destiny, *Bashert* [predestination]. We had a benefit performance at the National Theatre. Whenever there was a benefit performance, we used to invite stars from Broadway. Joseph Schildkraut was playing the father in *Anna Frank*. Beautiful performance. Schildkraut's father used to play in the Yiddish Theatre, you know. And when his son was a little boy, he was brought up in the Yiddish Theatre. That evening I was singing a duet from *Bar-Kokhba*, a magnificent biblical play by Abraham Goldfaden. I went to my dressing room and I changed clothes. At that time my hair was black. You hear of somebody turning grey overnight? I turned blond overnight.

[*Laughter*]

Schildkraut asked May Schoenfeld, the wife of Irving Jacobson who had the National Theatre (and I was playing in their theatre), "Who is this young lady?" She said, "Oh, that's our leading lady." After the curtain fell, he came over to me, introduced himself, and said in the way of a compliment, "Would you like to play the mother in *Anna Frank*?" I said, "Would I? Have tuxedo, will travel"—kiddingly. He said, "You'll hear from me." An agent by the name of Tim Goode calls me up. "Miss Kressyn? We'd like to send you the play. And we have a reading at so-and-so." I don't like to do a reading, because I never had to audition—outside of the union when I auditioned for the union membership. Because in the [Yiddish] Theatre, they knew who I was and what I could or would not do. After my reading, Schildkraut came over to me and said, "Miss Kressyn, I'm sorry, you can't play the part because Miss Hubert"—Gusta Hubert was cast originally, but her visa ran out—"got a prolongation on her visa and she will continue as the mother. You have to play the second part. Will you play the dentist's wife?" I said, "Mr. Schildkraut, not that the part is not good enough for me; I would only be too happy. But I don't think I am for the part. I can think of so many others that would do more justice to the part." So that's how I lost Broadway. And I knew there were other opportunities. Something always cropped up. Just a couple of months ago they were playing *Crossing Delancey* at the Jewish Repertory Theatre on 14th Street, at the Y. They sent me the script. And I read it and I said to my husband, "I don't like it. I can't play this. I've gotten away from that stuff. I cannot do it."

Besides, I'm always busy and I always have too much work. I do mostly radio now, and lecturing. I was teaching at Queens College for ten years. As a matter of fact, when they started to do the film of *Crossing Delancey*, they sent me the script again. It had been rewritten. Mr. Avni said, "The script is rewritten. It's much better now. And we have an excellent cast. And you'll fit in beautifully. And please, come and read." I said, "No, thank you." By that time I had a very serious operation.

Q: What about Hollywood?

KRESSYN: Stella Adler was on the way to go to Russia to see Stanislavski. Then she went on to Moscow. I went to South Africa. We came back, and we're sitting in the Cafe Royal. The Cafe Royal was the meeting spot. "Look at this letter. Warner Studios wants me to come for an audition. They saw my film *Der Purim Shpeiler* [*The Jester*]." She said, "Mirele, don't go. Here, you are a big fish. There, you'll get lost. Don't bother going." I went; we didn't like each other. I don't regret never having gone there because it was not *Bashert*, not meant to be.

Q: What about your relationship to money throughout your career? I know
   at the beginning five dollars a day was a great deal.
KRESSYN: For that time, yes. It was a good living. But a very hard living.
   For instance, in Johannesburg I was getting five hundred dollars clear.
   At that time five hundred was very good. Yet, when I was back in New
   York, I lived at the Union Square Hotel. It was fourteen dollars a week.
   And I didn't have that to pay. I lived on a cheese bun and a cup of coffee.
   And shared my cheese bun with the dog that I had. When I had to go to
   Africa, I owed the hotel in New York four hundred dollars. And I called
   a Mr. Schiff, a philanthropist who used to come to the theatre and sit in
   the first row. Every Christmas he used to send gifts to the ladies on
   opening night. At that time I was playing at the Art Theatre. The theatre
   closed and I was living at the Union Square Hotel. I had to pay the hotel.
   So I go up to Mr. Schiff and I bring my jewelry. I had very beautiful
   jewelry that was bought in Buenos Aires and in Antwerp. And he looks
   at it. He says I have to take it to an appraiser. I have to see how much
   it is worth. I said, "All I want is four hundred dollars. It's a diamond
   wristwatch—all diamonds. It's a pendant. It's a four-carat diamond square
   ring. It's a pocketwatch with diamonds. All I want is four hundred
   dollars." He said, "I'm sorry." Christmas, I was back at the Art Theatre
   and I received a pocketbook. And I sent back the pocketbook with a
   note. "I needed rent and not a pocketbook. And you refused to trust my
   jewelry." He didn't tell anybody why I sent it back. But there was an
   uproar in the theatre that Miriam sent back the pocketbook—she probably
   didn't like. It was embarrassing, but I had to live by my own credo, live
   with myself.
Q: What do you think you would say today to a young actor going into
   the field? First of all, of course, I'm sure you have much to say about
   the future or lack thereof of the Yiddish Theatre.
KRESSYN: Years ago, Don Appel—he was a young man—wrote *Milk
   and Honey*. He played in one of my plays. And he once said, "Miss
   Kressyn, would you mind helping me with this scene? I don't quite
   understand what this means." I always liked to help. That's why I
   enjoyed teaching for ten years. And I said, "Don, you're a young man.
   We'd love to have you in the Yiddish Theatre. We need young people.
   But don't waste it here. You have no future." You know how many
   years ago that was? Maybe thirty years ago. He went to Broadway.
   He started playing. He became a successful playwright. That's what I
   would say now, too, if I were honest. I love Yiddish so much, I hoped
   it would go on and on and on, even though I am not active anymore.
   I would say, "Yes. I'll coach you. I'll help you all." I taught at Queens

College for ten years—Yiddish Theatre and theatre history. And I had a workshop there. And every fifteen weeks as the semester ended, I put on with them a Yiddish play in Yiddish. And the students, by the time they were through with the semester, spoke about a thousand Yiddish words. I was awarded there for teaching. I had an eighteen-year-old student, and an eighty-year-old student—he was the librarian in Queens College. I had Professor Solomon, who was teaching Chinese at Queens.

If young people come to the [Yiddish] Theatre now, I say, "Yes, but learn the language." When they kill it, it hurts me. They don't want to learn! But that's how I learned, by listening and watching. The first time I played a mother, a young mother, I said, "Hannah, show me how you would do this scene, would you please?" That's how I learned. I wanted to learn. I'd come to the theatre and take a part; the director would say, "Oh, I never worry about you; tomorrow you'll know your part." Of course, I knew it. You know why? I stayed up a whole night and I learned it. I was an avid reader. I had two years of schooling at Northeastern University. When I was a little girl, there was a Sholem Aleichem's children's library of little tiny books. If there was a book that interested me, I took that little book and I rewrote it by hand on paper so that I would have a book of my own.

Q: So what would your advice be to a young person today?

KRESSYN: I would say—if I were honest—if you don't want to study, don't waste your time. You won't get anywhere.

Q: What do you think was your greatest satisfaction in your career?

KRESSYN: In the theatre, I think there're two plays that are really outstanding in my mind: *Anna Lucasta* and *Yoshe Kalb*. In the music, it was musicals about Ehrich Kalman's operetta. Or *Fledermaus*, which are on the verge of, you know, light opera. And of course, the early Goldfaden biblical operettas.

Q: What do you think were your greatest disappointments in your career?

KRESSYN: I wish there were more writers—to give us more to choose from. My illness, of course. That came at an age of forty-five. But that didn't stop me from playing theatre. Because I still went on. I stopped participating in plays about seven years ago. But my husband and I go on tour, lecturing to universities. We were invited to Berlin, Florida, Canada, California, Jamestown, and New York University. All over. Lecturing on Yiddish Theatre. And of course, radio—ours is the oldest radio program on the air, forty-four years. We began writing history of the Yiddish Theatre for Maxwell House. First they called it *Jewish Matinee Time*. Then we were invited on Channel 13 for four years—in

English, but Yiddish subjects. I took the same stories that I wrote in Yiddish and translated them in English. How did we get to television? An agent came to the Maxwell House and said, "What's Jewish radio? Television is the thing now. And you speak to your public in English."

Q: Well clearly, you have taken advantage of everything that has come into your path your entire life.

KRESSYN: I chose it because I know no other. Yiddish is my world.

MARCIA JEAN KURTZ

B. Bronx, New York City. Attended Juilliard School of Music (B.S.).
Trained for stage with Uta Hagen, Stella Adler, Liz Dixon, and Harold
Guskin. Company Member: Peter Brook International Center of Theatre
Research; Jerome Robbins American Laboratory Theatre; Joe Chaikin's
Open Theatre. Directed: Evan Handler's *Time on Fire*, Second Stage
Theatre. Awards: Obie, Drama Desk Nomination, *When She Danced*, 1990;
Obie, *The Loman Family Picnic*, 1990.

Q: Tell me a little bit about your initial experiences in acting.
KURTZ: My initial experiences were actually in dance classes, because
   that's where my mom took me first.
Q: How old were you?
KURTZ: Probably about the age of four, four and a half.
Q: She took you at your request?
KURTZ: I can't figure that out. I just remember going to tap dance very
   early on. And she said I sang and danced on the subways a lot and that
   people used to give me money [*laughs*] on the subways. I always
   seemed to be in some class, and I remember—around seven or eight
   years old—being in some improvisation class, in some acting class
   associated either with the public school or somewhere in the neighborhood in the Bronx and doing some improvisation about stealing cookies.
   And somehow it really went over big. And I was taken to lots of different
   kinds of modern dance schools. I remember the Blanche Evans School

of Interpretive Dance when I was eight years old. That was a big influence on me. We wore Isadora Duncan–type tunics and we did "antibomb" dancing. And this woman had drums and all kinds of odd instruments in the studio, and it was all very glamorous. That was kind of my introduction. It was more of a dance-oriented childhood than acting.

Q: How did your family feel about all this?

KURTZ: They seemed to love it. My mom used to take me to the Museum of Natural History to see things like dances from around the world, so I was always being taken to these cultural places.

Q: And you have a sister?

KURTZ: I have a younger sister.

Q: Your father was at home?

KURTZ: Well, he worked. And he used to drive us downtown Saturday mornings to Blanche Evans or, later on, Eve Gentry or Hanya Holm School of Dance.

Q: What did your parents do when you were growing up?

KURTZ: My father worked as an advertising salesman. My mom was a housewife and a bookkeeper at some point.

Q: What do you think in your early education provided you with validation or resistance in the world of the arts?

KURTZ: I think it was those very free dance classes where I did a lot of improvisation. There was so much imagination involved, if you were playing a leaf or a tree or a mood thing or just responding to music. And these people must have been on the cutting edge of stuff, because the music was, like, Music Concrète; it was very modern stuff that was being thrown at me.

Q: When do you think you became an actress? And how did you know?

KURTZ: I didn't become an actress until I graduated from Juilliard as a dance major, and I was dancing for a few years. I fell into acting quite by accident. I was working with Felix Fibich and his Hasidic dance group. And I was doing some Chanukah festival at the Waldorf Astoria, and some guy was walking around backstage and I was kibitzing with him and he said he belonged to this theatre group called the Open Theatre, and I guess I was becoming a little disenchanted with dance because I didn't know what my future was going to be. I said, "Oh, can I come visit?" And he said, "Sure, come down." It was Joseph Chaikin's Open Theatre, you know, in the 1960s, and it looked a lot like dancing to me 'cause these people weren't talking much at that point. It was mostly sound and movement. I thought, "Boy, I could do this." And I started going to the workshops. Peter Feldman had a workshop for people who wanted to become acquainted with Open Theatre. I was making my living playing the piano for dance classes at that point, also. I also studied piano all the time.

And when I was about ten, I got the lead in a drama group up in the Bronx. The Amalgamated Housing Project had a drama group, and I got to play Pinocchio. And that was a big thing too. So I was always acting a little bit. But maybe, for a Jewish girl from the Bronx, acting was—like—movie stars and Betty Grable, and though I remember you would play things like "I want to be Betty Grable. I want to be Roy Rogers and Dale Evans," I never thought of myself as somebody who could do that. It seemed other people did that. We did modern dance, you know. [*Laughs*] To save the world. Somehow it was all tied up with social work or whatever the political movements were at the time.

Q: You went to Music and Art High School?

KURTZ: I went to Music and Art as a voice major, having gotten in on piano. But still continued dancing. Sang with Leonard Bernstein in the chorus on television in a Villa Lobos piece and Copland's *Second Hurricane.* There was so much coming at me culturally all the time. And there was always music in my house. My parents gave me a lot in terms of culture. But I think the dancing always held. I choreographed the graduation show with a jazz piece, and I was teaching in camps: I was teaching folk dance and modern dance. I went to Surprise Lake Camp, the Jewish Federation camp; and every Friday night for Oneg Shabbat we put on plays and dances. So every week you were inventing a new show. Then, from Music and Art, I went to Juilliard, graduated as a dance major.

Q: Had you been formally training in dance at this time?

KURTZ: Well, yes. But I wasn't that happy as a dancer. So when I fell into acting, it seemed I could breathe better. I was never a great technical dancer. I was a good actress dancer. So when I found Joe Chaikin in the Open Theatre, that seemed natural. And then I heard about Uta Hagen, the HB Studio; and I went over there and took a class with Herbert Berghof and Bill Hickey, and then I auditioned for Uta and got in. And that was the beginning. The years were—twenty-three, twenty-four, twenty-five, something like that. And that's when I knew I wanted to be an actress. I think it took that long.

Q: Did you have peers in high school who were influential, who mattered in this whole process to you?

KURTZ: No. It was my dance teachers. Those were the people who I always looked up to. And the legends, you know. Like Martha Graham. No, I wouldn't say it was peers, at all. It was probably my family and teachers.

Q: Your sister had similar training in the beginning?

KURTZ: She had the same thing. She went to Music and Art, and then instead of going to Juilliard she went to the Oberlin Conservatory as a music composition major. She finally left it to become an early childhood education teacher and then got married and had kids. So she stopped.

Q: Who do you think were your most significant mentors and role models?

KURTZ: I think Uta Hagen was a big one. I guess it's the force of her personality, her integrity, her love of theatre, her love of teaching, and her love of seeing people develop. [*Pause*] I stayed with her a long time. I think I was with her for thirteen years. I was working as an actress too, all the time. So I would go in and out of class.

Q: After Uta, did you continue to study with anyone?

KURTZ: I went to Stella Adler, who opened up a whole other world to me. And I sort of observed at the Actors Studio, tried to get in, didn't get in. When I didn't get into the Actors Studio [*laughs*], I went to Stella. And studied a little bit with Mira Rostova. And then a wonderful vocal teacher named Liz Dixon who I worked on voice with for many years, as an acting coach also. And then found a man named Harold Guskin, who is one of the best-known acting coaches today—who, I would say, took all the training I had as an actor and just helped me to put it all together and just to free me up to be—me.

Q: Do you use acting coaches when you're in a part? Do you use them when you're not in a part? How do you use an acting coach?

KURTZ: When I went to Harold, I was a bit confused because I had so many influences and I felt I had so much technique that I couldn't move on my own. I had forgotten my own impulses, my own spontaneity. So I went and I studied with Harold every week, alone, one on one, for about a year. And now I just use him basically when I have a part for an audition. And then when I get a part that really matters to me, I'll take it to Harold and we'll pull it apart and go over it and explore it and—it makes me feel much more secure about going on that set if it's a television show or a movie, or the theatre. Because rehearsal times are so short and so fraught with tension, if you can do that work beforehand it makes it much better, I feel.

I was with Jerome Robbins's company for about seven months. Jerry Robbins had a company of actors. He got government funded for about three years. He had a big company on 19th Street called the American Theatre Lab—or the American Laboratory Theatre—and it was actors and dancers. With that and the Open Theatre, I started my professional life. And at Judson Poets Theatre also, because the whole '60s scene was so vibrant. You got to work a lot. There were all these little theatres. So I was at the Judson Poets Theatre. The Open Theatre was performing every week at Sheridan Square Playhouse. We were improvising in front of people. We were doing plays with Megan Terry and Jean Claude Van Italie. People like that. Sam Shepard. It was a hothouse of experimentation. I did *Viet Rock* and I did *America Hurrah*. And then, I think, after that I did *NYPD*, my first television show, which was also shooting down in the Village on 4th Street. I became an itinerant actor. I would audition for things and get little Off-Broadway plays. And then this Jerome Robbins thing looked interesting, so I got that and I was in that for several months and Anna Sokolow was teaching dance there. I also had her at Juilliard, and we would be doing strange things like the Japanese tea ceremony. Jerry was interested in all kinds of rituals and we'd be working on the Kennedy assassination as Noh drama, as dance theatre, as naturalistic theatre. Just about everything. Then I did a Sam Shepard play and a John Guare play. I did *Red Cross, Muzeeka*. And I had left the Open Theatre by that point, and Joe Chaikin got an invitation from Peter Brook to take five of Joe's actors. And Joe Chaikin was on tour with the Open Theatre, so Joe called me because I was free. And I went over to France and England to work with Peter Brook and his company. It was the first year of his international company. Glenda Jackson was in the company, Sammy Frye, Delphine Seyrig, Bill Macy from New York, Ronnie Gilbert, Roy London, Paul Boesing. Those are the Open Theatre people. It was a time of Grotowski, Brook, Chaikin. All these people were working in a somewhat similar way. So you could go back and forth and you'd have something to contribute and you'd understand each other's theatrical language. I played Miranda in Peter Brook's *Tempest*. It was the 1968 French students' revolution and we were guests of Jean-Louis Barrault, so we had to leave because the students took over the theatre; and we went to England, and the Royal Shakespeare Company put us up. We worked at the Roundhouse and we did *The Tempest* there. It was wonderful. It was the precursor of Brook's *Midsummer Night's Dream*. I mean, all this stuff that we did in that Roundhouse up in the air on scaffolds and with music and running around and strange Japanese songs, it all seemed to fit.

Q: Do you think your training finally prepared you as an actor?

KURTZ: Oh yeah, most definitely.

Q: Did you give yourself certain benchmarks during your career—such as, you know, "If I haven't done this in five years, I'll leave the profession or do something else"?

KURTZ: No, I never did that, because I think I never saw myself as part of a business. I guess it was more of a way of living. I mean, every year something wonderful in this profession happens—either a wonderful film role, maybe now I direct something, or a great play comes along unexpectedly.

I just never did that. I just kept going.

Q: And you always trusted that there would be something wonderful that year?

KURTZ: There were times, like every actor, I think, "I'll never work again." You know. And you get depressed. You just always do. But at the bottom you always think, "I'm not going to lose my talent."

Q: What were the first organizations you joined as an actor?

KURTZ: Actors' Equity, Screen Actors Guild, and AFTRA. Ensemble Studio Theatre—I became a member only about three or four years ago. But I had been a member of all these groups. After that I didn't want to join any more groups. I'd had it with groups. I just wanted to be on my own and just see what came up.

Q: And most of your benefits—like health insurance, life insurance, things like that—have come from the union?

KURTZ: Always came from the union, which I'm tremendously grateful for. Don't know what I would do without it.

Q: What do you think about unionization for actors?

KURTZ: I can't imagine the world without it.

Q: Why?

KURTZ: Because of health benefits. And all the stuff backstage. I mean, everything, the clean dressing rooms, the hours; nobody's exploiting you. I came in when this was all fought for already, so I take it for granted. But I can't imagine it without it. It would be horrible, I would think.

Q: When do you think you first received professional recognition as an actor?

KURTZ: I think probably in the Open Theatre. I could feel the audience responding.

Q: Do you think that now you have a group of peers that you rely on for support, opinions?

KURTZ: No, I rely on my coach mostly for opinions. Sometimes my agent. But more and more on my coach. And more and more on myself.

Q: When did you first get an agent? How many agents have you had during your lifetime?

KURTZ: I've been with two agencies. It's a difficult relationship. I would guess each actor and each temperament is so different. If you're somewhat retiring and not that pushy, you hope your agent's going to do it for you. But I have tended to go with agents who were not that bombastic, either. And I think I like them because of their integrity and—and their style. And sometimes you wish you really had somebody with a big cigar, making deals. But there's something in me, too, that shies away from it also. I'm with a good, reputable agent. You just never know if it's you who gets the work. If you would be out more, would you get more work? If the agents understand who you are. If they're seeing you in the way you want to be seen. It's a tricky relationship.

Q: Is there a standard percentage that they take?

KURTZ: Ten percent.

Q: How would you describe your occupation? And is it different from your career?

KURTZ: I have a job that's not acting. I work as a photo researcher for Macmillan Publishing Company. And I've had that job now about thirteen years. It's a full-time job. I go in five days a week. Now, it's a freelance job, so my hours are my own. But that's how I earn most of my living. And I teach acting once a week at the Ensemble Studio Theatre Institute.

Q: What is your occupation and what is your career, and are they the same?

KURTZ: I think my occupation and my career are both the same. I'm an actress. That's how I think of myself. I think I could make a living as an actress. I don't think I'd have trouble because I'm always asked to do something somewhere. But I say no a lot because I don't like to go out of town to do a role that doesn't excite me. I've been out of town. I find that your career stops. You come back to town and nobody gives a damn that you've been out there. Now, if it was a huge stretch of something—I wanted to go do *Medea* once, and I would have gone. I didn't get it, but I would have gone because, hey, how often are you going to get to play Medea? And there was a time I went a lot, when I was younger. I went to Cincinnati Playhouse to do a Schisgal play. I did do the Yale Repertory Winterfest thing. I did Long Wharf. I don't know if that's out of town, because that's too close, you know. I did Boston twice. I did *The Effects of Gamma Rays on Man-in-the-Moon-Marigolds* with Eileen Heckert and Mel Bernhardt directing. That was wonderful. Then I went back to do *Slow Dance on the Killing Ground* at the Charles Playhouse with Werner Klemperer and Clarence Williams III. I went down to Baltimore to do Sonya in *Uncle Vanya*. So there was a time when I went. I don't like it. It's lonely, for one thing. And then you do come back and nobody's heard of you.

Q: So then, what's your view of the whole regional theatre movement that's grown up—in relation to your own career?

KURTZ: I think it's wonderful. I worked in it. It gave me training, experience. I don't think it helped me get anywhere, though. I have to tell you that, for some reason, I enjoy more working in an office at my photo research job than being in a play that bores me.

Q: Let's talk about the teaching, as well. How often do you teach?

KURTZ: I've been teaching for about the last ten years, I think. Now I teach once a week—advanced scene study. Jack Garfein at the Actors–Directors Lab saw me at the Actors Studio once, when I was doing a scene there, and got interested in me. So he brought me on as a teacher and also as a director. He gave me my first directing experience, which I loved and am very good at. When I don't act much, I think, "Well, maybe that's what I should do." I think because I had such a wonderful experience with my teachers, and got so much from them, that I enjoy giving it back! So I taught at the Actors–Directors Lab, and then kids from Manhattan Class Company. I was with them for about two years, teaching.

Around that time I decided I needed a group. I had always heard about the Ensemble Studio Theatre. I applied for membership and got in. You are just a member there and you can do whatever you want. You can direct. If you are a good teacher, you can teach at the Institute, if you can get a class together. You can act in their productions. You can write if you're writing. I also wrote a screenplay. One season I took a screenwriting class at Hunter College and won a Writer's Guild grant— one of like six people in America. [*Laughs*] So I became a screenwriter for one year, also.

Q: Do you feel any responsibility to the marketplace and its condition, when you send actors out there?

KURTZ: I often look at them and I know how hard it is and I think, "Boy, I hope they're going to find a niche." It was easier for me when I was starting up because of that whole Off-Broadway scene. But you know, Uta Hagen said it: "Find your niche. Find your place. Somewhere there'll be a place for you. It doesn't matter how big, how little." And I think everybody does, in some way. Or if they don't, they leave the business. But that's such an individual thing.

Q: How old are your students? And where do they come from?

KURTZ: A lot of them come from college drama programs. They've graduated as theatre majors, And now they have to learn to act.

Q: Let's talk about how you see yourself being cast, and how you are most often cast.

KURTZ: That's the hardest thing. When you're in Uta's class or in Stella's class, you do everything. You never think of yourself in one way. That's to me the hardest part—that people will box you in and not see that you could play Shaw or this or Shakespeare or that.

Q: Have your career aspirations and your career opportunities differed greatly?

KURTZ: I think now I'd like to be offered much more than I'm offered. I won two Obies for the last two things I did, and a Drama Desk nomination, and was drawn by Hirschfeld in the *New York Times*. I won lots of wonderful critical acclaim across the board. I don't know—I've never gone to California. Which may be the big thing. It's very very bad, I think—1991.

Q: How would you describe your relationship to the marketplace and to money, throughout your career?

KURTZ: Terrible. Just terrible. I guess I came up in that era when women were not taught about careers or money or anything. I mean, all that training was for self-improvement. You know, you learned to dance and it would make you a better person—and maybe get a better husband, I don't know. But I didn't know about a career or career choices. Even the people five years behind me, I could see, knew how to start making a career for themselves. The people that I grew up with were not thinking in terms of money. I didn't see that. Certainly, the Open Theatre wasn't. They would turn their backs on it, if anything. I guess I just always loved it so much that money was an afterthought. I have managed. But I am managing also because I have a job now.

Q: Are there specific people who were gatekeepers in your career? Either positive or negative?

KURTZ: I don't think so. The worst thing is the stereotyping that goes on in our business. It's all about plastic surgery so much now. It seems that there's a greater emphasis on superficiality.

Q: What do you think has been the major turning point in your career up to now? Or maybe there is more than one.

KURTZ: I think finding Harold Guskin.

Q: Why?

KURTZ: Because it's like he freed me. He freed me to be me. It sounds so corny, but—I have a great deal more confidence in everything that I've learned, everything that has been given to me or put into me by all the people that came before. I feel now that I'm whole.

Q: Have grants or competitions or emergency funds in any way affected your career throughout it?

KURTZ: No, just my grant from the Writer's Guild. When the phone rang, it was three thousand dollars. I didn't even know how to type. I had to get myself a typewriter. It didn't affect my career at all. I just had a couple of months at the typewriter totally immersed in the writer's world—and when the phone rang for an acting job, I was almost disturbed.

Q: What kind of control do you think you exert over your destiny as an actor?

KURTZ: Boy, that's a tricky question. I think it depends on your personality. I think you exercise a lot of control. In your choices: in your choice of agent; where you keep yourself; what you'll do or won't do to get somewhere or not get somewhere; where you'll put yourself socially or engage yourself or not engage yourself. I think you exercise a lot of control. Now, where there are few plays being produced, I mean, that's another thing. That's the part you have no control over. People say there are not too many plays being produced now. What's opening is mostly closing. Also, this is the time of such huge technological change for the theatre. With the VCR, and HBO, we're going through a big change. People who really were trained for the theatre—I don't know that we know where we are, so much. Although I love television and movies, too. It's a very different world. It's hard to know how those changes have affected things.

Q: Do you think people can be trained for television or film without being trained for the theatre?

KURTZ: No, I don't.

Q: How have you interacted with the public during your career?

KURTZ: Well, it's been wonderful. I was going home from the office the other day and I'm going through the turnstile in this crowded subway at rush hour, and this woman rushes over to me. She says, "Oh—I saw your last television show." She says, "You're one of my favorite actresses. My friends just love you." I get that a lot. I mean, from people in the street. People come up and say, "Your last play, what you did for me. And you're *some* actress."

Q: What do you say to this?

KURTZ: I say thank you. I mean, it's wonderful.

Q: What are your criteria for success, Marcia, as an actress?

KURTZ: [*Pause*] It's so difficult, because you're dealing with marketplace success. I think I've had success as an actress. Winning those Obies for Donald Margulies's *The Loman Family Picnic* and Martin Sherman's *When She Danced* meant a lot to me. That Drama Desk nomination for *When She Danced* meant a lot to me. People say, "You should have gotten it years ago." And I can't say I wasn't proud of it.

I am. It was a nice recognition. It was a lovely recognition. And they were roles in which I felt I had really achieved something. I used myself in a way that I was proud of and felt very complete and knew I had communicated a lot to people with those roles. That television show, too—*Law and Order*—I played Hedda Nussbaum, and people were very moved by it. People said, "You know, you changed my life with that role."

I feel successful. I wish I was offered a wider range of roles. I wish that there was more being written. I wish that there was more attention to what a person can communicate from their emotional internal existence, rather than just a physical thing. I wish there was more of that need out there in television, I suppose. I wish it wasn't such a star thing. I wish it was a little easier to get roles if you're not a big name. But I do feel successful. I feel good about what I have accomplished. I'm ready for the next thing.

Q: Do you think that other actors have similar views of what's successful as you do? Or very different views?

KURTZ: I don't know. I don't hang out with actors that much. Actors kvetch a lot. I don't know—getting your name in the paper and having your face in the paper and being talked about—if that means success to a lot of people. I think it does. I think one would lie to say one doesn't want to be more famous or more well known. But it's about getting work. It's about using yourself for what you've trained for. You feel tense when you're not being creative.

Q: Were there certain periods of work in your career that you feel more satisfied with than other periods of time—or periods of work?

KURTZ: Yeah, I think the latest period is the period I have been most satisfied with. I think it has to do with personal maturity, also. I think you come together in your work as you come together as a person.

Q: What about critical review? What are your feelings about critical review of your work? Do you read reviews of your work?

KURTZ: I do read reviews.

Q: What do you think about them, generally?

KURTZ: They're scary. There's something that is mighty about the pen.

Q: Do they ever teach you anything? Do you ever change your mind by reading a review?

KURTZ: No. I don't think I ever, really, learned anything from a review. I think what made me happy was that what I think I was setting out to do was acknowledged—that what I was intending to do, it came across.

Q: The major frustrations—resistances to your professional development—

center around this lack of roles being offered and the kind of roles that you think you're worthy of?

KURTZ: I think also my—own—shyness about—pushing for things.

Q: What do you think is your greatest disappointment in your career?

KURTZ: Maybe not getting one or two roles that I wanted. That's about it. People talk about roles having your name on it—that mystical thing that actors say: you pick up a script and say, "That's my role." I have felt that way. Most of the things I have gotten, I said, "That's my role." You feel stupid saying that, but there's a music that communicates from that page. It just resonates and you become single-minded in getting that part. Somehow there's a match there.

Q: What about your greatest satisfaction?

KURTZ: My greatest satisfaction is a well-acted part.

Q: Could you describe a little bit how your technique has changed from your early career to now? What you see as the major differences?

KURTZ: It's not textbook anymore. It's really just doing it. It's not stuck in the head anymore: if I do this, I'll get to this. It's a much more— throwing yourself [*laughs*] into it. And trusting it. But I think you have to go through all the textbook stuff. I don't know if everybody does. A lot of it is going through that and learning. I don't know that there's anybody like Uta Hagen to give you the basic tools about how to live on a stage, just live like a human being. You know—drink that coffee so it looks like you're drinking that hot coffee. Sitting in that chair. Going through that door. That's terrific.

Q: Do you try to give this back to your students, this kind of thing?

KURTZ: Yes, I do. I do it in a very different way, though. Uta has worked up such a system about it all. I don't have a system. I do it in a much more integrated way within the scene. I get a lot of satisfaction from my students, seeing them grow and change. That tickles me no end. When I see people—with mannerisms or fears that I recognize in myself. And I'll share that with them. I'll say, "I'm the same way, and I know what you're doing. And stop it, because I do it, too. And you don't want to do that."

Q: You've talked very strongly about teachers who gave you some wonderful things. Do you think teachers can be a destructive influence, too?

KURTZ: I had some dance teachers who were insulting, who diminished people.

Q: What would you say—or what do you say—as advice to young actors today?

KURTZ: I think I was too sheltered as a young student, that not enough was said to me: "You should go here and learn about this agent, or this television thing or this movie. If you know these people, it will help you." And that was what my early training, I think, was not good for. It was really a cloistered world of "great art." I try to tell my students, "Well, go to that audition. Are you seeing people? Go to the agent." I try to get them out there much more. You know—"Oh, good, a soap? Terrific!" It was kind of looked down on when I was learning. I think that's terrible, because you become a snob about things and you don't learn how to make a living. You close your world out.

Q: So your own choices that you were describing earlier about saying no to work don't have to do with this hierarchy of where it is? Really, they have to do with the roles?

KURTZ: Absolutely. And the vehicle. First of all, you only do it once. You're not in it for six months. You're not bleeding every day on the stage in something that you can't stand. I won't do things that I think are demeaning or insulting. I've said no to roles that—as a woman— I thought were making a woman seem like a clown or a buffoon. And you just don't want to be seen that way. You don't want to have a woman portrayed that way.

Q: So what will you tell a young actor today—as a kind of rule of thumb?

KURTZ: I think the only thing is, find out your strengths, who you are, and find out your potential as an actor. In whosever class you can find it. In whatever company you can find it. Whoever you can find that helps you find out your greatest potential.

SUSAN NUSSBAUM

B. Chicago. Attended Goodman School of Drama at the Art Institute of Chicago (Certificate 1978). Ensemble member of Remains Theatre in Chicago. Awards: Jefferson Award Citation, playwright, *Staring Back*, 1984.

Q: What were your initial experiences with acting?

NUSSBAUM: My father's an actor, although he was an exterminator for twenty-two years before that. He became a professional actor after that. So I was attracted to it, I guess. I was exposed to it. After a long time of being involved in the antiwar movement and the women's movement, and in some social/political-type street theatre groups, I ended up going to acting school here in Chicago.

Q: Where did you go?

NUSSBAUM: Goodman School of Drama. And my third year I was disabled in a car accident. I was walking to school and a car hit me. So now I use a wheelchair. I thought at that point that I would not be able to do any more acting. I had absorbed all the kinds of discrimination and mythology surrounding disability that everybody else in our society had at that point. So I thought, "Well, I won't be able to do anything but sort of stare out the window." That was a real bad time, obviously, because I hadn't politicized the experience. I didn't know that there was just the beginning of a movement of disabled people that was intended to mainstream this whole population of people that have been segregated for all these years. It was especially strong in California. But it hit Chicago very soon after my disability. Right after I became disabled, I recalled a thing I had seen on the nightly news about a whole bunch of disabled people in chairs and blind folks and deaf people taking over and occupying a federal building in San Francisco in protest about a piece of civil rights legislation that the government agency refused to sign. They were just sitting on it for four years. All these disabled people spent a month occupying the building. A month! Severely disabled people. It's not an easy thing. I've been to a lot of demonstrations and jail, and it's a very taxing thing when you've got a lot of physical conditions on your life. I remember thinking, "My God, disabled people advocating for themselves." But that was just the tiniest fraction of information I had about what that whole world was going to be like. Mostly I thought it was just going to be real bad. I gave up acting.

Q: What made you change your mind after the accident and get back into acting?

NUSSBAUM: Partly it was this movement. I had always been a political person, as I mentioned. I had tried to see my life in a context and tried to analyze the way stuff worked in society. And tried to figure out how to change things. When I discovered that I belonged to this minority that also had a civil rights movement that was burgeoning, I became part of it. Through that, I took the burden of responsibility off of my shoulders of thinking I was icky and bad and unattractive and not worth much, and just said, "Society has to change. This is craziness." I was exposed to tons of disabled people that were doing all sorts of stuff, living independently and having marriages and children and affairs and jobs that meant a lot to them. Slowly I began to start writing. I was never a writer. And honest to God, I don't recall the exact circumstances, but I was commissioned to co-write a comedy sketch as a fundraising effort for some rehabilitation hospital here in Chicago. This was years and years ago. We did it at Second City [Theatre]. The thing was so incredibly successful that, when the run at Second City was over, another theatre wanted to produce it—the Organic Theatre. Then I began to see that there was an audience for this stuff and I had something to say, that I had a talent for writing, and that even though no one would ever in a million years be interested in a disabled actress, if I wrote plays and there were parts for a disabled actress in it I could cast myself. And that's what I did.

Q: When you were growing up, you said, your father was an actor. Was anyone else in your family in the arts? Do you have brothers and sisters?

NUSSBAUM: I have a brother and a sister. And my mom is not involved in theatre. It's only to the extent that my whole family is interested in what each of us does and is supportive of what each of us does.

Q: Did your father influence you as far as his experiences? Or was it something you always had a desire to do?

NUSSBAUM: I always had a desire to do it. It's just pathetic, because it's such a ridiculous thing to want to do. But I always had a desire to do it, and so did he. He didn't influence me, but he didn't discourage me. I think he did encourage me a bit. Even as unrealistic an aspiration as it may be, he probably wanted it to happen.

Q: Was there a particular time when you decided, "Yes, I want to become an actor"?

NUSSBAUM: I don't think there was a specific time. And I also don't think I ever saw it as an exclusive thing. I grew up during a very turbulent era. So to me, any kind of art would have to have some political content. I lot of people disagree with that. They say that you run the danger of becoming preachy and stuff. I don't think I've had that problem.

Q: You said you studied at the Goodman. Can you tell me about that? How did you feel about your training?

NUSSBAUM: I didn't think it was that great. It was a very small school. There was a lot of focus on the social relationships between the students. They had a technique of sort of stripping people down, unlearning them of whatever they thought were bad habits, and then building from that. I think it translated too often into people feeling like what they were doing was not good. So, people would start censoring themselves as young actors, and start saying, "Oh, I better not do that 'cause I'm going to get criticized." But there were some good things. Voice. There were a couple of great teachers. There were wonderful movement things. I found there were different ways of getting to know a character or getting a handle on a character. You didn't have to have something bubble up inside of you; you could maybe pick up a prop and suddenly you knew what you were doing. There were all sorts of tricks that I learned that I think are real useful.

Q: What about your friends?

NUSSBAUM: I've always and still continue to have friends in lots of different worlds. A lot of friends who are real political. A lot of friends who are apolitical. Who do theatre or other stuff.

Q: Did you have any role models or mentors? Or do you now?

NUSSBAUM: Well, I admire a lot of writers and a lot of people that try to have a vision of a society that's transformed. I sort of am amazed by

Helen Keller. We used to make jokes about her. I still make jokes in my work—Helen Keller jokes—because it's such great material. But Helen Keller was very severely isolated by her disability from all sorts of stuff—very much marginalized and discriminated against. She was a socialist and she was a great speaker and a writer and a teacher. The older I get, the more I realize the significance of her life. I read this poem a long time ago—the poet Christy Brown that they made that movie about called *My Left Foot* has a poem that he dedicated to her. He was sitting out in the backyard one day and the news came over the radio that Helen Keller had died. And he wrote this amazing poem about her. They had never met—but still.

Q: Can you describe what your technique is like?

NUSSBAUM: I try very hard to do as much as I can and then to cut away as much as I can. In other words, not to leave possibilities out for choices that you might make, no matter how outrageous or embarrassing they may be, or incorrect. And then to try and simplify it to the point where the kernel of originality is there. But it's not about you; it's about the writing. That's so hard for an actor to do. I think you really need a director to trust. Unless you're a really good actor, which I'm not. I'm not experienced enough to be that good of an actor, to know that much.

Q: What kind of acting organizations are you involved with or a member of?

NUSSBAUM: I'm a member of the Remains Theatre Company here in Chicago. I just was asked to join. It's a company that's been around for a number of years. And it's really a wonderful group. I'm the only person with a disability in the group, which is a breakthrough thing for me and for disabled people.

Q: Have there been any other organizations that have helped you as far as your career?

NUSSBAUM: No. I've always had to have other jobs. And as far as health benefits are concerned, you know, I'm a member of Equity. And we all know the sad state of affairs of those benefits. It's just really tragic.

Q: How do you feel about the acting union? Do you think it benefits the actor?

NUSSBAUM: I've always been pro-union. I don't know much about Equity, but I think the health benefit stuff is the most critical stuff. It's very sad that people are being fucked over in that area. There just isn't enough money. Actors are very poor. There isn't enough money in that insurance pot to cover everybody's health needs. And Equity is the worst. SAG has great insurance, I'm told, although Equity has now adapted themselves to this way of doing things, too. You have to work a certain amount of time every year and earn a certain minimum of money every year. There's a lot of pressure on people—especially as they age—to keep pumping it out so that they can keep getting those benefits.

Q: Have there been other periods of professional work that you see as particular highlights in your career?

NUSSBAUM: After I did *Staring Back*, I didn't do anything for a long time. I wrote a couple of plays that weren't produced, although now one of them is going to be produced, in L.A. Something I wrote many years ago. Then suddenly I got a call from the Goodman Theatre here in Chicago to audition for a play that Frank Galati was directing, called *She Always Said, Pablo*, about the relationship between Gertrude Stein and Pablo Picasso. I went and picked up the script. I had never been called and asked to audition for something. I never audition for things, because I rule myself out, number one—incorrectly—and number two, I hate auditioning. Unless I'm really prepared. I went down there and I picked up the script and I thought, "Oh God, what the hell is this about?" I went to the audition and I got the role of Gertrude Stein, never imagining that that's even what I was auditioning for. That was just incredible for me. To work with this wonderful group of people—Frank was the one who saw how right it was to put me in that part. But he had great designers and great movement people, and those people are still connected. Then about three years later, it went to the Kennedy Center. It was really quite a remarkable production.

Q: Did you get to go with it?

NUSSBAUM: Yeah. So it was a turning point in a couple of ways. Acting—I learned a lot. Particularly what happened to me was, I was cast in a role that nobody imagined in 50 million years. Especially because I was cast in a role that should have gone to a nondisabled actor. I mean, obviously, it shouldn't have. But Frank was the only one who had been able to see that. So that began a period of believing that it was reasonable to put myself out there as an actor for all sorts of roles that didn't necessarily call for a disability.

Q: Tell me more about other things that you've done. You said after your accident it took about three years to get back into acting?

NUSSBAUM: Actually, I did do a little radio drama right after my accident. But I was so disconnected from the whole experience that I barely remember it. After this play at the Goodman, I started getting offers to do different shows. I continued to write. I continued to work a regular job. I worked with Steppenwolf [Theatre Company]. I worked with Northlight Theatre. I wrote a couple of shows for Remains. I did a one-woman show there recently called *Mishuganism* that was auto-biographical—and that my father directed, actually.

Q: What's it like working with him?

NUSSBAUM: Oh, it was great. Once we decided to stop fighting with each other, it was wonderful.

Q: How do you support yourself if you're not acting or writing?

NUSSBAUM: Well, I'm lucky because I was able to cash in on the insurance policies of the people that hit me in that car accident. So to some extent I have some financial independence. Right now is the first time in many years that I haven't had a regular job on top of all the other stuff. I think it's reasonable to imagine I can live off of royalties within the next couple of years. I've been asked to write for a bunch of different theatres now, and people take me seriously now—at least in Chicago— as an actor and as a writer. So that's really kind of great. I even write stuff that I'm not in, now. And that's a whole different thing. That's kind of a good thing to do, too, and I wrote a screenplay last summer. So I'm branching out. I have a couple shows that will be opening this year that I will have nothing to do with. I wrote them so I'll collect the money. They're going to be in other cities and I don't know if I'll even see them. And it feels good. Especially when the money comes in.

Q: I want to ask you a little about casting, because you said you've written a lot of your roles. How do you see yourself being cast? And how do you most often get cast by other people?

NUSSBAUM: Well, I haven't been cast as an ingenue lately. [*Laughs*] I really don't know. I think people cast me in strong roles. And that's a good idea. But the other way would also be fine. I think that people make the mistake of believing that because you're a woman who speaks out, and because you've had a tiny bit of adversity in your life, people think, "Oh God, a wheelchair. That must just be so difficult." So they would tend to see me in roles that are stronger, more forceful. *But*, you know, I think it's going to open up more and more.

Q: What about yourself? When you're writing pieces, what kind of parts have you written for yourself?

NUSSBAUM: All kinds. Mostly funny. But, you know, lots of romantic stuff and political stuff and thoughtful, you know. I'm really drawn to humor. I think partly it has to do with disability being so mysterious that approaching it from the standpoint of humor is kind of surprising to people.

Q: Have there been other people like Frank Galati who've been gate-keepers?

NUSSBAUM: I'm sure—there have been so many people, although I can't think of anyone who was more important than Frank.

Q: What about your relationship to money?

NUSSBAUM: I think it's real important for actors to write, if they possibly can, for the exact same reason that I began writing. You know: you can always write for yourself. But also because you can always be creative. I mean, you're not going to be in a play all the time. It's very painful for actors to not be in plays, and that is the reality 99 percent of the time, for most actors. To be able to still be creative is key, I think, in continuing to keep your acting skills together.

Q: Is writing as much a release for you as acting, or is it a different creative release?

NUSSBAUM: Acting is easier. Writing is lonely and it's in a room. Acting is—you're out there and there's millions of people and it's great. It's fun. Acting is much more gratifying, in a way.

Q: What kind of control do you want over your career—that you don't have now?

NUSSBAUM: I want my stuff to get out there more, because of its political content, because of my disability, and because some of it can be controversial—there's a lot of fucks and shits and stuff like that in what I write. You know: I haven't made that leap. I can do almost whatever I want to do in Chicago—which is a wonderful thing, and I should be thrilled with that, and I am. But I would like to go to New York, and I wouldn't mind doing a little something out in L.A. where the weather is nice in the winter. And making those big bucks and then doing what I want. Now I'm real afraid, though, because I know that you do have to compromise like crazy and you do have to be pliant. That may be a problem, particularly in L.A. I think in L.A. there's much more of an emphasis on people's physicalities and also on sort of a homogeneous kind of acceptable political view. For them to do a sitcom about the life of a socialist or a communist would be kind of hard to imagine.

Q: How have you interacted with the public in your career? How do they affect your work?

NUSSBAUM: I just want them to like me, like everyone else, and then I get mad if they don't.

Q: How do you feel about critical review of your work?

NUSSBAUM: I understand very well that critics are just people, that they have their own opinion and they may have a stomachache that night and stuff like that. And often I'll read stuff that they've written. I don't make my decisions based on what they do. And yet I know that most people

do. Of course, it's very painful if you do something and you pour all
your energy and sweat and blood and tears into it and then it's sort of
flippantly tossed off—as being superficial or not very interesting—by
a critic, and then nobody comes to see it. And if you get a good review,
then everybody comes to see it; you're okay. So I don't really like the
system. I was just thinking the other day: wouldn't it be interesting if
there was a moratorium on all criticism—theatrical criticism and movies
and everything for one year? Would people still find their way to the
theatre and movies, somehow? Of course they would. Although it's not
like they don't have a role to play. Nobody has all this money that they
can go see every goddamn thing without knowing anything about it.
I think all actors have really mixed feelings, or else really negative
feelings, about critics.

Q: What are your own personal criteria for success as an actor?

NUSSBAUM: Oh, you want to be in stuff. You know, you want to get
better at it. You want to have more of a variety of roles offered to you,
and the experience of working with different people that are wonderful
to work with. And you want to make some dough at it—enough to
survive. Some people want to make much more than that. They're
entitled. I would have liked to be really well known, too. That's the
horrible truth of it.

Q: What about for other people? What are your criteria for considering
another actor a success?

NUSSBAUM: I don't know. I see people on stage who just give and give
and give to the other actors and to the audience. And every night, the
same thing—it's the same amount of energy and commitment. Those
are, to me, the most successful actors. Except those people—they love
it so much, they'll do anything. They're not jealous of other people; and
if they are, they don't show it. But a lot of times those people are not
celebrated people. And they're often unemployed people, no matter
how talented they are. In my own romanticized, personal, subjective
kind of fantasy world, I would say those people that just keep giving
are the most successful, and they must get just so much joy from it.

Q: Are there central ideas that you're continuing to work on in your
career? Or goals?

NUSSBAUM: All these contradictions that we deal with every day.
Mostly because it is political. Not overtly so, always, but my very
presence as a disabled person on stage is sometimes political. And the
language that you can choose—the words you can pick from—talking
about ideas and being a woman and living in a patriarchy and talking
about being a socialist and living in the capitalist empire of the world.

Those kinds of things interest me, and I like to find ways of incorporating them into my work so that they're accessible to people, so that they're real, so that people really are going to want to think about the stuff instead of being turned off by it or feeling like they're being lectured.

Q: How satisfied are you—overall—with your career as an actor and writer?

NUSSBAUM: You always want the bigger fix. It doesn't matter who you are. God. Nothing is ever enough. After you finish something that you're really proud of and it's great, you're happy—you're just on Cloud Nine for a couple days and then you start thinking, "Gee, what am I going to do next? I got to figure out what I'm going to do next."

Q: What about frustrations or resistances? What have been the biggest obstacles in your career?

NUSSBAUM: I guess some people would say that I myself have been the biggest, but I have a problem dealing with agents and people in positions of power, business people. I don't always make a good impression, as much as I try. I'm told I'm abrasive, and that I have a chip on my shoulder. Not by everyone, but by enough people in power so that it's been a problem, casting people.

Q: Is it scary when you're sort of in the middle of working on things, or things are pending?

NUSSBAUM: It's okay. There's lots of different things in life that are important. That's probably one of the greatest things that becoming disabled taught me. You know, being on stage and pretending you're somebody else is not the most important fucking thing in the world. It's just not.

Q: Do actors just starting out ever ask advice from you?

NUSSBAUM: Yeah, they do.

Q: What do you tell them?

NUSSBAUM: Isn't that funny? I just tell them how great they are, if I think they are. And I try and help them figure out how to enjoy themselves. And then also to be prepared.

Q: What if someone should come and ask you whether or not they should pursue a career in theatre?

NUSSBAUM: You know, they're going to make the decision on their own. I guess I would ask them what they want in their lives. Do they want financial security? If so, this is probably a bad career to choose. Is the need to do this so overwhelming? Is there anything else that they can do and still pursue acting, too? You know, there's so many things. You don't have to just be an actor. You really don't. You can have another kind of a career on top of it. And then if the acting thing takes off, great. But I think most people are either going to do it or not. And there comes a point when the circumstances of their life make it clear to them as to whether or not they can continue—not advice from somebody else.

Nine

JOHN RANDOLPH

B. Bronx, New York City, 1915. Attended City College of New York, 1936; Columbia University, 1943 (summer session). Trained for stage with Stella Adler, Erwin Piscator, and William Hansen at the Dramatic Workshop. Founding member of Actors Studio. Military: U.S. Army Air Forces, corporal, 1942–45. Awards: Peabody, *Come Back, Little Sheba*, 1951; Tony, Drama Desk Award, *Broadway Bound*, 1987.

Q: Mr. Randolph, would you tell me your very first experiences with acting?

RANDOLPH: First of all, I didn't think I was an actor. Second of all, I do remember, in retrospect, that there was a wonderful English teacher in the sixth grade in public school who talked a lot about Shakespeare. She used to recite the works of Shakespeare; Hamlet, she played Hamlet. She was a little, very ugly, old lady with a great passion for it! And of course I remember her saying that people should never commit suicide; it's a crime. And then she would do Hamlet—"To be or not to be"—and she did it with such feeling that, even though I was only a kid, it affected me deeply, as if she said, "I thought of committing suicide, and I didn't." Then I wrote a newspaper article about Shylock and Antonio. She said, "Do whatever you want to do, to dramatize that period." And I became a newspaper editor and I interviewed Shylock; I interviewed Antonio, and Portia, and all those people; and I told the atmosphere in the courtroom.

Q: Where did you go to school?

RANDOLPH: It was Public School 70 in the Bronx. Later on when I became an actor, where I actually started was when my brother made a date for me, for an audition that was held at [radio station] WMCA in New York "at the top of your dial." I was going to City College [CCNY] at the time. I was a lower junior, and I was class of '36; but I only went up to about '35, and I went to this audition! I don't know why. I cut classes.

Q: What were you majoring in in college?

RANDOLPH: Sociology, economics, and speech. But basically, I had no idea what I was going to do. So I went to this audition, and I was not nervous. My younger kid brother just thought I should be an actor! I don't know why. It was during the Great Depression, and nobody was working; college students were going nowhere. When I walked in there, I saw all these very nervous people. And these were people from the streets of the City of New York. That's what they wanted: they didn't want any actors who were trained; they just wanted people who were from the streets of New York to read for them and maybe form an acting class. I saw people crying and nervous and everything, and I walked in, and they said [*mimicking formal speech*], "Won't you sit down." I said, "Oh, my God, they're using heavy voice sounds." I said [*in dramatic voice*], "I certainly will." I sat down, and they said, "Read this." Now I tell you, if you did it to me today with all my experience—in movies, television, radio—I would say, "Let me look it over." Well, I didn't bother saying that. I read it cold! I looked at it: it was a gangster talking to his mother on the telephone. I'd just seen Paul Muni in *Scarface*, so I did Paul Muni! [*Laughs*] And I saw that they were very impressed, and they asked when did I get interested in acting. I said, "All my life." I lied completely. Matter of fact, probably the first acting that I really did. "All my life. I dreamed of it, but I didn't believe it was possible." I was very poor—came from a poor middle-class family; lost everything in the Depression. I felt perfectly at ease there, and normal and excited, and I got in the class! Now, I was studying philosophy in CCNY. I also went to Columbia. I was interested in psychology; I was interested in history; I was interested in anything that had to do with sociology and background of people; I was interested in speech; I was a very good orator and I was a very good debater—everything that I was interested in seemed to come together as far as acting was concerned. So, on the test I got the highest marks. I won a pair of tickets to see Helen Hayes in *Mary, Queen of Scotland* at the Theatre Guild. It was the first play I'd ever seen.

Q: How old were you at that time?

RANDOLPH: About twenty. I must say that that kind of kicked me off! I met some wonderful people in that class; one was a young woman that you might know as Helen Beverly, but her name was Helen Smuckler and she was in the Yiddish Theatre, acted opposite Maurice Schwartz. She was an ingenue, and the name of the movie she was in was *Green Fields*. Her father was a former prompter at the Moscow Art Theatre— always wanted to be a director—and then was editing a tobacco magazine in New York; and the mother was a Polish actress, a background in theatre. He [the father] wanted to have a theatre group, and he formed a theatre group; and those of us who Helen liked and felt were good ended up working in theatre, in a little flat in the Bronx. Doing Ibsen—doing *A Doll's House*; doing *Ghosts*. And the old man was our director! And that was the first feeling I ever got about theatre—first real training.

I did several radio programs with this group at WMCA, where I learned that I would have to know different accents. They had a show called *Five Star Final* that was like the *March of Time, The News of the Week!* But this was every day! Taught me things that I would never have studied anywhere.

I approached Liggett's—a very famous drugstore with a counter— and I applied for a job there. So I got this job in Liggett's as a soda jerker, and I didn't know how to jerk anything—so I just watched them, while drinking Coca-Colas. And then I went to work. And some lady in front of me said, "I'll have a Lime Rickey." Now by that time I'm in college and I knew how to make a Lime Rickey—with ice, and with a little syrup, and then squeeze a lime in it, and then the soda, and then just give it to her. And I had done that, and they're all watching me, and I slid the glass—to be professional—slid it along, and it fell right in her lap! And I will tell you that one guy [*laughs*] said, "Listen, Lippman" (that was my name at that time), "you better stick to washing dishes for a while." I got fired after that. I would work twelve hours a day, three days a week, one way split shift. It was a terrible terrible thing! But I made eighteen dollars a week! And it was a lot of money at that time! Then I became a paint salesman. I was also making deliveries for a hardware store, and I saw this wonderful paint! I fell in love with it! It was called Alkaloyd. I never forgot the name of it! It was stronger than iron; it was resistant to stains; it was resistant to acid, resistant to alkali; it would never wear out—

Q: How long did this career last?

RANDOLPH: One week.

Q: You had to become an actor! How did your family feel about you becoming an actor?

RANDOLPH: Oh, terrible! My mother used to say to me—when I really got started a little bit, working in the Bronx for nine months, one play, no money coming in—"Look at Orson Welles. He's your age, and he's making a living and you're a bum." I said, "Ma, give me a break! I'm just starting!" I didn't know how I would go about it. I had no way of knowing how you make the rounds or doing any of that; but the thing was, you were with other people who also lied—said that they never wanted to be an actor until they auditioned. And some of them knew more about the business. I found that I fell in love with every woman automatically who was a lead. I was a very handsome guy, and very enthusiastic about all of it! And moody at times. I would leave the rehearsal—knowing my part didn't come up for about a half-hour or an hour—and then just walk out, leaving a little note behind: how I just could not concentrate for a minute; I needed some air; the world is in a state of chaos—and all that kind of crap! And when I came back, everybody understood this handsome, moody young man! I felt, "My God! My mother never cared!" My mother—when she saw me upset— would say, "What's the matter? You feel bad?" I'd say, "Well, I'm just thinking about all those seventeen million unemployed." She said, "Listen, eat something. You'll feel better." That was my mother's reaction to all of it, anything: eat a little bit; maybe you'll feel better. But if I said I was moody or upset, the other actors all understood.

Q: Tell me about your peers when you were first starting out.

RANDOLPH: Well, I had no other friends who were in the theatre! I didn't know anybody in the theatre! By this time I'd read almost everything about theatre that came out. And once working with Smuckler and Helen who came from the Yiddish Theatre—the great Yiddish actors brought wonderful culture to America! Though I was Jewish, I didn't understand much of Yiddish! But my mother talked about those people— and theatre—how they went down to see theatre. So, even poor people loved the theatre! And the theatre came to them! Second Avenue had eighteen theatres! Yiddish theatres with very famous people. I was surrounded by that attitude towards the theatre as an important part of life. Stella Adler, Piscator—all of the people I worked with talked about the theatre as an important part of life, a contribution that the artist makes to society without which there's nothing rich in the society.

Helen picked me because, I guess, I was the juvenile, or the leading man. But I played only character roles! I never played any leading men with them! I played Krogstad in *Doll's House*; I played Engstrand in *Ghosts*. And I was around nineteen or twenty.

Q: When you were starting out, did you set certain benchmarks for yourself?

RANDOLPH: Nothing. No illusions. And I think that was healthier for me.

Q: Would you tell me about other people who were role models or mentors to you?

RANDOLPH: I think as I worked, of course, the Russians became great role models: a great actor name of Cherkasov who did Peter the Great, Alexander Nevsky—did all of these great parts—Don Quixote. He used different makeup in everything he did! He was a character actor! So, the character actors are where I was going, 'cause the life is longer. I reacted to the challenge of character, not to whether I was good-looking and tall and very attractive in many ways. I was a nice guy. I wasn't belligerent. I began to love the whole atmosphere of the theatre, and it gave me an attitude that went through rough periods. And now I see that my nature prepared me better than anything else. My nature, my political philosophy, my attitude towards life came out of the Depression! I'm gonna live! I'm not gonna be down. If they move the furniture out, we move it back! Ideas were the most important thing in the world! The world was not very pretty at that time. I never gave in to that! I will tell you that it was the best thing to prepare me for the most trouble—that included the blacklisting.

Q: When do you feel you first achieved professional recognition?

RANDOLPH: I think I felt that most in the Federal Theatre. Now, the Federal Theatre's another ballgame. Life itself is so different from anything I could predict. When I was in the Ibsen Theatre—which really had practically no audience, but it had a ticket price and we had a program and your name was in the program—at that time my name was Mortimer Lippman. Prior to that it was Emmanuel Cohen. My real dad died when I was four years old. He died in the 1919 flu epidemic. And my name was Emmanuel! The family's name was Cohen. These are all fine names; there's nothing wrong with them. But my stepfather, Joseph Lippman, married my mother a couple of years after my dad died, decided to rename me from Emmanuel to Mortimer. He thought that Mortimer was more like a banker! He thought Emmanuel was too Jewish. Then I was known as Mortimer Lippman at a time when Edgar Bergen had a character called "Mortimer Snerd" and it was sweeping the country. So the "Mortimer" became an object of ridicule in high school, and even in college, though I could hardly take it! I was known by that name in the air force. I was a control tower operator, and I was known as Snortin' Mortin or Slippy Lippy. By that time I already had ideas of changing the name. But I had no idea what I would do. I think that it was actually going into the Federal Theatre when I found out what I would do. The Federal Theatre, during the WPA [Works Progress Administration] days, was the greatest surge of creative work in the United States. It was a phoenix rising out of the ashes of the Depression, and the greatest outburst of creative work in this country, in the arts. And it was the first time America had ever subsidized an actor! You got twenty-three dollars and eighty-six cents a week; it was enough to support your family and have money left over! Enough to pay the rent. And you were with other actors, and directors and producers, and suddenly this country took off. The actors had nothing to restrict them. Some were from Broadway. Some were from regional areas. Some were like us, just struggling actors; all of us had some record of proof that we were actors. Actors' Equity said, "No, they don't want that! Only professional actors who were members of Actors' Equity could be in the project."

Q: Were you a member of Actors' Equity at that time?

RANDOLPH: No! No, the main thing was to put money into circulation! That was what it was. Hallie Flanagan and the people who worked in the Federal Theatre basically made it a dream world for us. We had two Black Theatres; we had a Jewish-language Theatre; you had a German-language Theatre; you had a Classical Theatre; you had the Orson Welles Mercury Theatre; you had a One-Act Play Theatre; you had a Suitcase Theatre, where you carried a suitcase from one engagement to another. It was everything that you ever dream of as an actor. The dancers—all of whom were poor—became very famous, every one of them. Whether it was Anna Sokolow or Helen Tamiris or Danny Negrin—they all flourished! Martha Graham! Well, there was no way a dancer could make a living! Suddenly they were getting paid! Artists who couldn't afford the oil and the canvas, suddenly got oil and canvas! And the tools to work with! And twenty-three dollars and eighty-six cents a week. And no restrictions. Censorship didn't come in until later when the cries of "Reds!" and all the rest of it came into it. Other than that, that was the most glorious part of my life. Ah! I loved it! I was smart enough to know that it was something special. Once I got into the Federal Theatre, I was in the Children's Theatre. The Children's Theatre had almost four hundred people. The Living Newspaper had 450 people—writers, directors, and actors. They tried to blend all these different skills. One of the theatres that came out that was terribly creative was the Living Newspaper—the dramatization with a clown, and wonderful imagination and voices!

Q: Did you go into the schools? Or did the students come to the theatre?

RANDOLPH: We did even more than that. Forget about Joe Papp! The first theatres in the park were the Federal Theatre! And the Children's Theatre had a truck that was built specially for that: one side came down; it was a platform. Then they had canvas on the top that uncurled and was pegged into the ground, and that became our dressing rooms. They had a generator; and the sound system was part of the equipment, and lights. And we would do plays in front of twenty-five/thirty thousand people in all of the parks all over New York City, and Brooklyn, Manhattan, Queens. And it's all free!

Q: How long did this period last?

RANDOLPH: Two and a half years. It was between 1935 and '39. It was all over the entire United States. There was a show called *It Can't Happen Here* by Sinclair Lewis, known as "Red Lewis." He was one of the great dramatists, and it was about the building up of fascism in the United States! Anti-Semitic, antiblack. Terrifically powerful—and the title *It Can't Happen Here* is where it can happen. And it played in twenty-six cities in the United States, with a cast of sixty people in each city, and opened up simultaneously one night all over the United States.

Q: You've always been very politically active in your career. Is this where it started?

RANDOLPH: It started in college. I never believed that my acting was divorced from society! I never believed in theatre, *just* theatre—just to do Noel Coward or do Shakespeare. Because Shakespeare was political, too! As I began to read and study, to me the most exciting theatre eventually became George Bernard Shaw, Sean O'Casey, Ibsen, Bertolt Brecht—things that had something to say that could change society! Luckily I was able to get involved in the Federal Theatre. You sat with a hundred and fifty or two hundred people who were thrown together! Some of them, actors from Broadway who said [*mimicking haughty manner*], "Well, I'm only here for a short time. I have an engagement"— they didn't have any engagement! The terrible hurt feelings of being paid by the government, 'cause you had to be on Home Relief to get into the project! I knew what they were talking about! They all had to be on Home Relief! And somehow, being a newcomer to the theatre I was able to see things more objectively. I had no false pride; I had already known what being on Home Relief is. We were on Home Relief! My stepfather lost his business. Gangsters were coming to the house. So, I saw people with false pride disappear after a while.

In the Federal Theatre you had everything! You had vaudevillians; you had acrobats; you had legitimate actors who did classical work; you had actors from different shows who all had worked and had been in the theatre where there was a program and they got paid something. *We* never got paid; but to qualify we had to show a program from the Ibsen Theatre, and that admission was paid to see you. That was the only qualification. And you had to be on Home Relief.

Things change. But basically, at that time, what happened to those of us who were involved in this experience—to hear, for example, an actor getting up and saying, "Well, I don't think we should use the term 'nigger.' That's no good!" I never heard anybody talk like that. I figured the script calls for Passe-Partout, in *80 Days Around the World*, it's called a "nigger"! "My nigger man." That was part of the French interpretation! Then arguments took place! Over terminology. And actors say [*mimicking*], "We have no right to change the words of the playwright! We are only hired to do the works of the writer!" That kind of thing. And I'd listen to them, and listen to the old ladies who were behind a wonderful guy, name of Wayne Ayrie. I've never forgotten him. He had blue eyes. He looked like what an actor should be. Wonderful grey hair. The voice was like a trumpet! And the old lady actresses all loved him! He got up and he said [*mimicking quaking actor voice*], "I too have never heard the actors protesting about a word like 'nigger,' but they're right. It is a shameful statement. It's a shameful term, going back to the days of slavery, and I think it is *wonderful* that these young actors are saying that!" I fell in love with that guy! I didn't know at that time he was a member of the Communist Party. That was the kind of thing that was going on. I was prepared for that! I'd been arguing all day in every year in my classes in college. It was just continual. It didn't seem abnormal to me to have these discussions.

By the end of two and a half years, the Red-baiters had forgotten; they got mad: "What are we doing spending our money for all these communists, the writers and the actors and all?" There was a famous hearing of Hallie Flanagan being called down to Congress and asked by the representative from Arkansas, I think it was, about "all the communist infiltration [*mimicking Arkansas accent*] in the Federal Theatre" and how "we've got to get rid of these things." "And now, for example," he said, "Miss Flanagan, you got a play called *Faustus*, written by that communist Christopher Marlowe!? How do you let a thing like that get by?!" She said, "Well, Congressman, Marlowe was a contemporary of William Shakespeare. [*Laughs*] And he knew nothing about communism, and we believe in freedom of choice"—and so forth and so on. "There is no attempt for Reds to dominate it; and Mr. Welles and Mr. Houseman who are the producers and the actors, like everybody else, are poor and became part of the project. We have no control over people's thoughts and ideas." There was a certain amount of carefulness, because it was government money, and she tried carefully to avoid conflict. You had to walk a line. A lot of fights went on. Suddenly I had a way, and suddenly I was occupied with people. That's where I began to meet directors, producers, actors, musicians; we all stuck together. We had a big rally to maintain the fight, to avoid being cut off the project when they began to cut the funds. They didn't care what Hallie Flanagan said. [*Light Southern accent*] "She's just a little Red from Vassar College." And that was kind of the whole attitude. They're all a bunch of Reds, see? I led delegations down to senators. And Hallie Flanagan—as if she were the villain, when people were getting what we called "pink slips." When somebody committed suicide, there was a big picket line around 23rd Street—the Flatiron Building where the WPA had headquarters. Twenty-three thousand people picketing! And some of them were not actors; some of them were supporters of the City Project Council and the Workers Alliance! I had never picketed! I was a leader. I was so ashamed of carrying a picket sign! All I could think of was—if my mother were watching—"Don't make waves!" I was tall, so I carried a picket sign. But I was not a very brave leader! That was my first time ever I did that.

Q: What happened with your career after that?

RANDOLPH: When the Federal Theatre began to fire everybody, by that time I had done Shakespeare. I did the Children's Theatre up until a point where the Children's Theatre was being disassembled, and by that time the writing was on the wall.

Then I was co-opted by another branch of the Federal Theatre: the Theatre of Four Seasons, where they did plays like *No More Peace* by Ernst Tuller—again, political—[and] *Captain Jinx and the Horse-marines*. I did *Coriolanus*, Shakespeare, for the first time. I loved the idea of the repertory company. I only had that for a very short time. Then I went to Boston; you could also work in some theatres where they didn't have a leading man. It's like jobbing out.

They had stock companies, part of the Federal Theatre! And so I played Maine in a show called *Sure Fire*, but there were no theatres! There used to be theatres; there used to be symphony orchestras—but they all were unemployed! So there was no more orchestra. Suddenly you had orchestra; you had actors; and I was a guest star. So I got thirty dollars a week, instead of twenty-three dollars and eighty-six cents. I had to pay for my own room and board and all that kind of stuff, and send money home. We would play in a gymnasium. And at the end of the first act, the people'd go home! They didn't know there was a second act! So then we had to have a vaudeville group that came into the thing. We finished the first act; the vaudeville groups came on, song and dance, a fast-trick violinist; there were tap dancers. So they stayed there. Then we started the second act! We trained people again to go back to the theatre! We played all over Maine!

Then in Boston, there was this play called *Created Equal*. By that time the project was almost ending. *Created Equal* was a part of a Black Theatre project in Salem, Massachusetts. In Harlem, in New York, two black theatres opened up! Some of the great black writers! A guy, name of Gus Smith. A guy who did *Big White Fog*, Ted Ward. Fantastic writers that came out. Orson Welles did a black *Macbeth* up there that was incredible—a voodoo *Macbeth* that you've never seen anything like! It was that experience—it was that total explosion—I'm talking about! It's hard to convey it except the enthusiasm in my voice—and that doesn't go on a piece of paper. But that was the growth. In Boston, while I was still in *Created Equal*, there was a guy, name of Frank Silvera, who became one of our finest actors—a black actor who was from the West Indies. He and I became really close friends; and when I got fired, I stayed with Frank! He put me up, didn't charge me any rent; I didn't have any money. And I made the rounds as a radio announcer in Boston. I'd lost my Bronx accent and had worked on speech enough, and then—when I was unable to work any more—instead of going home to New York I stayed and I made the rounds of every radio station in Boston. I couldn't get in under the name of Mortimer Lippmann. You smelled anti-Semitism! You just smelled it! And then when I went to the last station—which was WHDH, the "Voice at Home to the Fishermen at Sea"—I had the name of John Randolph.

I'd written an article in a left-wing magazine, by that time, that exposed a program called *America's Hour* as being really supported by the National Association of Manufacturers. I passed myself off as a reporter. They gave me an office, gave me a secretary; I investigated this program. I said I was doing an article on the role of the artist—of the actors, the performers—in a different wonderful program that NBC was doing—particularly, this program. And CBS the same thing. And so they gave me a secretary! And after one week, I got everything! I know how to read. I mean, I studied in CCNY; I knew how to go to the library, I knew how to do research. I was a good student and I did it all, and I had a wonderful article. Then I got a letter in the mail that said, "You have been passing yourself off as one of our reporters of *Time* magazine"—which is an extension of *Fortune*/NBC. "This is a crime that would sentence you to three years in jail and a ten thousand dollar fine. Have your lawyer contact us." I'm poor! I have no money! I mean, it was in the Bronx! Who had a lawyer?! I called up and said, "I was just doing a college paper. I didn't have any idea; I just thought it would be a wonderful idea for a college article." They said, "Well, you come right down, and you bring everything that you've written. Otherwise, we'll pursue this course of suing you!" So I put on a CCNY Letter. I had a white team shirt: "CCNY." (I'd been on the fencing team.) And of course, I was not going to college anymore. I came down there in the highest voice I ever had—with all my enthusiasm—and gave them all the papers!

Q: They didn't sue you.

RANDOLPH: No. But I had written the article. And shortly afterwards I wrote this article *"America's Hour,"* and it went to all the magazines— *New Masses, Nation, New Republic. New Masses* was the only radical magazine that had wonderful people in it, but I had no idea who they were. They accepted it. And when it went out, I got a lot of fan mail. I got over about a hundred letters. And one was from a guy—and they had said, "Do you want to use your name, Mr. Lippmann?" And I said, "No, you better give me a pseudonym"—because I was still working in radio! And I got a letter from a guy, J. R. Atkins. Now, in Jewish we don't have any middle name. It's Emmanuel Cohen; it's not Emmanuel Hersh Cohen. So, I had only one name. And I never knew what "J. R." stood for; and certainly, "Atkins" was nothing to do with me! I got this letter from this guy, name of John Randolph Atkins from New Meadows, Idaho! Written on a nickel pad that he'd been given a home from Government Grant, and he'd come over in a covered wagon, and he found this place in New Meadows, Idaho, and he had a huge cabin and then it became a big, big house, and he was seventy-eight years old, and he was looking for ancestors who might have come over from Scotland where he came from, and he thought maybe I was one because he had written to me when I ran for mayor forty years ago in San Francisco and I didn't answer! Now, I'm only twenty-three! [*Laughs*] All I can dream of is, I can get out of the Bronx; I'll have a home in New Meadows, Idaho! I don't even know where New Meadows, Idaho, is! And I write back, "I'm so sorry. I was so busy campaigning. I apologize for ignoring you. But I certainly have time now, and I am one of your relatives, and I'm very curious to meet you too!" Hoping somehow I would get out of the Bronx and I would be able to go see the rest of the world. And I never heard from the old man. All I got is his letter to me and his name.

Q: When did you get back into theatre?

RANDOLPH: I came right back to New York and began to go to classes at the American Theatre Wing. I went back and I acted in a show called *Kate Smith Hour* with a very good man who directed it—a director who was in the WPA with me in the Children's Theatre, Jules Dassin, who later married Melina Mercouri and did *Never on Sunday* and all those other things. Jules Dassin afterwards directed my first professional job. That was called *Medicine Show.* It was the first "living newspaper" outside of the [WPA] Project. Martin Gable and Arlene Francis were the producers.

Q: What were the first organizations that you joined?

RANDOLPH: I joined Actors' Equity Association. Later on I was one of the first people to form AFTRA, the American Federation of Television and Radio Artists. And Screen Actors Guild didn't come until just before my blacklisting period. Just prior to that, I was in a show called *Come Back, Little Sheba* with Shirley Booth in New York, on Broadway. Shirley Booth and Sidney Blackmer. It won a lot of awards. I won the Peabody Award as the actor with the most potential to succeed in comedy.

Q: How old were you at this time?

RANDOLPH: I think twenty-three or twenty-four. It was pretty exciting when I realize it. Just before I was blacklisted, I did a thing called *Naked City*—a movie with Joan Blondell—and I joined the Screen Actors Guild. That was the first movie for that period. I could not work for fifteen years.

Q: What did you do during that fifteen years?

RANDOLPH: Stage. Theatre was the only place where we had no blacklisting. Once, I was in a live television show; I was playing Anthony Quinn's brother. It was called *Danger.* (During that time I had already been in the left-wing movement and demonstrations in Madison Square Garden—packed to twenty thousand people—and represented the young people that came back from the war.) Sidney Lumet was directing. And then suddenly—just before we did this show—Lumet was called up by the vice-president of CBS, and the producer also was called up. We had a half-hour break. Never occurred to me there was anything wrong. We knew the blacklisting was coming, but we didn't know how it would work. We were already seeing people being blacklisted, and I wasn't on that list. I was challenging blacklisting. But I myself was not blacklisted.

And then they came down and the producer called me aside and he said, "John, I want to tell you that Sidney and I were called up by this vice-president and he said, 'Get rid of John Randolph.' " And Sidney said, "Why?" He said, "Well, we got a call from Young & Rubicam, an advertising agency, and they got a call from a guy name of Johnson in Syracuse who owns three supermarkets there, and he's the head of the American Legion, and he said, 'John Randolph is a Commie. He marched in the May Day parade. And you better get rid of him; otherwise, we're going to boycott your product. We'll put under every Amadent toothpaste that's being sold in my stores, 'Amadent toothpaste sponsors Communist activists.' "

Q: Did you know who this person was?

RANDOLPH: No. All I know is that he mentioned his name; but it never meant anything till later on in my life, when we fought against guys like Johnson. And Sidney said the vice-president at CBS didn't know who the hell I was. He was just in charge of clearing people considered radical. Young & Rubicam said, "You better get him off, because our client is sponsoring *Danger*." And Sidney said, "We can't. John has a big part, and this is live television. We have nobody that can replace him. We're going on the air tomorrow." He said, "Well, if you hire him again you're finished with this network." That's gangster talk.

But nobody knew that that was the way it was working. I knew, and I knew from investigating blacklisting already, that the CBS loyalty oath—if you didn't take it, then you could be put on a blacklist. I had to take an oath that said I was not a member of all of these organizations—150 organizations. The Nazis, the Communists, the Socialists, the NAACP—you mention it. If you'd been a member of any of those organizations, that was considered Red. Once I found out how it worked, I got together with people like Ossie Davis, Ruby Dee, Sarah Cunningham (my wife), Eli Wallach, Anne Jackson, Lee Grant. And we worked out an antiblacklist clause. Already we saw the writing on the wall. It was spreading like wildfire. In New York—CBS, NBC, you mention it. Four hundred actors eventually got on that list. I had meantime gotten a job in *Paint Your Wagon*, Lerner and Lowe, in Boston. But I had already written an antiblacklist letter—I knew how the blacklist worked. So when there was an Equity meeting, I sent my letter in to be read by Clarence Derwent, the president of Actors' Equity at that time. So there was an antiblacklist resolution. The membership meeting voted on it. It was a clause in the contract of Actors' Equity—

which is in it today—that nobody can be discriminated against for political, economic, religious, or any other reason. We had a lot of actors who were against the blacklisting. And we knew on Broadway that this was hitting hard. 'Cause live television was there; commercials were there; industrial films were there. I could not make a living in anything where you could generally make a living as an actor. Except the stage. And it was the only time that the League [of American Theatres and Producers] and Equity agreed: on this antiblacklist clause. They reopened negotiations only on that clause alone. And it is now in our union contract.

Equity was my only home. And Broadway was my only home. And any theatre that I could work in. Nobody gave me a job because I was blacklisted or that I had a wife and a kid and another one coming. You just had to read for every part. That was the task. And the other task was to fight blacklisting. I had a wonderful wife by this time: Sarah Cunningham, from the South—Greenville, South Carolina. Family were signers of the Declaration of Independence and the Bill of Rights. Daughters of the American Revolution. She was blacklisted. Not just because she was married to me. She was pretty liberal herself. Sarah also had ancestors who were presidents of the United States. We were called before the House Committee on Un-American Activities—the first investigation on Broadway, of the Broadway theatres. This was when we began to organize to defeat the people who advocated blacklisting in the union— the leadership of Screen Actors Guild and the leadership of AFTRA, and TVA (Television Authorities). We were beginning to win in fights against blacklisting.

Eventually I ended up, now—as I am now—on the board of directors of Screen Actors Guild. On the board of directors of AFTRA. So the world has changed around since that time. And I will never let the membership forget, and they never have. We have an antiblacklist resolution now in both those unions. Never again will that union leadership send a telegram to an actor who's called before a committee like the House Committee on Un-American Activities and told, "You must answer the questions of the House Committee, or any committee of Congress. If you do not, you can be fined, suspended, or expelled." It's bad enough that you couldn't work anywhere except in the theatre. Then your union is going to ban you, so you can't even work in theatre!? That was when you had right-wingers in leadership in Actors' Equity Association. But not that strong. But at Screen Actors Guild and AFTRA—particularly out here in Hollywood—right-wing kissed the ass of the industry, played ball, and threatened their own actors.

When Sarah Cunningham got on the stand right after me, and she was asked her name, she said, "I want to make a statement." They said, "Well, you can't make a statement. Leave it here. We'll put it in the record." She said, "No, I have to tell you that my ancestors, who were presidents of the United States and signers of the Declaration of Independence, would not look with favor upon this committee." And Sarah had a Southern accent and she was an actress who had learned perfect speech. She had a big white hat—looked like a Southern belle from *Gone with the Wind*. They got her off as quickly as they could. They didn't know that the presidents were really schmucky presidents. One was William Henry Harrison. He died three months after he caught cold at his inauguration. And the other one, Benjamin Harrison, didn't make much of a contribution. Didn't make any difference. My son's name is Henry Harrison Randolph, named in honor of those guys because that name scared the committee. I was then acting in a show called *Much Ado about Nothing* at the Brattle Theatre in Cambridge [Massachusetts]—my first big Shakespeare production. When I was called in front of the committee, Sarah was crying. We had a lot of hate people in the courtroom. The first six rows of the courtroom where the hearings were held were given to the right-wingers. I'm talking about horrible cameras all over, and radio things. It was like a circus. It was like a kangaroo court. Our lawyers couldn't say anything. We did not know what the charges were.

Q: You were not allowed to know what your charges were?

RANDOLPH: That's right. There was no way of knowing. Committee made a weak statement of why they were in New York about the actors on Broadway supporting the Soviet Union communists. But they had no real statement. Therefore they had no real reason why they were there except to witch-hunt and get people to give names. Now, you cannot give names without jeopardizing the lives of other people. You cannot legislate names because a committee is only organized by Congress to do research and come back with recommendation for legislation. How can you legislate in the area of names? And so it didn't make any sense. Later on, it was thrown out—eventually.

But what happened was that when I got up—she said, "I was so frightened, John, because you're my husband, and you're one of the first people to be called." And then they asked you a question: "Where do you come from? What's your name?" And you give them all your names. And, "Where'd you go to school?" And what shows you've been in, and how many weeks—and they didn't know what you were talking about. They really didn't know. I went through everything—every single show. And then finally I said, "And at the present moment, without any criticism of the committee, I'm in a show called *Much Ado about Nothing*." And got the first laugh.

Q: You talked about your background, and you grew up without much money. What has been your relationship to money over your career?

RANDOLPH: The relationship is that I've never got over it. It's almost like a Pavlovian experience. I owe nobody any money. Everything I buy I pay for. I will not have furniture taken out of my house, like they did when I was a kid. I will not kiss anybody's behind because I don't have any money. I will not crawl. And when I began to earn some money—it took a long time—I knew how to save it. So did Sarah. I knew how to cut everything immediately so I could survive. My children didn't understand it in the beginning, 'cause they went to the High School of Music and Art. We gave them an education. Whatever money we had. They had musical education; they went to ballet, went to the theatre. So my daughter just took it for granted. Went to summer camp. Went to all those things. We believed the children should have all that. And later on, it became a difficulty because they were used to having money.

Maybe I put too much emphasis on money, I don't know. I always worried when a job was ended; I was really looking ahead for the next one, especially after the House Committee on Un-American Activities had called me up. And by that time I was known as a fighter against all of that crap, and I was "radical." And I had nothing—thirty-eight dollars in the bank just about this time. I was finished. I was picketed in a show called *Wooden Dish* 'cause I was the first actor to have a job on Broadway who had defied the Committee. I lost the job because the show closed. At that point I only had thirty-eight bucks. I was hustling for a job. Sarah was pregnant by that time with my son Hal. And Martha Eoline was three-and-a-half years old, going on four. Sarah was not working. And I just went from one place to another. Eventually I went to read for *Inherit the Wind*. There was a national road company headed by Melvyn Douglas. Paul Muni, starring as Clarence Darrow, had lost his sight in one eye. Melvyn replaced him on Broadway, and Herman Shumlin was sending it on national tour. I got a tip-off. In those days we could go into an office; you didn't have to have an agent send you. I went in to see Herman Shumlin and I waited like all the other actors, and he saw me, and I told him I was interested in being in *Inherit the Wind*. And he said, "Have you seen the show?" And I said, "No." He said, "I'll get you a ticket for it." Then I saw the show. From what I saw, there was nothing that I could tell him I would be right for. But I called him and said I thought it was the most wonderful experience to hear a man say on the stage, "An idea is a greater monument than a cathedral." When I heard that ideas must be exposed to the sunlight to live or die, you know, that's all I heard. I heard me fighting. And everything I wanted to say about freedom of speech, religious freedom, all the words that Darrow had brought up at that monkey trial—which I just did.

Q: When the blacklist was finally over, how did it feel to start working again in places and with people that you could not at that period?

RANDOLPH: I brought a great deal of resentment. When I came to do *Seconds* with Rock Hudson, I had a big part. It was the way to come to this town [Los Angeles]. I knew what I was doing. I've been fighting all my life. Rock Hudson and I played the same character. I played an older man who goes through plastic surgery and becomes Rock Hudson. And it was a break, a great part. Frankenheimer broke the blacklisting for me. I didn't have to sign any papers. I would not sign a paper.

Q: Was that a major turning point for your career?

RANDOLPH: Oh, yes. I did this wonderful part. I had four or five weeks when they were shooting Rock Hudson. I demanded that the agents— who I didn't know—take me around. I mean, I was going to face these sons-of-bitches. I know what they did. They cooperated with the union to get rid of actors. They weren't hiring anybody who was considered a lefty or a radical—or a supposed radical—or a liberal. I went around with these agents. I finally got a television job in between waiting for Rock Hudson. I know I'm in a position of strength. I knew. Working in Paramount, co-starring in an important role. They didn't know my face. They didn't know who the hell I was. 'Cause they didn't see me on television. They didn't see me in movies. So when I went around, eventually I got this call for a television show. My first in fifteen years. Really, with one exception my first job out here. And I got a call from the agent, said, "John, the vice-president of CBS—thought it might be a good idea if you kind of write a little note that they can put in the files that, you know, I mean, I don't know anything about your background, but something about your background." I said, "You mean if I was a radical and a Red, a Commie?" "Well, I don't know. I guess so." Nobody knew how to talk about this. It was over. But they didn't know it here. Still living in fear. I said, "Well, I can't do that." I said, "Have the vice-president call me." By this time we had won a big trial against blacklisting. John Henry Faulke won a suit against Aware Incorporated, and this guy Johnson in Syracuse died the last day of testimony at the Faulke Trial. He committed suicide in a Bronx hotel. And the vice-president said, "Well, you know, Mr. Randolph, we know you're a very distinguished actor. You're playing a big part here. But, you know, we have a problem—a lot of nuts in this town are going to accuse you of being kind of radical, and we'd like to have it on record that you disavow all that." I said, "If I disavowed that, I'd be doing something I've never done in my life. And we just won a suit against CBS, against blacklisting, against Aware Incorporated, of three-and-a-half million dollars. John Henry Faulke." And he said, "Well, uh, it's not me, I mean, well—forget about it. It's all right." That was the last. That was tackling it straight, and tackling straight was the only way I knew how to do.

Then I did this television show. And then I left as soon as I finished the movie. Couldn't stand it. Couldn't stand it. I saw all my friends that were not blacklisted who had to see me. I mean, the acting fraternity out here was wonderful. They all knew I stood up. They knew I fought back. They knew I fought all that stuff. They were wonderful. Jimmy Whitmore and Arthur Franz and all the guys at the studio—working, making a lot of money. I was making no money. And when I came out here, invited me to their houses. I was getting the lowest salary any actor would ever get working for a movie. My agent at that time, Harriet Kaplan in New York, and Lily Veidt—two wonderful people—just said, "We want to sign you up, John. We don't care what they are offering. If you don't mind." I said, "I don't give a shit. Just put me on that film." They wanted to break the blacklist pattern. It was a big part. I had no idea how important it was, to be a lead in a film. I was in the first forty-five minutes of the movie. I mean, that's a lot. I did *Seconds*. And I left immediately.

Q: You went back to New York?

RANDOLPH: Right. I didn't trust 'em. You got to understand who I am. This kind of mentality—of McCarthy, of anti-Semitism, of antiblack— is something that I know will always be there. And it has to be continually fought. If you want to protect other generations. If you're an actress and you are protected, [it's] because I fought for an antiblacklist resolution with other actors—not alone. And I got rehearsal pay because actors who came before me by the name of Sam Jaffe and Phil Loeb fought for junior Equity members to get the same wages— anybody. We got twenty-five dollars a week rehearsal pay. But if you're a senior member of Equity, you got forty dollars a week. You had to have fifty-two weeks—or fifty weeks—of work as an actor before you become a senior Equity member. You had to have a beard a mile long before you got fifty weeks of work in our industry. I learned from them. I listened to them. And they fought for people like me. Those people fought for me. And for me not to fight for the next generation would seem to me indecent.

Q: You've been so active in social issues and politics in your career—how have you interacted with the public?

RANDOLPH: People were my strength. People are my strength. I didn't believe that I had any strength alone. Maybe there are people who had that power, but it wasn't me. But if I had a lot of people and we had a chance to win, that's when you fight. If you lost, okay, then you try to reorganize. But it was a fight. It was a struggle. And I think it kept me alive. I think it kept me healthy. I try not to forget those days. And I'm still fighting it. I mean, I'm still involved in so many different things now, at seventy-six. I wasn't arrogant; I just know who I am. I know that I could take all of the crap that they deliver in this industry that makes you negative and makes you self-critical—you think it's your fault. And all the rejection that we go through as performers—every audition is a rejection. For stars, as well. I don't care who they are. If they talk about the past, they got to talk about that one part where suddenly you're not called. We have rejection syndrome. We have all the syndromes that have to do with anxiety and ulcers, you name it. I never had any of that. I think it's because I took a more positive attitude.

Q: It seems like you controlled your career, almost. You really controlled your destiny.

RANDOLPH: I learned. I learned how to read. I had to learn. I became a better actor when I finally studied with Stella [Adler]. I was a good actor, but—she taught me how to break down a script. She taught me how to use an audition piece and make it come alive, better than anyone else who ever taught me. There were holes in the Stanislavski Method for the American actor. When I was in *Medicine Show*, when I was in *Hold onto Your Hats* with Al Jolson, I was very young. How do you handle a musical comedy? How do you handle an Al Jolson—Method? Screw the Method. He don't even talk about that. How do you handle Martha Raye singing and dancing on the stage while she was drunk? I mean, how do you add up all those things? There was no way that I knew how to solve certain problems. And when I studied with Stella, I'd been in two Broadway shows, one musical comedy on the road, and *Native Son* with Canada Lee, directed by Orson Welles.

Q: She was a real mentor to you.

RANDOLPH: Oh, she was. Because she taught me what self-criticism was. She was against a negative approach to acting. She was able to say in the class—when we finally learned how to criticize—"What did you like?" Not, how you would do it. "What was good? What didn't you believe in? And be specific." But Stella would never permit you to make value judgments.

Q: What is one major point that you would make to a young actor entering this profession?

RANDOLPH: I would tell you what I would tell my own child, my own boy. Get involved with other actors. Get involved with people in any benefit—in any way. Work to clean the theater. Do anything to be around that kind of atmosphere. Volunteer to do anything. And don't expect money. Find another job to keep you alive. And find a place where you can live cheap. 'Cause you're going to do it anyway. If you really want to go—if you come from out of town to New York; come from out of town to Hollywood; come from New York to Hollywood— they're all going through the same problem. But recognize it. And it doesn't mean that you don't have talent. It doesn't mean you can't grow. It doesn't mean you won't find places to work, and you won't find places to volunteer to work. And if you can do that just to get started, then you will begin to audition. You'll know where to go. Not like me. Once I got into the Federal Theatre, then I met all these people. I had to learn how to stay on the third floor of NBC and collar directors. Past the NBC desk. Got on the third floor. Director would come out—grab a hold of him: "My name is John Randolph." Didn't make any difference. He never heard it. Send him a turtle in the mail, with my name on it, so he would remember—a little baby turtle for ten cents. Have pencils with your name on it—anything!—for them to know who you are.

Finally you passed the audition, goddamn it. Maybe you could get one line, or two lines—whatever it was. You learned how to do that. You learned how to make the rounds. Sometimes, as I told you, on Broadway you could walk into an office—a producer. You didn't need an agent. Slowly, the agent was something that came along, when you were famous—when you did two lines in a show, or something. So I think that there's only one answer. How can you get it from any mysterious guide? Now they have papers, they have magazines, they have bulletins that tell you who's casting and all the rest of it. Even then, it's tough. The basic job of the union—as a change from just wages and working conditions—has changed, because people realize that the union has to do more than fight for wages and working conditions, has to find a way of opening up the theatre for people. Giving them a chance—if they become an Equity member—to be able to have a chance to audition, whether your agent can get you the job or not. How to meet agents. How to open up the doors out here to agents. Without agents in L.A., you're almost lost. It's almost impossible. So, we have an Agents Committee in the Screen Actors Guild. How can you find out unless you get involved in any way with people or acting? Whether it's street people, or Joe Papp—when he first started. All these groups starting with actors who have no contacts, and they're trying the best they can to get together. When you go to a college—the chances are, if you went to Yale, you were looking for Yale graduates. Carnegie Tech, you look for people—there are a lot of people from Carnegie Tech here. You find out there are other people who went to your school, who would welcome you into the Alumni Association.

Basically, what I'm saying to you, there's a time in your life. Don't try to organize your life completely. Leave the road open for adventure, for romanticism, for accidents; and be able to move in. You should know your craft. You should be ready to do the best that you can do to jump into it. And if you do that, don't put yourself down, because there's always somewhere where you can study. Always somewhere where you can work. Always somewhere you can at least use the tools of your trade. But whatever it is, be prepared.

JASON ROBARDS, JR.

B. Chicago, 1922. Education: American Academy of Dramatic Arts. Military: U.S. Navy, 1936–46. Awards: Obie, *The Iceman Cometh*, 1956; Tony, *The Disenchanted*, 1959; Academy Award, *All the President's Men*, 1976; Academy Award, *Julia*, 1977; Emmy, *Inherit the Wind*, 1988.

Q: What were your initial experiences with acting as a young person? How did you start?

ROBARDS: My father was an actor. So I was born on the road, in a show called *Lightning* that he was doing, playing the lead in it. It was a New York show; we were out of New York. My mother was pregnant, went out there to Chicago to meet him, to be with him; and I was born in Chicago. So I guess the acting was around me all the time. And for the first four years of my life, I was in New York and on the road with my father. I remember vague things of traveling on trains with actors. The Cliff Hotel in San Francisco. I remember going up in an elevator there as a little kid. Of being on stage in a taxi in a play that he did; they took me across the stage in this taxi that was used in the play. It was a fake taxi, but it was exciting to a little kid.

And then we moved to Los Angeles. He was under contract; he'd been on the stage for about fifteen years and he signed a contract out there in the '20s, and we all went out there. My brother and sister were born out there. But my father was always in the business. So I think the awareness of acting was always around. It was good and bad in my mind, because as he continued in Los Angeles and did not continue on the stage he started deteriorating—his work got worse. Like James O'Neill in *Long Day's Journey*, he started in a way just selling out for everything. And then the work didn't come, and then he got depressed, and I said, "Gee, this is a terrible profession." So I went the whole other way: I became an athlete. Which I suppose in a way is part of showing off or being in front of a crowd.

Then I went in the service, and never thought about acting. I went in before the war, before the draft, and went to China. I was at Pearl [Harbor] when that happened. I was in communications—which, in a way, is acting again, I suppose. Anyway, I got out of the service; that is when I went into the American Academy. I didn't know what else to do when the war was over. At one point I had entertained the idea of staying for twenty years and retiring at thirty-seven and doing something else. I'd have had twenty years in if I'd stayed till I was thirty-seven. But I didn't. The war drove me out. I then asked my father, you know. I wrote to him, and said—I thought I might try it. And he said, "Well, don't go anywhere in Hollywood. Go back to New York. Go to the school I went to, the American Academy of Dramatic Arts." And I did. And some of his teachers were there. And they remembered him.

And then I fell in love with it, fell in love with the theatre. It was nothing to do with movies; it was all about the theatre. I loved it, and we did plays there, besides classwork. And we covered makeup and dance and sword fighting and rehearsing and voice. They had many things— but with all that, they did plays. That's the best way to learn of all. We kept doing plays.

Q: So you learned on the stage.

ROBARDS: That's how I got really started. And then the guy that ran the place said to me, "Look, they need a guy in a stock company this summer. You don't need to come back to this school. Here's fifty bucks to get down here, to Delaware. They need you to play the lead one week and the second man the next week. A fifteen-week season." So I went. I went down and then I started acting, did fifteen weeks of stock. A new show every week. See, there you don't have to think about class or anything like that. You just get out and do it. Boy, did they let you know it, 'cause they're paying, you know. They'll boo you off the stage or throw stuff at you. In this particular company, every year they did an old-fashioned melodrama as their last show of the season. And they'd sell things to throw at the actors. I played the villain in it! I got hit with everything in the book! Besides bad acting, I got hit for being a bad man in a bad play!

Q: How did your family feel about your going into acting at this time?

ROBARDS: My dad?

Q: Yes.

ROBARDS: Oh, I'm sure he was very pleased. He just told me that it was a very chancy thing, and very heartbreaking. It had been very heartbreaking for him. And he felt that the chances were few and far between. And there were no chances for me out on the [West] Coast, just being a young guy out of the service and trying to get a job in a studio. At that time they still had a few of those contract players. That was '46, when I got out. They'd give you a leading man or a character man. They had signed character people, too. And they had these companies. But television was coming in, and it forced the closing of all those kind of things. At first the studios were not willing to admit that television was anything. They didn't even want to know about it. They knew it was the thing that would eat into their product. There were a lot of studios: Columbia, Paramount, Warners, Metro, Goldwyn, Selznick International. Each of those studios—especially the Big Five—would put out between seventy-five and eighty pictures a year. Think of the hundreds of pictures that were put out! Television removed all the class-B pictures, because you could do it on television. So then there were only really the A pictures, even though there were a lot of lousy pictures made, too. But it was never on that scale of the late '20s and through the '30s and part of the war years. They were doing an awful lot of films.

And early on in movies, most of the actors were stage actors. Almost all of them. Not all: Cooper is an exception. Gable was—all of them had been in the theatre in New York, you know. It's amazing. And that's really, I suppose, the core of their ability to handle a full feature in three weeks. They'd just shoot a whole feature. It wasn't like now.

Q: Did you have any role models or mentors during this time? Was your father a role model, do you think?

ROBARDS: I suppose—in a subliminal way. He never really told me anything, but I'd seen him on the stage when I was eleven. *That* I remembered very well. And I remembered that—seeing him on the stage—he was wonderful, and he put me at ease as an audience. I felt— secure. People say they feel secure with me, as an audience. And I feel that, once you're secure, you can then sit back in the audience and enjoy the play. But if you're up there wondering what the hell is going to happen every minute—a lot of things happen like that, nowadays; people that don't do the play, they do themselves, they only are interested in how they feel—then I feel the play suffers. I know a lot of actors, they shouldn't even be acting with other people! Acting is a cooperative business. It's not competition; it's cooperative, and it's the giving and the taking. And it's really interpretive business about the play. The play is the thing; it's not you. It's the character in the play. A lot of people don't realize that.

Q: Did you have any other role models that influenced you?

ROBARDS: I had a teacher named Eddie Goodman, who was at the American Academy, who really first encouraged my work. He criticized, but it was the first constructive criticism I had that I felt that I had a chance to be an actor. I did a couple of scenes from *The Little Foxes* in a class and he was able to see through what I did in it—to explain to other people and to me what was going on, what I'd done for the play. And that gave me a little hope. Of course, I made stupid mistakes later, and that doesn't matter—but at least I was learning.

Of course, [Charles] Jehlinger was still there. Jelly was somebody that we still talk about. I was doing a thing with Kirk Douglas a couple of years ago. He'd gone to the Academy. And the first thing we started talking about was, "Jelly was really tough on me"—and we were all still talking about him fifty years later. He had started the school.

Cecil B. DeMille was in the first class. It was then called the New York School of Acting, but for some reason they didn't like that. Somebody who put money in said, "That sounds too risqué. I think we should call it the American Academy." Imagine how restrictive thinking people were. Anyway, he was at that school. And when I got there, he was still there. He wore a hearing aid; and if he didn't like you, he'd just turn it off. But the few things that he gave me were wonderful. Yeah, he told me I was a bigger idiot than my father ever was! I understood what he meant!

Q: Were there other people who provided you with a kind of critical review you respected throughout your life?

ROBARDS: Yes, my first wife did. And my present wife, too, is very very good about that. I respect her views. She knows.

José Quintero was very influential to me. And he was—critical, but in a right way: that he knew that you'd find it. But he could get you there without telling you you're an idiot!

Q: Did you give yourself certain benchmarks through your career?

ROBARDS: No, I didn't. But I did say, "What am I doing wasting my time here, after eleven years of really near starvation, a wife and two children, and thirty-four years old? What in the hell am I doing with my life?" It wasn't a benchmark; I just said I'm going to stop this and go take that job that I was offered. There was a radio station, they wanted me to do some announcing—an NBC affiliate—because I'd done some and I knew the chief announcer at NBC, Pat Kelly, and he said, "I found this job for you if you want it, up in Torrington, Connecticut." And I said to him, "I think I better take it." Because, you know, you can't live starving all the time.

Q: Did you take it?

ROBARDS: No. My wife said, "No, I think you can hold out a little longer. We'll hold on a little longer." We did. And then I got *The Iceman Cometh* right after that. I had been in things, but it was not a steady income. It was this income where I had to do other things to supplement it, and always on the edge of not making the rent, or paying the gas or the light or stuff. We never starved; I never missed a payment. But it was always on the edge. There was always that worry.

Q: Were there any organizations you joined? I assume you joined Equity when you started.

ROBARDS: Oh, yeah. Equity. AF-TVA, that was the first television union. And AFRA. Not AFTRA, AFRA. AFRA was the radio union. Equity and SAG. Those were the three unions. And then there was a fourth union came in—was TVA. And that union then joined with AFRA and became AFTRA, which we have now. Those affiliations. But the only thing Equity gave you was the shoes, you know. That guy left money for the shoes, you remember that? I got a pair of Thom McCann shoes that were as heavy as—I could have been sunk in the East River! You know—like the gangsters used to put cement on your feet and throw you in the water. That's what those shoes were like! They never wore out.

Q: How do you feel about unionization and the theatre?

ROBARDS: I feel it's fine—if they don't go overboard with it. I was, strangely enough, in what they call the "Lockout," or the actors' strike of 1960. In fact, right at the Edison Hotel is where we kept having our meetings, which was when chorus joined Equity and I was not for it. A lot of us weren't for it.

Same thing's happening now with SAG; they want to have Screen Extras Guild join SAG. What happens if you've got people that have longevity in their union? Chorus longevity is five years. They take them in and that's it. And yet they get all the pension funds, the medical, the this, the that, and they don't participate. It's hard enough just for the Equity members—we're 88 percent unemployment all the time. It's hard enough for us to pay the money into our own funds to have that to be covered. Now you got all this coming in, and it destroyed our union, by the way. Equity's one of the weakest unions. When I was injured in an accident, Equity couldn't come up with anything. Now, SAG was the best. I don't know what's going to happen to SAG now. See, I think they should have "Chorus Equity," and have their own union, and that's fine. But I don't know what all this joining was about. Also, not everybody's an actor. You either got it or you ain't got it, you know what I mean? I don't know what it is that everybody says they're an actor.

Q: And other unions have entry requirements, and Equity has none—except, get a job.

ROBARDS: Yeah, but that's a tough requirement, in a way. You can't if you can't read for things if you're not an Equity member, and it's a catch-22. Now, I'm not running down Equity, but I do feel that the joining of it did hurt it a lot. I guess Colleen [Dewhurst] would be turning over in her grave if she heard me say that, although at the time of the strike—she was our president [of Actors' Equity], you know—at the time of the strike, Colleen and I and Maureen Stapleton and all of us didn't want them in there. We said, "No, no, they should have their own union." And it was a big lawyers' fight. Seems the lawyers got all the money out of it. My father, by the way, started Equity. And the Screen Actors Guild. He was the original member of Equity, in 1919—the Equity strike then—and the Screen Actors Guild right after talkies came in, in '33. He was a charter member of both unions, from the beginning. So I'm not against unionism or anything. I just don't like unionism out of hand, in any field—newspapers, mining, anything.

Q: Can you describe a little bit the time when you first felt you received professional recognition as an actor?

ROBARDS: Well, oddly enough, there was a theatre here, and a teacher at the American Academy that developed a thing called the "Children's World Theatre." It was at the Barbizon Plaza Hotel in New York, which is a very good theatre of about five hundred seats at 58th and Seventh Avenue. We took that over; they created this thing; and we did original children's plays which were very, very successful. Brooks Atkinson reviewed them for the *New York Times*. He'd bring a child and he would write the child's review with his own comments. And that was our first recognition, really. Tom Poston was in the company; Bernard Cates, myself, Juleen Compton, Lila Scala was in it. There were a whole lot of people in it, and they were very well done productions. I did *Many Moons* by James Thurber, an original play we did for children. We did *Jack and the Beanstalk* and all those things. Then the company toured. Philly; Stamford; Bridgeport (which at that time was not the city that it is now), it had a theatre; Brooklyn. There were weekend shows, by the way. They were not done all week; we only did them on Saturday and Sunday. But we had a little recognition out of that, as actors. You know, I went up to an agent, and she said, "What are you doing?" You know, we always used to keep making the rounds. And I said, "I'm playing the wolf in *Little Red Riding Hood*." She said, "No, we don't have any wolves; nobody's calling for wolves this week." All I was ever interested in was working in the theatre. I was not interested in being a star or going to Hollywood. I never really have been. Because, as I grew up out there, I don't want to go back! So the whole idea of recognition: it was to be in something and be working, and that was the most fun of all.

Q: How would you describe your peers then and now? And have they changed? Or are they the same?

ROBARDS: Well, some are still around! Maureen's still around. Colleen was, up until—see, she went to the Academy with me; we were at the Academy together, forty-five, forty-six years ago. But I was a little older than those girls, too. Because most of the guys at the American Academy had come out of the service, and the girls were all eighteen or twenty— they were younger. But Charlie Durning was in my class. Don Murray— he was a juvenile then. Grace Kelly went, too; she was behind us, but we used to see her in the Green Room. She became a big Hollywood star. She went on the stage first; I saw her in *The Father*. But how would I describe my peers now? Well, you mean Liz Wilson and—I love her. She and I work together a lot. George Hearn. Judy Ivey, who I work with in this [*Park Your Car in Harvard Yard*]. She's thirty years younger than I am, yet she's like out of our time. She's absolutely wonderful. She knows what the play's about. She knows. She's bright she is so smart about writing and what's in the play, much more than I am. She can spot—and also she's a marvelous actress.

Q: What about gatekeepers? Are there markers in your career that you remember, where people were letting you in or keeping you out?

ROBARDS: I think that if people kept me out, it was later—that there was a reason. I think it's up to you, really, to get in. I don't know that they keep you out. Now, people would let me in, but I was down there pounding on the gate. I wasn't giving up when they closed the gate. I was stopped—on the way home from work, and I stepped in to have a beer right near my house. I was working at Brown's Steno Service; I was working for them. And I stopped in on my way, because I knew the gal who tended bar there was in stock with my wife and I and a whole bunch. And I said, "Mary Ann, how are you? Give me a beer." And she said, "Listen, why don't you go down to Circle in the Square and see José Quintero." I said, "Who's he?" she said, "Well, I'm in a play with him down there, and he's looking for somebody to go into *The Grass Harp*"—a Truman Capote play. "Why don't you go down and see him? You ought to meet him anyway." So I went down there, and I met him. And I talked with him, and he said, "Well, you're too young for this part, and thank you very much." But we had a nice talk. And he called me up about two or three months later, and he said, "Listen, that play's over; I'm doing a new play. I've got a part for you. You want to come down and do it?" So I did. It was called *American Gothic*. But he did not close the gate. But in a way I opened it myself.

I mean, unless you're drunk and you beget a reputation, which I had for a while—saying, "Geez, this guy's crazy. He's crazy drunk! On the pictures, you know!" Then they say, "Oh, well, let's close the gate on him." But that's up to you. That was my own doing for a while. But those things happen. I mean, that's part of growing and learning. And also to be able to afford to drink. For eleven years I couldn't afford anything but a beer. Couldn't get a lot of booze in. Never had the money! [*Laughs*]

Q: Do you think in your career that there are ways you should have been cast that you weren't cast? Are there still ways you see yourself being cast that you're not cast, usually?

ROBARDS: No. There are parts you want to do. Now, I can't judge that I'm right for them. For instance, I wanted to do a part in *The Desperate Hours*. So I wrote to the director, but he cast Dewey Martin in it. But I wrote him and I said that I knew I could—and so forth and so on—in the movie. I hadn't even done a movie at that point, I don't think. But I would try. You know, I wouldn't let the gate be shut; I'd at least try to get a letter in.

One of the first big cattle-call auditions I went to, *Mr. Roberts*, I was over at the automat—that's where we used to hang out to plan our day, whatever actors were around. And we were sitting there with Ralph Meeker, and Tom Poston; and Ralph said, "Listen, there's this cattle call for *Roberts*. Let's go over there." I said, "Fine, let's go." So we went over to the theatre west of Broadway; we got in line with about three hundred guys; and we were marched up the alley and onto the stage and Josh Logan looked at us. No reading, nothing, just to be in the play. Well, he picked Ralph! I'm standing next to him. You know, Ralph was a big strong wonderful-looking guy. And I said, "How come you picked him?" He told me to go on. I said, "How come you picked him?" I said, "I just got out almost seven years in the Navy. I really know what this play is about." Rah-rah-rah-rah. . . . [*Laughs*]

Q: What'd he say?

ROBARDS: He sent me two tickets for opening night. Logan. "Thank you very much. Yes, I know, I'll keep you in mind." And I thought, "Well, that's it." I had two tickets to opening night! He sent them to me! And I went opening night to *Mr. Roberts*. I sat in the mezzanine— fabulous seats!

Q: Do you think there have been discrepancies between your career aspirations and your career opportunities? Did you want something different than you got?

ROBARDS: I really wanted to be on the stage—Jane Fonda said to me once, "The trouble with you—see"—we'd done *Julia* together, and then we were doing another picture afterwards. We were on a shoot, and she said, "What are you doing now? You know, you're right on the threshold. You ought to go up really big." I said, "But I'm going to do this O'Neill play. I'm doing *A Touch of the Poet*." She said, "You and that O'Neill! You always go back and do those things and stop your momentum!" But it's true: it does stop you. Then you turn down jobs or something, and you could go to other things. But I was much happier doing *A Touch of the Poet*—and in fact, it's one of the happiest experiences I had in a play.

Q: What do you think were the major turning points in your career up to now?

ROBARDS: *Iceman.* Yeah. Yeah, that turned things around. Mrs. O'Neill gave us *Long Day's Journey* after that; and I did *Iceman Cometh*, then *Long Day's Journey*. That was the major turning point. Then I got a lot of offers and movies and this and that and the other thing. But I went up to Canada for three hundred bucks a week to play Shakespeare. I didn't go do the movie; I wanted to play in Stratford—and I did. But in a strong way, that prepared me to be able to carry a play, which I did right after that season: I did *The Disenchanted*. That enabled me to play that kind of a lead and carry the play. By doing that Shakespeare. I don't know why I did it, but I did it. When Michael Langham invited me, I said, "Yes, I'm going. I don't care—I'm going. That's it. I don't care that it's not any money." Well—I did *The Iceman* for twenty-five dollars a week! Five dollars to rehearse.

Q: How long did it run?

ROBARDS: Two and a half years, and I didn't stay with it. José pulled me out of that and put me in *Long Day's Journey*. Because that went into rehearsal about six months after we opened. We got that play, and he said, "You've got to go into that play now." That was good.

That's a big turning point. Now, other turning points are—I was going downhill very fast, and the other turning point was meeting Lois twenty-five years ago, and that really changed my life and got me back on track. And I had an accident, you know. It was very bad; and she pulled me through that. And then I started to change a lot of things in my life. I have a nice family. That's the turning point that made all these last twenty-five years—quarter of a century—worthwhile.

Q: What's been your relationship to money throughout your career?

ROBARDS: I've always paid my debts. I've never been in debt to the tax department. I've even paid my alimony and child support—everything. It's broke me, but I've never reneged. But that's all over now. I don't have to worry about those things. And I still feel that the Depression's going to hit us again, 'cause I lived through the first one. I feel I'm in it now, in a strange way. I don't know what it is: banks haven't closed yet, but they *are* closing. You know, when I was a kid, when they *all* closed, my dad said, "Geez, I've got fifteen dollars down in the bank!" And that was a lot of money then, you know. "I wish I could get that out," he said. "I wish I could get that fifteen dollars out." Money has not been that important to me. I don't like to owe money. I don't like to borrow, go in debt. I pay my mortgage. I've helped other people— I give money, I give [to] people, if they need it.

Q: But from what I'm hearing, it has no relationship to the work. The work is the work, and money is money.

ROBARDS: Money is money. And you go do a picture sometimes. You know, I did a picture, once, called *Raise the Titanic.* You try to do the best you can on those terrible things, but you do it. My wife said it's called *"Raise the Bathroom,"* because we had done something with our bathroom—remodeled it or something. But it also was for school and—you know, you have to have cash flow. But oddly enough, I'm still in the same old spot: I have to look for a job. I was on the phone today. And I said—now, this job's come up—I said, "If we can hold that to June, we can get that job. We need that then." And, you know, endless. At my age. I feel it's obscene that people make fifteen million dollars a movie. Or even five million. I don't know what they're talking about. It's Monopoly money! It doesn't have a reference to me. What is that going to buy you, any more than if you have a nice house and you educate your kids? I don't know what fifteen million's going to do for you. If I had it, I'll tell you what I'd do with it: I'd put it right back into the theatre. I'd build a theatre, or I'd give it to a theatre. Like Paul Newman. He's unbelievable. All that money he makes he gives back to people. That's what you do with it. You make it do more. Give it to the needy. Give it to these kids that are dying of cancer. I went up there, you know [to Newman's camp]. Did the "Shooting of Dan McGrew." And they acted it out, and I recited it, up on the stage with these little kids. It was great fun. It was wonderful! But you see, that's what you do with it. You give it that way. Or help other people with it. Maybe these guys do, I don't know. Where do all these people come from? We're all in the same—well, I guess we're not in the same business.

Q: When you work on a role, is there someone that you talk to in your mind when you're working?

ROBARDS: No. Only the author. Took me months to figure out. As José said, "Look, it's like when you see Spanish dancers with all these petticoats. And you'll see one color go by. But the more you find, there are more and more colors to that: there's orange and purple; there's red, white. And you keep working on the play, keep going to text, go to the text, go to the text, and something will come out."

Q: Do you think you have any control over your own destiny as an actor?

ROBARDS: No. I don't. Once we've rehearsed the play and all, I have control over the timing and the thing of it. But the destiny as an actor—no.

Q: What are your own criteria for success as an actor?

ROBARDS: To enjoy what you're doing. I think you must have an enquiring mind, an ability to learn—to know that you can learn something new all the time. You never can stop that.

If you don't enjoy what you're doing and you feel a knot in your stomach—not out of fear, because we, we all have fear about going out on the stage the first time in a new play; you say "Geez, where are we going out here? What's gonna happen?" Those are things you take for granted. But if you have a knot for other reasons so that things aren't working, you've gotta either talk that out or find out what it is or get out of the play. And you have to recognize it's not from nervousness or anything; it's from something else. There's something that says, "That's not right!" What was it Walter Matthau said?—"My shit detector tells me that that's not good!"

Q: What about critical review of your work? Do you read reviews?

ROBARDS: No, I don't read them. I can't—because even if it's a good review, then you go out and try to do all the good things they said about you, and it stinks it up. And a bad review doesn't matter. Because everybody has a different opinion of you, and you're not there for that. You're there to fulfill the play—and that I must do every night! I have nothing to prove, and the reviews don't prove anything to me. I mean, our proof is going out. And the minute the people stop coming, we have to close—which we're doing Saturday night! Then that's it! Then we have to look for something else.

Q: So who's your final arbiter? You? Your own performance?

ROBARDS: Audience.

Q: Your own evaluation, and the audience?

ROBARDS: Yeah, and the audience. The audience—that's what you're there for! The three of us—the play, the audience, and the actor—once we've joined together and you hear the silence and the breathing in the audience, then you know that that's it! That it's working, true! It doesn't happen a lot of the time.

Q: No. It also has to do with what you said at the beginning, about the audience being comfortable that you're fine.

ROBARDS: Yes. They're secure! And then they start working! We all pump each other up with this idea of this play!

Q: How satisfied do you think you are with your career as an actor?

ROBARDS: I wish I'd done *Hamlet* when Lillian Hellman wanted me to, but I didn't. I was doing her play *Toys in the Attic*, and she wanted me to do *Hamlet*. She said, "You must do it." And I didn't. I don't know—went on to something else; I did *A Thousand Clowns* or something. I'd like to do *Lear*. That I think I might do shortly, before I really fall apart, because otherwise—I gotta have the energy for that, you know. I don't know—I'm pretty satisfied with what I've done! I've had a lot of fun and done a lot of things. You can always do something better: "Geez, I'd like to go back and do that play again. Now I really know what it's about"—you know?

Q: What are your major frustrations in your career as an actor?

ROBARDS: I'll tell you: those years of making the rounds and being turned down a lot and doing other work and getting little bits. I got just enough to keep me spiritually alive.

Frustrations, in a way, that I've had to do things to take me away from the family—I don't like that. When the kids were in school, I'd be gone; and I've missed them and am frustrated I didn't see them as much as I could have. But I have to work, so, I mean, everybody understands that.

Q: What have been the greatest satisfactions that you've had in your career?

ROBARDS: O'Neill. Doing O'Neill stuff. And Shakespeare. Those two. They give me the most satisfaction.

I liked *A Thousand Clowns*. That was a nice play.

Q: What advice would you give a young person? I mean, this is a very different time—the stage is very different than it used to be.

ROBARDS: There's hardly any stage left! I mean, there's a lot of Off-Broadway. A lot of good stuff. To be an actor on a stage? You gotta get on the stage! Get out there and do it! That's why that teacher said to me, "Look, don't hang around here in this school anymore. Here's a job. There's a job, they need somebody, and I recommend you. Go down there! Get on a stage! Fifteen shows in fifteen weeks! See what it takes." And that's what you gotta do! And if you want, then you say after a few years, "Maybe I need to go to class to pick up something here." Or, you know, "I need a speech thing."—"I'm not moving right, and I'll go to a movement class." But this examining your navel and this self-concern that so many of these actors I see—young actors—have. Self-aggrandizement. They don't give a shit about the play or about the other actors; all they care about's themselves and how they feel! This is a wrong sort of attitude to have in the theatre, because we are a loving and sharing group! We're not this! And I hate to run into these people—and I do! And I've had to work with them sometimes, and it's absolute murder!

But my advice is to stick with the play and the character. Don't change because you feel like it! Change because the character does or the play tells you to! I don't know how you can drum that in strong enough! Serve the play! That's what it's about, and there's a lot of people serve it: the actors, the director, the scenic designer, the lighting—everything that we have. Stagehands. Everything is all serving these words that were put down. It's all there for that. I don't go for these star turns and all that business, and no good actor I know does!

I don't care if it's a non-Equity waiver house in L.A., in San Diego, wherever! I don't care where they are! They gotta get out on the stage and do it. And you can't do it in your room; you can't do it and say somebody's coming; you're not like a writer or a painter where you can do it alone and send it out. And you're rejected in a much different way than any other profession: you're rejected on your nose, on your weight, on your age. The little thing that holds you together as a human being is constantly being slapped down. And you've gotta be able to take that and say, "I don't give a damn!" Listen, a critic like whatever his name is on the *Times*—these slap-downs are nothing compared to what we've had to go through just to even get a job, and live in this life! And you've gotta be able to take that—and criticism then doesn't matter! The only good kind of criticism, anyway, is from somebody that can stand out that knows the play and knows the business. You know, like Kerr knew, because he was a teacher and a writer and he wrote plays and directed and he knew a lot. And Brooks Atkinson knew, and

Harold Clurman knew more than anybody! They only give you things to help you! They never give you things to tear you down.

MERCEDES RUEHL

B. Queens, New York City. Attended College of New Rochelle (B.A.). Trained for stage with Uta Hagen and Tad Danielewski. Awards: Obie, *The Marriage of Bette and Boo*, 1985; National Film Critics Award, *Married to the Mob*, 1988; Tony Award, Outer Critics Circle Award, and Drama Desk Award, *Lost in Yonkers*, 1991; Golden Globe, Academy Award, L.A. Film Critics Award, and Pasinetti Award, *Fisher King*, 1992.

Q: What is the first experience you remember about acting in theatre?
RUEHL: Probably the very first was, when I was about four years old, we lived in some new garden apartments in the foothills of the Pocono Mountains. My dad was an FBI agent. We moved around a lot and we always lived in apartments. And these apartments were actually built into a wood that went into these hills, you know, foothills. Out behind our house, there was a high hill and then there was a huge forest. It was a little severe but, in front of the huge forest, there was a long light wall of a parking garage—a long white brick wall. It was actually kind of beautiful—but it represented to me, I guess, some kind of stage. And I used to go up this hill, up behind our house—and they were all red brick apartments that were kind of a U-shape around it—and I used to sing opera. But I would make up the words, of course, because I was only four and didn't know *Rigoletto* then. So I would make up these words, and the only themes that I knew how to sing about were stories of Baby Jesus, because I was brought up a strict Catholic and already

was deeply into the phenomenon of Baby Jesus. So, they were religious songs, and I improvised them and I sang them in some insane soprano, and I never knew at the time that all the women who lived in that building would watch me from behind their windows. I think, on the one hand, I had no idea there was an audience but I had every idea that there was an audience—because I knew I was singing behind these buildings, so there was a sense of theatricality to that.

Then, when I was in grade school, I remember being an angel in a white dress with tinsel—a tinsel halo and tinsel wings—in the Christmas pageant in first grade. And that was extremely exciting. I remember being excited by the smell of the tinsel and the gold paint you had to paint your little slippers with. I think a good sign is if you're hooked into the smells of your vocation. I mean, if you're a painter and you really love the smell of linseed oil, you're well on your way. I have always loved all smells associated with backstage theatre.

And the first theatre I ever did was a backyard show in third grade. I played a clown and I did skits with my best friend Mary Lou, and my brother was the second part of the show and he did bicycle-riding feats, in a large parking lot for gathered multitudes of at least three children. I remember one time I decided that I would tell everyone that I knew an Indian fairy princess who brought me candy whenever I wanted. I just started telling people that. I don't know why. I was six years old, maybe—so this is in that same place in Scranton, Pennsylvania. I mean, we're talking about an audience that still believes in Santa Claus, so it was a possibility that they would believe me. And as I've discovered all my life, if you tell the outrageous with great force of conviction, you can get cynics to believe you. I had them curious, but they demanded to see this princess, at some point. So I decided she was going to make an appearance one day, and I threw caution to the wind. I had this Dale Evans costume—little cowgirl costume—and I turned it inside out so that you couldn't see the Dale Evans logo on it and I put my hair back and a band on it, and I appeared in the backyard, and everybody wanted to know where Mercedes was, and I said, "Well, she's inside, but she sent me out." Then, of course, they demanded to have some candy, and I had to say something about not delivering candy on demand—that would happen to them by surprise. And my brother, at one point, came up to me—and this is the power of the well-told lie—and he said, "I know you're Merce, but I won't tell anybody if you just admit it to me." And I said, "Me no know you, white boy." And this has become a story that has been told by my family for years now.

Q: What about the rest of your family?

RUEHL: My brother is a journalist. My father was an FBI agent, and there's a certain aspect of drama and excitement in his work. My mother was an art student turned grade-school teacher and homemaker. But she always had a sense that she was *au fond* [in her soul] an artist, so that I had those two strains. And apparently there was somebody back there—a generation or two ago—who did vaudeville, named Lucille LaVerne, who was related to me somehow. But in recent generations, there were no actors. They were just hardworking Spanish and Irish immigrants who got through a life in the Bronx, basically.

Q: What happened as you got older?

RUEHL: I did school plays. I created school plays. When I look back on it, there was an undeniable impulse. There were signs to everyone, including myself, that there was something in drama—in presentation; in drawing attention to myself in the way that an actor does—that appealed to me from my youngest years. I think one of the things that inspired it was, I was brought up in a strict Roman Catholic household and we observed all the Catholic holidays and holy days. When I was little, Christmastime began with Advent, the first Sunday of the four Sundays before Christmas. And an increasing excitement, if you're a little child in a Catholic grade school, evolves in you as you move through Advent. We used to have little Advent calendars that we would open. On each day there would be a special little toy behind a little window in a calendar. And so, the rituals of the church—Lent, the Stations of the Cross, High Mass. There were songs in Latin and candlelight processions on Christmas Eve. The smell of incense, and these beautiful, beautiful Gregorian chants. And the hallelujahs, the beautiful music of the Resurrection and of Easter. All these things are romantically theatrical because, in the Western world, theatre emerged out of religion. It emerged out of the Greek temple. The origin of theatre was the chorus and the priest in the Greek temple. And then it was brought out onto the steps and then other people got into the act. So it has a deep religious root, too, in my mind.

Q: Were there any other art forms that particularly appealed to you?

RUEHL: Well, my mother and painting. There was a period of time when she tried to teach me how to sketch and draw and paint in oils, and that was something that I got obsessed with for a while. I studied ballet for a long time, and there was a point—after I decided I wasn't an opera singer, at seven—when I thought about dance for a while and became totally obsessed with ballet. But I had the weakest feet this side of the

Valley Nile so I finally had to give up on dance. And I'm tall. I mean, I have a dancer's build, in a way; but it's just too elongated. And then I finally, by about ninth grade, settled down to the place that I had been aiming for—yearning toward—all that time, which was just theatre, theatre.

Q: Did you know that early that's what you wanted to do?

RUEHL: Absolutely knew it, by the time I was in high school. I remember asking everybody, "What about theatricals? How many plays are done here a year? How do I get in them?"

Q: How did your family feel—your parents?

RUEHL: Well, they come from certain traditions where fear, worry, concern about making a living is very strong—as it should be—and so they really wanted me to go and do graduate work and teach eventually. And I wanted to do some graduate work just to stay in a place where I could still do theatre. Because I was twenty-one when I graduated from college and I would have been very happy to just do theatre in a graduate program for a while. But nobody would accept me. I auditioned at Columbia, at NYU, at Yale, and Juilliard, and everybody said no. Then I eventually got out into the streets, and I met with Sanford Meisner at the Neighborhood Playhouse. I auditioned for the Actors Studio. Nobody would accept me.

By this time, when I was twenty-one, I was in love with the grand English actresses—the Dame Edith Evanses and Zoe Caldwell. I'd recently seen Maggie Smith—when I was in school—in *The Prime of Miss Jean Brodie*. That grand, enormous thing. And it works if it's supported by truth. But at twenty-one—a skinny, dark-haired, can't figure out even what her nationality is, really, because I'm Irish and Spanish. I look Latin. I didn't know what I was. At twenty-one, I had no idea. Was I a girl? Was I a woman? I had sort of grown up with this sort of tomboyish mien, so there was still a lot of that tomboy thing and I wasn't coming across as a sex kitten or an ingenue. And I was always too, somehow, a kind of intelligence. Not too intelligent, but I had a breed of intelligence that disallowed that kind of ingenue sort of thing. So nobody knew what to make of me—least of all myself—and I couldn't get myself placed anywhere in a school, given the fact that I was doing this crazy acting at the same time.

So I had to get an apartment in New York with some friends and go about it the long hard way. I had a full-time job for about six months and then I realized I wasn't going to get anywhere working nine to five, so I decided I would begin what became a several-year-long career as a waitress. And study at the HB Studio, which was one of the few places in town where you didn't have to audition, except for Uta's class. You paid your money and you picks your choice. I studied with Bill Hickey there for a couple of years. And eventually did study with Uta Hagen, and that was my first introduction to acting classes—technique classes, per se.

Q: When you went to college, did you major in theatre?

RUEHL: Majored in English literature. The only way I could get away and go to a college near New York was to go to a Catholic one, so I went to a college—an Ursuline college—called the College of New Rochelle, in New Rochelle, New York. It was a small Catholic liberal arts college. The Ursulines are a very old teaching order, and one of the best departments at the school was the English department and I got quite an incredible education in English literature there. Another great love of mine is literature and poetry. At that point, I was very happy to stay in an area of broad education. As long as I could be near New York and go to the theatre and work in the theatrics. I was delighted to go into classes and read medieval literature about the Grail—which then figured much later in my life in *The Fisher King*. I wound up lecturing the entire cast and crew—until they were ready to kill me—about the Grail legend in *The Fisher King*, because I had gotten so fascinated with it.

Then when I came out, it was time to study acting. And as I say, everybody rejected me so I had to go to the one studio in town that accepted you if you paid money. And I lucked out and studied with two extraordinary actor-teachers, actor mentors, Bill Hickey and Uta Hagen. And that was where my education began. During that time I did a showcase—modern adaptation of *King Lear* called *KL Lear*, with a guy named John Ryan (who is in *Hoffa* right now), a good actor. He played Lear. I was twenty-one. I was just an extra in this production, and one of the fellas who was an extra with me was Harvey Keitel. There were some wonderful actors who have since become quite well known, at the [HB] Studio at that time. For about three months, I sat in on all of Lee Strasberg, the great mentor at the Actors Studio. Then I studied at the Lee Strasberg Institute for about six months. Didn't really buy that. Lee was one thing; but the Strasberg Institute were former students—sort of a watered-down version of Lee—and I didn't want that. I wanted the source or nothing.

Then I got into a fabulous workshop with a man named Tad Danielewski, and that man probably was the great mentor of my acting life. Like most of the things in my life, I happened on it quite by accident. I had a roommate at the time who was also an actor. We had met doing summer stock and we were sharing this cheap little apartment in New York. We were glad to have a roof over our heads and we were just going looking in the trades, taking any non-Equity audition, whatever we could get. And she got some auditions. She sent her picture into something—she couldn't remember where or when. But suddenly she got a notice she had an audition for this workshop, and she said, "They want a scene. Do a scene with me." We went in; we did this scene. I got called back. So I am now called back to this workshop that I know nothing about, and I meet for an interview with this totally strange, unexpected, small, intelligent, very keen-eyed Polish man, early sixties. His name is Tad Danielewski. He was born in Poland. He was a member of some kind of underground youth group. He was captured by the Nazis in 1943 or '44. He spent a year in Dachau. After the war he was released and went to Italy for a while and then found himself in London. In London, he saw a production of *Oklahoma!* that had come over from the United States. He was so bowled over by this lively, explosive, beautiful production that he decided that he was going to America to study theatre and perhaps television—which in the late '40s, early '50s, was becoming this explosive new area for directors and performers. So he went and he studied at the University of Iowa for a while, and then he came to New York and he became a director in television—very popular one, for a while. Directed the *Hallmark Hall of Fame* and the *Playhouse 90* and *Omnibus*. When television turned, in the '60s, to a different kind of venue—the sitcom thing—he no longer worked, because he was not interested in doing that kind of television, essentially. So he had had a workshop, out of which came James Earl Jones and Martin Sheen and some really fine actors. That workshop dissolved; and it was a couple years later, and he was forming a second one.

And I found myself, finally—after several auditions and strange interviews and meetings with this guy—in a workshop with Sigourney Weaver and Jim McLure and some really extraordinary actors and writers. I stayed in this workshop for about four years. It was free. ABC donated the space, and it was sponsored by the Television Academy of Arts and Sciences. They were the most extraordinary acting classes I've ever been in in my life. He had four essential exercises, and you did them with a monologue; and the monologue could be a piece of prose from a novel, it could be a Shakespearean monologue, it could be a sonnet, it could be anything—language. You could do half a page of the telephone book if you wanted. But with a monologue, you had to do four exercises: a fast, a slow, a whisper, and a shout. And bring them in when you had worked on them. The class would then determine whether you had done a successful fast, a successful slow, a successful whisper, or a successful shout. And success depended upon you didn't stop shouting for a syllable, or you didn't speed up the slow even for a second. Or if it was fast, you didn't slow down even for a second. Or if it was a whisper, you never ever never used voice. And the thing was to make these monologues seem like that was the only way it could be done. It became such an incredible challenge to find material that could be made to work this way.

When we started to get good at it, then he added an activity. The whole time you had to be sewing something or painting something or chasing a butterfly. And I discovered from him something that could be compared to five-finger exercises for a pianist—certain exercises that work the actor muscles of concentration, imagination, relaxation, freedom, experimentation, risk taking, balance. All of these things were brought into play by these exercises.

You had another great exercise where you would have to do a character sketch. You would study somebody on a subway, or a bus, or walking down the street; and the first thing you would do is, you would take them in. Like, I would notice that you're sitting with your leg crossed; and you're not looking at me straight on, but slightly at an angle. And that there is a smile, and that you wear lip gloss and that you have a very bright, keen, scrubbed healthy face and the long hair. And I would notice how your clothes make you sit. And then you have to get close enough to see what they smelled like. Every sense had to be involved in this character sketch. And if you didn't hear them talking, you would have to engage them in a conversation. Then you would have to watch how they gesture when they talk, and you would try to get just the timbre and the rhythm of their speech, and the accent. And as you were describing this person to the class, you would be incorporating every characteristic as you described it. What you were going for was a transformation—that thing that hooked you finally into the life of this other character.

He got us doing exercises I'd never heard about in Stanislavski or the Method. And largely, they were coming from the outside in. Now he did do emotional recall. It's also called "emotional memory." It goes by different names; but what it is is, when you have to leap to an emotional moment on stage, sometimes the story will take you but more often than not—especially in long runs—you have to flash on an image that will open up the wellsprings of laughter or grief you know, and the image has to be from your own past. And he did those exercises, too. Inside-out exercises.

Q: When you first started working here in New York, or training, did you
    set certain benchmarks for yourself?
RUEHL: Set all the benchmarks, and blew every one of them along the
    way. It took me forever. I remember announcing at twenty-one, when
    this guy I went to college with came up to me, and he said, "So when
    are you going to be a star, Merce?" And I said, "Give me two and a half
    years, okay?" Well, it took me seven or eight years before I started working
    in regional theatre. And about twelve years before I started working in
    New York and started to get the breaks which eventually led to Off-
    Broadway, Broadway, films. Around '86, I started working with the
    Public [Theatre]. The Public led to Broadway. Broadway led to small
    parts in films. The small parts in films led to larger parts in films, which
    led to another Broadway show, which led to bigger parts—and
    suddenly, I got into a place where I was on my way to critical mass–hood,
    and nothing could stop me, you know.

    A friend of mine (in that same workshop that I told you about)
    years before said, "Don't worry. Don't worry. Just stay in one place and
    eventually they'll find you." I'm sure she meant to give me encour-
    agement. She had no idea how much encouragement she gave me—
    because I thought, "If you believe that of me, then I'm going to believe
    that of me, too." And in a way, I really did. The only thing, I didn't
    know how to schmooze agents. I didn't know how to schmooze
    producers. I was never good when I was begging or trying to sell myself.
    Always blew it. I just stayed in acting classes. I studied with Wynn
    Handman. I studied with Joel Friedman, when the workshop broke up.
    I got in other acting classes. I did Off-Off-Broadway showcases. I just
    kept my stuff out in front of some audience. If I wasn't in a free
    workshop, I was in an acting class or an acting seminar that ran for
    twelve weeks and I paid money—just to stay up in front of people,
    acting. It wasn't even so much that I had anything to learn from these
    teachers anymore, although I did learn from every single one of them.
    But I just knew I had to keep acting in front of people. And as long as
    my stuff was out there, and there were two people in the whole city
    talking about me, somehow it might get to somebody. It was the only
    thing I knew how to do.

    And finally it came and got me, right about the time that I was
    thinking, "I can't live like a graduate student anymore." I was thirty,
    thirty-one, and I said, "This is it. I'm going to look into either teaching,
    or maybe directing industrials for some big corporation." That was my
    father's brainstorm. And I actually told him I would make an appointment
    with a friend of his who worked for Baltimore Gas and Electric who

had a woman working for their company who was an ex-actress and directed industrials for their company. You know, I was poor. I'd been poor for ten years at that point, and I was tired of it. And I was angry at this damn business because I thought, "Finally I'm getting good. And it's resisting me still. I'm doing these auditions that people are applauding—and then I don't even get a callback." I remember I was very angry. I thought, "The hell with theatre. I'm getting out. It doesn't appreciate me." It was kind of like a love affair. It was like, "I've had it. I've done everything I can do. I've been a doormat for you, and— [*laugh*]—and now I'm leaving." And as in a relationship sometimes, that is the moment where the person either calls you back and says, "Please don't go"—or you keep walking. And in this case, thank God, the lover called me back, in the person of a writer named Albert Innaurato, whom I had known for a while.

Albert had written a play about a woman in her early thirties who falls in love with a seventeen-year-old boy who's a runaway. It was being done by a very talented actress, but it just wasn't working. They had already had it up in previews. So Papp said, "This story is autobiographical, isn't it?" And he said, "Yeah." And Papp said, "Write that story. I'm going to give you two weeks over Christmastime to rewrite it, rerehearse it, and get it up on stage. Let's go for the real thing." He changed the character to a man, and the second lead to a female. He had known my work from some readings, and he said, "You don't have to audition. You don't have to talk to anybody. I told them I want you. I want you to come in and do it. We've got twelve days. Just do it." Well, I've been breaking my back for seven years to get an audition at the Public Theatre—let alone hired in a play. And suddenly somebody just lays it on a platter and hands it to me. So I said yes. I was scared to death. My first Off-Broadway show—in the Public, at that!—and twelve days to learn this whole role and get it out there. Papp was in on all of the rehearsals and he did a lot of directing and he saw I was afraid. I think he saw I had some talent. He was very kind to me and he took a shine to me and he really helped me and encouraged me, and so did Albert. The two of them were very much in my court. But I think I did okay in that role.

I was then hired by Jerry Zaks to do a small role in a Chris Durang play called *The Marriage of Bette and Boo* that was done almost immediately afterwards, with Olympia Dukakis and Joan Allen from the Steppenwolf Company. I was in Seventh Heaven. During that, a great casting director named Juliet Taylor—who casts all of Woody Allen's and Mike Nichols's films—she saw me and put me in a small film that was written by Nora Ephron, called *Heartburn*, with Meryl Streep. Juliet's husband then saw me and asked me to replace a girl who had broken her leg in *I'm Not Rappaport*. All this happened within a period of four or five months. I was suddenly on Broadway a few months later in *I'm Not Rappaport* with Judd Hirsch and Cleavon Little. Played it for a year. Was asked to do a small film with Steve Landesberg that went straight to video. Then, a couple other small parts. I did a little role in *Radio Days*; small roles in *Secret of My Success* and *84 Charing Cross Road*. And suddenly came *Big*, through this same Juliet Taylor. While I was doing *Big*, another casting director introduced me to Jonathan Demme and said to Jonathan he'd been watching my progress. Jonathan gave me my first big role in film. This same Howard Feuer really put me into the major films that I've been in—really championed me and insisted that these fine directors see me and not cast anyone else until they did. But when the door opened, one opportunity after another flooded through, and I had been chipping away at a brick wall without success for eleven/twelve years. I would be hard put to say what causes were responsible for this breakthrough, but they were many. Some of them were deeply personal. Personal growth. Confrontations with some of my personal bugaboos. A certain kind of courage had entered into my personal life, and it made itself felt almost immediately in my professional life. A coming of age, in a way. I was now thirty-two. I was no longer an ingenue type. I could play closer to myself, which is, if anything, more of a soubrette—a sort of knowing, wry character. And I am more fascinated than ever with the process of acting and what it yields. It's a great journey of self-discovery, and discovery of the human critter generally.

Q: What about organizations you are involved in or a member of—like acting unions or any other acting-related organizations?

RUEHL: I'm in the Screen Actors Guild; AFTRA, which is the television actors guild; and Actors' Equity, which is the theatre guild. I'm a lifetime member of that workshop I told you about: Tad Danielewski's workshop. I'm part of a political group called the "Creative Coalition," which is actors, producers, directors, and writers from film and television. I'm not active in my unions particularly. But I do feel that the Actors' Equity is a fairly powerless union. This is because theatre right now is not a moneymaking industry. I don't think that the thrill of recognition—the communion that happens in live theatre, that happens between actors and an audience—will ever totally die out of culture. If it does, culture will be the loser. But you don't make money right now. You lose money in theatre. So any union protecting [stage] actors is not going to be very powerful, because we are pretty much at the mercy of the producers, and the producers are at the mercy of a dwindling audience. The Screen Actors Guild is a much more powerful union. You get a lot more money for a lot less work in films. And since I do very little television, I don't participate in AFTRA. I just pay dues, maintain myself in that union.

But one thing that has drawn me to Equity in the last few years is, Equity has very strong AIDS-related committees: Equity Fights AIDS, and Broadway Cares. The theatre union has rallied its membership much more aggressively behind active participation in AIDS groups, AIDS organizations, benefits, and things like that. Even last night, the reading I did of *A Christmas Story* at the Book Friends Café—the profits all go to Equity Fights AIDS. I mean, it was ever so: that those with only a crust of bread to give, split the crust. The film community, which has a banquet to give—the active participation of the members of the film community in AIDS-related activities is, I think, a bit lower. But it's not organized the same way either, in all fairness.

The Creative Coalition is a group of people who actually got together in the hopes of remaining nonpartisan to study social and political issues—to study them; to have panels; to have discussions; to disseminate knowledge, disseminate information, to people in the film and theatre community; to support certain causes that they espouse: pro-choice; the homeless problem in New York City and in Los Angeles—they have about six agendas that they're working on right now. I'm a fairly new member of the Creative Coalition. And during the recent conventions— especially the Democratic convention in New York—they sponsored a lot of seminars, meetings, and panels that just discussed the issues that were the major political and social issues that were going to be dealt with in that election. They're a wonderful group. And while they try to remain apolitical, as you know, the theatre and film community is basically a liberal bunch, with notable exceptions. Well, let me say at the outset I'm not, you know—I'm no political maven. I have great gaps of ignorance in every area of life, and politics is one of them. But there's this whole fascinating network of human activity, of which politics is often a very clear indicator of what's going on in people's hearts.

Q: You mentioned earlier that you were never really an ingenue. You never saw or felt yourself that way. How do you see yourself now being cast most often, or how do you want to be cast?

RUEHL: I can't answer that question in any kind of simple way. There's a great poem by Theodore Roethke. There's a refrain in it that goes, "I wake to sleep and take my waking slow. / I learn by going where

I have to go." And what I have discovered is, I do this one role—this crazy Italian harridan—and then it transmogrifies into the next role, which is an Italian girl but now she's kind of sexy. And while she's strong, she's got this great vulnerability too. And then that transmogrifies into this other role where I'm playing this somewhat retarded Jewish girl in a family in Yonkers in 1942, who's all vulnerability.

And now what people are asking me to do is all over the place. I've recently been asked to do the part of a Cuban refugee who comes from Havana to Miami during the Mariel boatlift, who's a borderline prostitute and she's got these *merengue* hips that never stop—sort of an earth mother. And in between, I've done Shakespeare's *Antony and Cleopatra, Much Ado about Nothing*, Molière, Chekhov, Noel Coward, and a lot of stage work. So I'm still in the process of discovering who I am. I think that now—as opposed to when I was twenty-three or twenty-four—I feel more confident about asserting a sexual person, about asserting an elegant person. Sometimes more confident about asserting an arrogant person. And much more confident about asserting a vulnerable person. As a matter of fact, those are depths that are always interesting to explore, because human vulnerability is endless and has endless manifestations. And a person in a state of vulnerability is almost always beautiful. And the varieties are infinite. So I don't see myself as any one thing. I'd love to play Saint Joan. I'd love to play Blanche Du Bois. I'd love to play Laura—which I'll never do now. I'd love to have played Juliet. I'd love to play Eleanor Roosevelt. I mean, it's all over the place. But I don't want to be typed. That's the kiss of death.

Q: How do you feel about the critics and what they say about you?

RUEHL: Well, no matter what you say about critics, if you're a human being, they make you feel damn fine when they say you "move from strength to strength" in a way that bowled them over in the course of a play. Which somebody once said about me recently. And as the Jewish people say, I *kvelled.* But then I got a review in the *New Yorker* a few years ago for a thing I did at the Ensemble Studio Theatre—just a small play in one of their Oktoberfests—and a critic in the *New Yorker* said, "Mercedes Ruehl was simply awful. There's no other word for it." My subscription to the *New Yorker* I abruptly canceled—I was reading it in bed one Sunday morning with coffee and just feeling all cozy and nice, and flipping through the *New Yorker*. And I come—"Oh!"—upon a review of my play, and all of a sudden: "Ehh!" Not only did it kill the morning; it killed the day and took a lot of joy out of the ensuing week. So I am very vulnerable to what they say. I am still too vulnerable to what everybody has to say about me as an actress and as a human being.

I'm trying to move away from it—but what people think of me, I'm afraid, is still a little bit too important. I've still got some work to do in that regard. But when you get a good review, you often think that critic is quite an insightful fellow; and when you get a bad review, you can also think, well, critics are the lackers and onlookers of greatness. Often they're wrong. Often they're moved only by very particular personal tastes. Or personal dislikes. One thing that I am gradually coming to terms with is the fact that you literally can't please everybody and find the essence of yourself. Because when you find the essence of yourself in a character, you are invariably going to alienate or disaffect somebody. You know, it's going to remind somebody of someone that they know and didn't like, or their mother, or a kind of vulnerability they just can't stand. Or a kind of childishness in an adult that they just can't stand. The only thing I can say for posterity, in terms of the critics, is that you've got to rise above them.

Q: Didn't you win a Tony?

RUEHL: I won a Tony for *Lost in Yonkers*. I had a very good year awardwise, I must say. I won the Outer Critics Circle and Drama Desk award, and the Tony; and I won the Golden Globe and the Oscar and the L.A. Film Critics award, and the comedy award, best supporting actress of the year; and Sci Fi Fantastic Films, they gave me an award for best supporting actress. I won the Pasinetti award at the Venice Film Festival—the critics' choice for best actress. Suddenly it's dropping like manna, and sometimes I just want to get up in front of some bunch of kids and just say, "You know, you have to stay with something past despair." Because that point where all of my anger and pain and hurt and tired of wearing coats that were too cheap and not warm enough for these New York City winters and blah-blah-blah. That was a point of a certain kind of despair. And I just finally thought, "It's not going to happen. I could have sworn it was going to happen, but it's not going to happen." And in my life, at least, that was the point that I had to bust through and get on the other side. I had to stay with it past despair. And I think sometimes, you know, in relationships, just when you want to despair of the person ever coming through, you stick with them. You don't close them out of your life. You don't close this theatre out of your life entirely. Don't close this dream out entirely. And sometimes that's when it happens. I guess you have to *want* to do it. As Tad, my great teacher, said, you have to be able to look somebody in the eye and unflinchingly say, "I would die if I couldn't do it." I remember him asking a girl in class—and she was good, but she was kind of holding back in the emotional work—he said to her, "Would you die if you couldn't act?" And she was very flustered and she didn't know what to say, but finally she said, "No." And he said, "You should do yourself a favor—all of you—and if you can't answer that in the affirmative, find something else." He's sort of the prefigurer of Joseph Campbell saying, "Follow your bliss." If this is not where your bliss is, then go and look for where your bliss is. Don't get so hung up on this thing that you throw your life away—and the great lifework that you might really do with joy and love and risk-taking abandonment. If you'd die if you couldn't act, then start acting like it.

B. D. WONG

B. San Francisco, 1962. Attended San Francisco State University. Trained for stage with Don Hotton and voice with Tony McDowell. Awards: Tony Award, Drama Desk Award, Outer Critics Circle Award, Clarence Derwent Award, Theatre World Award, *M. Butterfly*, 1988.

Q: What was your initial experience with acting?
WONG: My initial experiences with acting were related to different manifestations of creativity earlier in my childhood. I was always very nonphysical. I was always making things, and my parents sent me to art school at the museum in San Francisco where I grew up. They knew that I had a particular liking or affinity for creative things. I was not interested in playing any kind of sports; I was not into that kind of stuff. I began playing the violin when I was in fourth grade—I was nine years old—and I was apparently very good. This was one thing that people seemed to be responding to when I did it, you know; I got a lot of attention at school because I played very well, and I had solos in the school band. My parents were convinced by this music teacher that I should take private lessons, and I took private lessons until ninth grade. I got very good. And I don't really think that I was good enough to be a concert violinist or anything like that, but I probably could have worked as a musician, perhaps in an orchestra, in a large city. I certainly wasn't going to be a soloist. At any rate, in ninth grade I discovered— because of a strange chain of events—that I disliked playing the violin

a great deal. This was a great personal revelation, because I had been doing it, and I had been doing it so well. And I realized at that point that there were other things that you could probably do well and you could like them, too. And at the point in time when I was beginning to think about what it was that I wanted to do with my life, this was a great revelation. This came about because I was about to play in the orchestra for the high school production of *Guys and Dolls*. And a friend of mine said, "Oh no, you don't want to play in the orchestra. That's really boring. You really want to be in the show. Come to the tryouts with me." And I secretly really wanted her to make me go. And she did. And I got a part—I was in the show. And all of a sudden this thing happened where I realized I could be good at something, and I could enjoy it, and I could actually probably contribute to it as an art form—not just doing it and going through the numbers and doing it for other people, like my parents (who were extremely wonderful and supportive, but who weren't the only reason why I should have been doing it) and the teachers. This was a great thing.

Immediately, there was nothing else I could think of but theatre. I became obsessed with doing plays in and outside of my school, in the community, semiprofessional. And that was it. From the first moment I set foot on stage in that production (I was in the chorus and had little featured parts), I probably knew that I wanted to be an actor. Then I went through a whole lot of obstacles—regarding my parents; regarding the stigma of being an actor; regarding whether or not that was a realistic choice or whether it was just a kind of a pipedream—and overcame those things. And that's the short version of why I'm here.

Q: Tell me about your family when you were growing up.

WONG: They're an extremely influential and important reason why I'm an artist. My mom and dad are second-generation Chinese Americans. My dad's grandfather came to California. So I'm one-quarter fourth generation. My parents were Depression kids that grew up in San Francisco's Chinatown. They were very Americanized; but like most Depression kids, they wanted very strongly for their children to have a better life than they did. They were as reliant as most parents are on the concept of financial stability in choosing a career. I have two brothers: an older brother who is now a doctor in Seattle, and a younger brother who is a firefighter. We have these diverse careers simply because my parents nurtured our individuality and put aside a great deal of concern and fear and personal trepidation about what we might choose, and allowed us to forge our own path. As a result, we have these different careers. It's amazing to me that they could do that. Because of their

more you're required to know and to be able to do; and you need to be as facile as possible. And during the entire career, I have been dealing with the challenges brought on by my own ethnicity. That has required me to be better than most—if possible—in order to survive.

Q: Tell me about your peers in high school.

WONG: I was in a small clique of peers. You know, we all thought we were going to be great, wonderful actors. And for kids in high school, we did some great work. But I think I'm one of the only ones that actually pursued a career. I was what I would call a very odd breed of person called a "theatre nerd." I was popular because I was in the plays, but I was unpopular because I was in the plays. I was not a sports figure, and I wasn't particularly an intellectual figure. So I was in this strange void. The girls didn't want me because of it—and yet I was like everyone's friend. It was very strange. And come graduation, it seemed I was very popular. But when I was in school, I was also very involved in speech and forensics. I learned a great deal from competing (with monologues and cuttings from plays) with other kids from high schools all over the country. That was really very rewarding. The acting coach or the forensics coach at your school will coach you in ten-minute monologues, either from comedies or from dramatic plays. And you get up in front of three judges and five other people who are competing in your round and do these monologues. After three rounds, they post the finals; and you see if you made it into the finals; and you do the monologue again for a much larger group of people. It's a great way of learning the craft. I established—from dramatic interp and humorous interp for the National Forensics League in high school—a technique for multicharacter presentations which has been a major thing for my career, and a major sensibility that I have.

Q: After high school, where did you go from there?

WONG: I went to San Francisco State, very briefly, right after high school. I was also ushering at the Golden Gate Theatre, which is a large professional theatre where national tours—mostly musicals—come through. I ushered there, which was also a great training ground for me. I witnessed a great deal of classic musical theatre performances. My high school training prepared me and gave me a sensibility for and a love for the musical theatre. I wanted to be a musical theatre actor. I wanted to be a Broadway stock musical star. I went into San Francisco State University, studied what they called their "lyric theatre," which is musical theatre, and a little bit of acting; and—partially because of my own personality, and partially because of the laziness that I described to you—I was not interested in being there. I didn't want to be at

San Francisco State. Also there was a big problem with casting. I didn't get any parts. I felt like I learned by doing. Now, I *have* learned by doing, and it has been proven to me that I respond very well when it comes to learning by doing—as opposed to sitting in a class and learning from an acting teacher, in that way. I was saving all this money; I was ushering, and I was making chocolate chip cookies at Mrs. Fields, and I was a bank teller—not all at the same time, but at various times throughout this. And I also was directing high school productions for the San Francisco Unified School District, and I was on the payroll as a cafeteria monitor—that's how they gave me some money for it. I went to several high schools and directed some musicals.

Anyway, I had to go to New York. I just had to. But the reason why I dance around it this way is because I don't want kids to say, "Well, this person—look what happened to him, and he dropped out." I think that it's very important for most kids to stay in college. For me—I had to see what it was like. As a result, when my friends got out of college four years later, they had to learn a lot of stuff that I learned by having a career—about the professional experience of being an actor, which you really don't learn in a lot of colleges. Which is frightening. They didn't learn about getting their pictures taken or how to audition or carry themselves in an interview of anything like that. They learned acting, fencing; they learned juggling; they learned musical theatre techniques; and they were in some shows; and they learned how to make costumes. But they didn't learn these things about marketing yourself as a professional actor, which I did know. So as a result, it was a trade-off.

Q: Where did you go, when you left?

WONG: I came right to New York, after maybe a year at San Francisco State University. I knew one person, and I stayed with her, and I bounced around in a lot of different apartments. I got my Equity card in about four weeks doing a children's theatre production of a musical. And I worked quite steadily. I did chorus work in dinner theatre and stock, and I was solidly aiming towards a career in musical theatre. I got a national tour of a musical called *La Cage aux Folles* as an understudy. It was my first production contract, which is the big Broadway contract. It's reserved for Broadway shows and first-class national tours and stuff like that. And so that was a big break. It opened in my hometown at the Golden Gate Theatre in San Francisco. All my friends still worked there. It was a great experience: I was in the chorus of a Broadway musical. So it was a great homecoming. And that company went to Los Angeles. I was in Los Angeles for eight months.

When the show closed, I decided to stay in Los Angeles. I got an agent, and I began working in television and film. For the first time not doing musicals. For the first time dealing with going to auditions and just reading words, not singing. And the L.A. scene was very different. I realized—partly because of the racial barrier; partly because it was the first time I was ever faced with it—that I had to compete, and that I had to be really good to compete, and that I had no technique as an actor. I was a natural. I could pick up a script and I could read it with any amount of feeling, any varying palette of emotions—I could do that. But I couldn't tell you why, and I couldn't incorporate that into building the role if I got it. I couldn't discuss it intelligently. That was one of the things that I didn't like. So I nosed around a little bit, and I had met a young actress, and she told me, "Oh, I'm going to this interesting class, you should come to it. It's very very modest. It's in this, like, basement cellar theatre in Hollywood. And there's this old guy there that teaches acting." And I went for an afternoon. I was lucky, because I didn't try a lot of different classes. Coincidentally, he had the very technique that I was looking for. I responded to it very well. And he responded to me and I responded to him. His name is Donald Hotton. He was a student of Mira Rostova's, and a contemporary of Lee Grant's, and was in New York during all of those wonderful days that you hear about—when American acting technique was forming itself. And I responded and went to Donald faithfully at six dollars an hour or something like that, and he slowly and surely taught me how to act within a year, or taught me a technique. The technique is simply based upon recognizing that the play, the screenplay, the teleplay, is written by a person, the writer; the words are written for a reason, and your job is to illuminate the ideas and the messages and the meaning of those words. You are not to do anything but that. You mustn't be creative, and do anything which gets in the way of that message.

And that is one thing that I learned to do at auditions a lot, in order to compete. You had these words: "I'm going to the store now. I'll see you later. Bye." And you would choose—"Well, I'm going to cry through the whole thing, and that'll be really creative. And they'll like me because it's really creative." Cheesy casting directors might respond to it. Ultimately, it's such a false thing; it has nothing to do with what the writer intended and what the writer is trying to say and what the piece is about. Now, granted, in television you have to do things like that sometimes—that's how you get jobs, and that writing is not conducive to having any kind of message. But when you're talking about doing plays, and creating characters in plays, and working with Shakespeare, the message of the writer becomes the foremost thing. That is your job.

You're not more important than the writer. In fact, you're much less important than the writer; the writer had a blueprint for you, and you're supposed to build a house. When you're watching Donald's students, all of a sudden you're understanding what the scene's about, as opposed to how good the performance is. There's much less ego in it.

As a result, it prepared me for a certain political sensibility. As an Asian American, I was very dissatisfied with the industry and the way I was treated as a member of a certain ethnic group in the industry, at casting sessions or just in general—not being able to be seen for things. But I didn't really know what to do about that, or know that I could really take a stand and become a part of changing that or anything. And two things happened: I met Donald, and Donald taught me this kind of technique regarding accepting the responsibility as a messenger of a playwright; and then Donald helped me on this audition for this play called *M. Butterfly*, which I was fortunate enough that they put a call out to Los Angeles to look for people. To make a long story short, I got the part. And all of a sudden I was the messenger of a great Asian American playwright, who has a very strong sense of Asian American politics, and a sensibility that's built into the play. And I had to accept that responsibility—as a student of Donald's—to carry the message out.

Q: Do you feel he adequately prepared you for your career?

WONG: Regardless of how long I spent with him, I took very well to the philosophies of the technique, and they're very instilled in my work now, completely. I have a handbook that Donald wrote; it's like a Bible to me. So, yeah.

Q: Did you set benchmarks for yourself when you first started in theatre? Such as: "In five years I want to be a star."

WONG: Yeah. I think that we all do that. One of the plays that was very influential to me in my quest to become a musical theatre performer— a catalytic theatrical event, as far as I was concerned—was the original production of *A Chorus Line*, in which one of the characters said, "Gosh, I did that. I set a time limit for myself. By twenty-five I had to do this; by twenty-eight I had to be playing parts." That play was extremely influential and inspiring to me. And I did do that. I couldn't tell you what they were—and those things change as you go along, and they're not very valuable to you, unless they motivate you, which is good.

Q: Can you tell me about organizations and unions you're involved with, and your activity with these organizations?

WONG: My involvement—aside from being an actor—with Actors' Equity is as a member of a committee called the Committee on Racial Equality, which is pretty much a very frustrating group of people, because they really don't have any kind of power. But there are many actors of color within the union that have a lot of problems with the way the union deals with their equal access to parts and things, so that's what this committee is about. It meets to suggest to Equity Council varying things when it comes to negotiating contracts that are coming up or controversies as they may occur. Probably the talking about the issue is not going to be helped by talking about the union at all, because that's really almost a dead issue. The union can't do anything about the sensibilities of artists in this country at this point in time. It can try to, and at least it can nobly adapt certain policies, but it can't really change the sensibility of the artist. Not one organization can. A general sensibility about certain things—which is creeping about, I think—is what's in order.

For example, the controversy that arose over the musical *Miss Saigon*—without getting completely into the whole mishmash—is something that was an unprecedented discussion. The one thing that was left in the wake of the storm was that there was a problem in the industry with the way Asian Americans had access to parts. Not only Asian parts—in this case it was specifically an Asian part—but not only that, but in regards to nontraditional casting, which is the concept that, when the race of a character is not germane to the play or to the part, then any actor could be considered. I don't think anybody argues with that, but there is a great deal of trouble getting casting directors and producers and directors to understand that sensibility—understand the unbalanced playing field and competition that's existing in the industry. So the one thing about *Miss Saigon* was that a discussion arose about the plight of ethnic artists—which wasn't happening prior to that, and that was a very valuable thing.

I have also been involved in an organization which was formed because of the *Miss Saigon* controversy—called APACE, which stands for the Asian Pacific Alliance for Creative Equality, which is an organization that hopes to educate and advocate any kind of policy which helps to even the playing field. Including a broader understanding of what nontraditional casting is, and how to implement it, and how that is a valuable thing with regards to society. Just while we're talking about nontraditional casting, I think it would be helpful to try to kind of dispel any kind of confusion. It's an extremely confusing issue. The thing that probably a lot of people have trouble with (but which is a fact, and which is the nut of the whole confusion) is that nontraditional casting was defined and created so that ethnic actors could compete for jobs—not ethnically specific roles. So therefore, it only works one way. Nontraditional casting is not when you take a Caucasian actor and cast him in an ethnic part. People say, "Well, that's nontraditional casting, too. It should work both ways." It does not work both ways. It is a device concocted to even out decades of unfair access to parts. Part of my involvement in all of this is related to the fact that the media is extremely influential in our forming opinions about people of other races. And so you can't just say "No, it's just TV; it doesn't matter." No. It's extreme; we put our kids in front of the TV more than ever now, and they draw from the television—and movies—attitudes and impressions about people of other races. Especially if they're in areas where they don't have a lot of involvement with people of other races. And anything that is not a true reflection of society—as multiracial as it is—is then a mixed signal for these kids, and then they carry with them this idea that black people all smoke crack and push drugs. And then you realize that part of it is that people of color don't have access to parts, can't compete for parts, can't get the parts, therefore you have to break down some kind of door. Nontraditional casting is part of breaking down that door. It's not meant to exclude white people. It can only be understood and subscribed to by people who understand that, while we all have challenges in our careers, there is an ethnically unbalanced playing field. If somebody was doing a show with an Asian theme at this point in time on Broadway, they would look for an Asian cast.

Q: We were talking about casting. How do you see yourself being cast? And how do you most often get cast?

WONG: Well [*laugh*], I mean, the first issue that I would discuss in that area would be that playing a transvestite on Broadway for a year and a half, or what people called a "transvestite" in *M. Butterfly*—I never should have said that, because I always was very sensitive about her being called a "transvestite"; but that's what casting directors think I was, I was a transvestite—playing anything that specific is something that is very difficult for people to overcome.

More often than not, casting people are not qualified to be casting people. "Casting directors" they're called. More often than not, they misunderstand or overexaggerate their position in the process of casting. They don't really cast; they provide a service for the director which allows the director to cast. This is my impression of it. So therefore, they can have seen the play *M. Butterfly*; they can have seen the spectrum of emotions that were presented; they can see the spectrum of characterization; they can see the dual personality that occurred in that role—I played two acts as (hopefully) a very persuasive female and then, in a twist in the play in the third act, became (hopefully) a very persuasive male. And they were completely polar—the characterizations—and hopefully that was what was so great about that performance.

So, they see that, and yet they don't get it. They just see a transvestite—that's all they see, that's all they see. So you end up being classified in a very strange and uncastable void. And it becomes quite an obstacle. The play changed everything. I was automatically an actor who didn't have to go to the casting session prior to meeting the director. I could meet the director. But I didn't get a plethora or a selection of roles which were—worthy of that experience. I mean, I'm extremely grateful and happy about what it did do—and that was that it gave me a certain stature and it gave me a certain credibility. And also I'm very lucky that I made my [Broadway] debut—ironically enough—in a play that was not a musical. Because that is a very difficult thing to overcome.

Q: Tell me more about things you've done since *M. Butterfly*.

WONG: I've done a lot of small featured parts in feature films—luckily enough, films that did very well in the box office. Specifically, a movie called *The Freshman*, that had Marlon Brando in it; a movie called *Father of the Bride*, with Steve Martin. I did that for a long period of time and didn't do a lot of theatre. Immediately after *M. Butterfly*, I did do a production of *The Tempest* with Frank Langella at the Roundabout Theatre, which was lots of fun. And then I did a bunch of movies. And this year I've gotten back into doing a great deal of theatre. I did a play at the Actors Theatre of Louisville ([at the] Humana Festival) which was a world premiere of a new play by David Henry Hwang, who wrote *M. Butterfly*—a play called *Bondage*. And immediately after that, I did a one-person musical in Philadelphia at the American Musical Theatre Festival—called *Herringbone*, which was a play that I had wanted to do for ten years, just a play that I wanted to do desperately and was finally able to do. Then, just a couple of weeks ago, I did a production of the musical *Peter Pan* at the Kansas City Starlight with David Ogden Stiers. I also have recently taken on a subcareer as a lecturer at colleges and universities. I have an agent that sends me to these colleges and universities where I talk about everything that I'm talking about with you. Casting issues and my career and my awakening as a political messenger.

You know, it's very hard to be objective about your own career. You always want more than you have. That's natural and human, and I don't think there's anything wrong with that; but as a result of that, it makes it very difficult for you to be able to see clearly whether you should be having more, or whether you just want more. I have done Broadway-type musicals—I starred in this musical *Peter Pan*, a very conventional, traditional thing—and then I was able to do these parts in movies. And as a result, some of the racial problems come to my aid—which I can turn to my advantage. For instance, the fact that the casting people think that there is such a small pool of Asian American artists means that I get in on almost anything that I want to get in on. And because they think there's less, well, I don't have to worry as much as other people.

Q: Have there been other people who've been gatekeepers for you, either opening doors along the way or closing them?

WONG: Not necessarily. Not any that come to the top of my head. I hope to be a gatekeeper, though. I mean, I meet a lot of wonderfully talented people. And that's the other thing that I look for in the future: is not just acting. I've just opened a production company, and I think that's a very exciting thing and interesting.

Q: What kind of control do you exert over your career?

WONG: A great deal. I have taken four years to train the agents that sit on the other side of that door as to what it is that I will do, what it is that I don't want to do, and what it is that I require them to do. And I think that's very important.

Q: I have heard many actors of color that I've talked to mention that exact same thing. And it is a personal choice, sometimes a financial choice, isn't it?

WONG: Absolutely. A member of a certain community can't begrudge a person for putting food on their table and having to do something that they personally wouldn't do as a result of that. And there are a lot of undignified roles there for people of color, still—particularly in the Asian American community, because of the influx of black American filmmakers and the influx of the strength of that community. I mean, it still has a far way to go and a great deal of things to be challenged by. But the Asian American community is in a much weaker spot, and there are a lot of characterizations that are completely undesirable and embarrassing, and there will be actors that will do them, and they have to do them. I mean, there is also a creative challenge to that—and I have played roles that were potentially that, and have tried to manipulate the artistic process so that I can give the character a new spin.

Q: What's your relationship been, then, to money through your career?

WONG: It's very up and down, and very cyclical. I have been able to have a very good livelihood. I'm in a dry spell right now. I don't think there's anything wrong with describing that. This has a lot to do with my wanting to open up a production company, my wanting to write and direct and do lots of different things. Money, unfortunately, has a lot to do with how much you can play those games; and at this point in time

I'm not as facile being able to do all of these wonderful things, because I don't have that foundation. I look forward to having that in the next few years.

Q: How have awards helped you?

WONG: They're prizes, and they're little pieces of metal on your shelf. You're supposed to try to keep it in perspective that they are what they are. But they are very helpful in commanding a certain amount of professional respect. And I think money is one of those things.

Q: Have there been any other grants or financial awards—besides the Tony—that have helped you along your career?

WONG: I won the Clarence Derwent from Actors' Equity—which was a thousand dollars which, they hope, goes towards your training and life as an actor—and that's what it did. And that is a wonderful award. I mean, that's probably one of my favorite awards from the *M. Butterfly* experience, because I had been a kind of rank-and-file Equity member for a few years, and I was going to a lot of chorus auditions and stuff, and had witnessed people getting this award, and always wanted it. But that one comes with a thousand dollars, and that's very nice.

Q: How have you interacted with the public throughout your career?

WONG: I have always enjoyed a great deal interacting with the public. The public. Earlier on, I could tell you—with *Guys and Dolls* and going right up until Donald—I pretty much was an actor because of the ego gratification. I was an actor because I could act and because I loved the feeling of people clapping—and that's a rush that cannot be described. And many actors and artists do what they do because of that. As soon as I accepted the responsibilities as the messenger, and understood how profound that was, I had a completely different idea about what it meant to be an actor. You clearly were an actor, then, to give a thousand people (or whoever) a night a message, a gift. And the message didn't come from you; it came from this person that had the pen, or the typewriter. And you were just supposed to give them that message. Now, you could enjoy that you gave them the message. But you weren't giving them the message for you; you were giving it to them for them. And you could take a great deal of satisfaction from their receiving that gift. And the result.

I'm extremely into the public, and how they respond to my work, and what they have to say about it. It's not fun to be in a play and not be able to see the faces of people in the audience—to me, anyway. For instance, I took this job to go to Kansas City and play Peter Pan— partly because Peter Pan was a dream part for me; partly because Peter Pan had both never been played by a person of color or a man; and

partly because when I was at the Golden Gate Theatre in San Francisco
I witnessed this production of *Peter Pan* starring Sandy Duncan, and
I saw the audience, and I saw how it affected them, and I wanted to be
a part of providing that experience for people. As a result, I couldn't
have had more of an electrifying experience, even if it were on Broadway.
The situation in Kansas City is a tradition of people bringing their
children to the theatre—which is very unique. I mean, it is a problem;
and organizations like the American Theatre Wing in New York City
have as their main challenge getting young people to go to the theatre,
getting people to bring their children to the theatre. And here in Kansas
City is a decades-long tradition of people not only bringing their kids
to the theatre, but it's a big community thing with kids being in the
shows. They always pick a show that kids can be in. And, for instance,
parents bringing their kids to the auditions for the shows where they
were in the shows when they were kids and their parents brought them.
The tradition of it—and the whole ritual of the theatre—is something
we forget about. And that has to do with the message. That has to do
with people being rapt for the message—and *Peter Pan*, ironically
enough, has messages in it. So I went there, and I had this great
experience with the audience. I got to see the same look on their faces
that I saw when they looked at Sandy Duncan. I got to shake hands with
kids—little kids who thought I was a magician—and that was a
wonderful thing.

Q: How do you feel about critical review of your work?

WONG: If only people understood that, for the most part, you do it
because you're a part of this family of messengers; there's nothing to
be critical about. Everyone has taste, and everyone has different tastes.
Why someone's taste is more important than another person's taste is
not interesting to me, or not important. I do not understand the whole
consumer-watchdog kind of mentality about the theatre: "Well, I need
to tell people that they shouldn't spend their money on this. And these
days, at sixty dollars a pop, well, I need to be the person that says you
shouldn't go see this, or you should." That is just twisted to me. The
whole spirit of theatre is about communicating; and if people like the
show they communicate it to their friends, and the show exists and
thrives because it's worthy of a large amount of people that want to see
it. *It is a waste of time to put negative energy into anything in the
universe.* I mean, this is a metaphysical concept. But there are people—
whether you like it or not—that are busting their butt on that stage, and
you can't write off what they're doing. The universe will not respect
you for that! Ultimately, it's just a hollow thing. I mean, if a personality

of criticism now was constructive and, and the consumer aspect of it was really taken to heart, and when somebody said, "I didn't like something," they were intelligent and gentle, then I could respect it. But I do not respect the whole concept.

Q: What are your own criteria for success?

WONG: My own criteria for success are related to whether or not I feel that I have assumed my potential—say, if it's a performance, whether I put as much energy and as much commitment as I should have into something. If it's a career situation—I have a very specific and pretty definable moral code—and if what any aspect of my life we're talking about fits into that moral code, then I'm a successful person. It has to do with putting negative energy into something—or *not*; it has to do with assuming your potential; it has to do with trying to make the world a better place; it has to do with—being as generous as possible; it has to do with being optimistic; and it has to do with not being materialistic, or—I'm still wrestling with this—being materialistic for a socially relevant cause. I could be really kidding myself, but I do think that I want money for the right reasons. I think that I want money to put into my work—to do things and say things and to help people and to help make the world a better place, or to get us to reevaluate our prejudices.

Q: Are your criteria the same for others as for yourself?

WONG: Yes and no. I don't feel that you can always put upon others what you put on yourself, and yet I find myself doing that a great deal. There are times when I find myself critical of someone and have to evaluate that criticism—because I'm evaluating on my own terms, and that's not fair.

Q: What one piece of advice would you give to other younger actors just starting out?

WONG: I was told when I was that person that you described—the one thing that I remember that I think that I would pass along—was that you had to have in your soul the heart of the actor. That it just does not happen if you don't. If you're a good-looking guy, and someone says to you, "You should be an actor," and you go, "Oh, okay," and then you decide to be an actor, that's wonderful. And you might become a big movie star, I will tell you that. But that is not what acting is about. Acting is about having a desire to give something to people. Now, it can be something different for everyone. For me, it is the spirit of message and the spirit of joy. And the spirit of self-awareness as a person on the planet. What you get for that unselfish commitment is a great deal of satisfaction. A profound, lifetime kind of satisfaction for making that commitment. I mean, it's fun. Everything. *Then* when you're sitting at your makeup mirror and putting on the fake mustache, that becomes fun because it's part of the message. It doesn't become fun because it's make-believe or because it's fun and you look different. It's fun because it's part of the message—the costume becomes fun because it's part of the message. Doing the Gap ad is fun because somehow it's part of the message. So hopefully you will have that. If you don't have that, it's time to study the violin. What *I* think is that the world does not need actors who don't have that.

I think it's important to say, also (and this was *not* said to me), the life of the actor, the *career* of the actor—let's assume the actor accepts the responsibility as the messenger—the *career* of that person is viable and *possible*. And full of struggle and challenge, *but it can happen if you have that commitment.* Nobody told me that it was *possible* that it was a career and that I could make a living and that I would be happy. And I think that that's *possible*. I would add that it's not possible unless you have that thing, but it is *possible*. And I would say, "Work hard towards finding that." I was lucky to have the parents that I have, but you have to find support in yourself or outside of yourself in order to have this particular lifestyle and this choice of life. Because it's unique. And as a result, very rewarding because of its uniqueness. But it does have its own weird challenges. And I would also say, "Godspeed."

BIBLIOGRAPHY

Anonymous. *The Truth about the Theatre*. Cincinnati, Ohio: Stewart & Kidd, 1916.

Barrett, Lawrence. *Charlotte Cushman*. Boston: Dunlap, 1878.

———. *Edwin Forrest*. Boston: Houghton Mifflin, 1882.

Barrymore, Lionel. *We Barrymores*. New York: Appleton-Century-Crofts, 1951.

Belasco, David. *The Theatre through Its Stage Door*. New York: Harper and Brothers, 1919.

Bernard, John. *Retrospections of America*. New York: Harper and Brothers, 1887.

Bernheim, Alfred L. *The Business of the Theatre*. New York: Actors' Equity Association, 1932.

Binns, Archie. *Mrs. Fiske and the American Theatre*. New York: Crown Publishers, 1955.

Bobbe, Dorothie. *Fanny Kemble*. New York: Minton, Balch, 1931.

Carson, William. *The Theatre on the Frontier*. Chicago: University of Chicago Press, 1932.

Clapp Jr., W. W. *A Record of the Boston Stage*. Boston: J. Munroe, 1853.

Courtney, Marguerite. *Laurette*. New York: Rinehart, 1955.

Deutsch, Helen and Hanau, Stella. *The Provincetown: A Story of the Theatre*. New York: Rinehart, 1931.

Drew, John. *My Years on the Stage*. New York: E. P. Dutton, 1922.

Dunlap, William. *A History of the American Theatre*. New York: J&J Harper, 1832.

Eaton, Walter. *The Theatre Guild: The First Ten Years*. New York: Brentano's, 1929.

Flanagan, Hallie. *Arena*. New York: Duell, Sloan, and Pearce, 1940.

Frohman, Daniel. *Memoirs of a Manager*. New York: Doubleday, 1911.

Fyles, Franklin. *The Theatre and Its People*. New York: Doubleday, 1900.

Gagey, Edmund M. *The San Francisco Stage*. New York: Columbia University Press, 1950.

Gallegly, Joseph. *Footlights on the Border*. The Hague, Netherlands: Mouton, 1962.

Gillette, William. *The Illusion of the First Time in Acting.* New York: Dramatic Museum of Columbia University, 1915.

Goodale, Katherine. *Behind the Scenes with Edwin Booth.* Boston: Houghton Mifflin, 1931.

Grossman, Edwina Booth. *Edwin Booth: Recollections by His Daughter.* New York: Benjamin Blom, 1894.

Hapgood, Norman. *The Stage in America, 1897–1900.* New York: Macmillan, 1901.

Harding, Alfred. *The Revolt of the Actors.* New York: William Morrow, 1929.

Hewitt, Barnard. *Theatre U.S.A. 1665 to 1957.* New York: McGraw-Hill, 1959.

Hill, Errol. *Shakespeare in Sable.* Amherst: University of Massachusetts Press, 1984.

Hill, George H. *"Yankee." Scenes from the Life of an Actor.* New York: Garrett, 1853.

Hillebrand, Harold. *Edmund Kean.* New York: Columbia University Press, 1933.

Hughes, Glenn. *A History of the American Theatre, 1700–1959.* New York: Samuel French, 1951.

Hunt, [first name unknown]. "The Nashville Theatre," *Birmingham-Southern College Bulletin,* May 1935.

Ireland, Joseph N. *A Memoir of the Professional Life of Thomas Abthorpe Cooper.* New York: Dunlap Society Publications, 1888.

Isaacs, Edith. *The Negro in the American Theatre.* New York: Theatre Arts Books, 1947.

Kanellos, Nicolas. *Hispanic Theatre in the United States.* Houston, Texas: Arte Publico Press, 1984.

Kendall, John S. *The Golden Age of the New Orleans Theatre.* Baton Rouge: Louisiana State University Press, 1952.

Koon, Helene W. *How Shakespeare Won the West.* Jefferson. N.C.: McFarland, 1989.

Library of Congress Federal Theatre Collection at George Mason University Library, Fairfax, Va.

Logan, Olive. *Before the Footlights and Behind the Scenes.* Philadelphia: Parmalee, 1870.

McGlinchee, Claire. *The First Decade of the Boston Museum.* Boston: Bruce Humphries, 1940.

Mackay, Constance. *The Little Theatre in the United States.* New York: Henry Holt, 1917.

McKay, Frederick E. and Wingate, Charles E. *Famous American Actors of Today.* New York: T. Y. Crowell, 1896.

MacMinn, George R. *The Theatre of the Golden Era in California.* Caldwell, Idaho: Caxton Printers, 1941.

Morris, Clara. *Life on the Stage.* New York: McClurg, Phillips, 1901.

Morris, Lloyd. *Curtain Time.* New York: Random House, 1953.

Moses, Montrose. *Famous Actor Families in America.* New York: T. Y. Crowell, 1906.

Mowatt, Anna Cora. *The Autobiography of an Actress.* Boston: Ticknor, Reed & Fields, 1854.

Murdoch, James. *The Stage.* Philadelphia: J. M. Stoddart, 1880.

National Archives Federal Theatre Project Collection, Washington, D.C.

Northall, William. *Before and Behind the Curtain.* New York: W. F. Burgess, 1851.

Odell, G. C. D. *Annals of the New York Stage.* 15 vols. New York: Columbia University Press, 1927–49.

Patterson, Lindsay, Ed. *Anthology of the American Negro in the Theatre.* New York: Publishers' Company, 1967.

Poggi, Jack. *Theatre in America.* Ithaca, N.Y.: Cornell University Press, 1968.

Pollock, Thomas C. *The Philadelphia Theatre in the Eighteenth Century.* Philadelphia: University of Pennsylvania, 1933; reprint, Westport, Conn.: Greenwood Press, 1968.

Skinner, Richard Dana. *Our Changing Theatre.* New York: Dial Press, 1931.

Smith, Solomon. *The Theatrical Apprenticeship of Sol Smith.* Philadelphia: Carey and Hart, 1846.

————. *Theatrical Management in the West and South for Thirty Years.* New York: Harper and Brothers, 1868.

Theatre of the Thirties Collection, Special Collections and Archives, George Mason University Library, Fairfax, Va.

Wemyss, Francis C. *Twenty-six Years in the Life of an Actor and Manager.* New York: Burgess, Syringer, 1847.

Whitman, Willson. *Bread and Circuses: A Study of the Federal Theatre.* New York: Oxford University Press, 1937.

Willard, George O. *History of the Providence Stage, 1762–1891.* Providence, R.I.: News, 1891.

Wilson, Francis. *Joseph Jefferson: Reminiscences of a Fellow Player.* London: Chapman and Hall, 1906.

Winter, William. *Life and Art of Edwin Booth.* New York: Macmillan, 1893.

————. *Wallet of Time.* Vols. 1 and 2. New York: Moffat, Yard, 1915.

Wood, William B. *Personal Recollections of the Stage.* Philadelphia: H. C. Baird, 1855.

Woollcott, Alexander. *Mrs. Fiske.* New York: Appleton-Century-Crofts, 1917.

Works Progress Administration. *San Francisco Theatre Research.* 20 vols. San Francisco: WPA, 1938–42.

Zacek, Dennis. "The Acting Techniques of Edwin Booth," unpublished dissertation, Northwestern University, Chicago, 1970.

INDEX

ABOUT THE EDITOR

JOAN JEFFRI is Director of the Research Center for Arts and Culture, which she founded in 1985 at Columbia University; Director of Columbia's Master's Degree Program in Arts Administration at Teachers College; and former Executive Editor of the *Journal of Arts Management and Law*. Her books include *The Painter Speaks* (1993) and *The Craftsperson Speaks* (1992), both published by Greenwood Press; *ArtsMoney: Raising It, Saving It, and Earning It* (1989); *Artisthelp: The Artist's Guide to Work-related Human and Social Services* (1990); and *The Emerging Arts: Management, Survival, and Growth* (Praeger Publishers, 1980).

ABOUT THE RESEARCH CENTER FOR
ARTS AND CULTURE

The Research Center for Arts and Culture is both a service and a resource
for arts institutions, policy and decisionmakers, funders, scholars, individual
artists and managers. Committed to applied research in the disciplines of
arts management and arts law, the Center provides the academic auspice
so important for exploration, education, policy making, and action.

In addition to the vast resources of Columbia University—including the
considerable cooperation and participation of the faculty—an advisory
board of artists, administrators, and members of the legal and business
professions offers continuous support to the Center, helping it to
provide services and expertise. Collaboration and cooperation with
service organizations, trade publishers, and arts institutions strengthen the
Center's unique position and enable it to translate its findings into useful,
practical forms.